2005

The Jack Ryan Agenda

The JACK RYAN Agenda

Policy and Politics in the Novels of Tom Clancy: An Unauthorized Analysis

WILLIAM TERDOSLAVICH

FORGE®

A TOM DOHERTY ASSOCIATES BOOK

NEW YORK

THE JACK RYAN AGENDA:
POLICY AND POLITICS IN THE NOVELS OF TOM CLANCY:
AN UNAUTHORIZED ANALYSIS

This book is printed on acid-free paper.

Edited by Brian Thomsen

Book design by Mary A. Wirth

A Forge Book
Published by Tom Doherty Associates, LLC
175 Fifth Avenue
New York, NY 10010

www.tor.com

Forge® is a registered trademark of Tom Doherty Associates, LLC.

Library of Congress Cataloging-in-Publication Data

Terdoslavich, William.
The Jack Ryan agenda : policy and politics in the novels of Tom Clancy : an unauthorized
analysis / by William Terdoslavich.—1st hardcover ed.
p.   cm.—(A Forge book)
Includes bibliographical references (p. 253).
ISBN 0-765-31247-6
EAN 978-0765-31247-1
1. Clancy, Tom, 1947-—Criticism and interpretation.   2. Politics and literature—United
States—History—20th century.   3. Political fiction, American—History and criticism.   4.
Clancy, Tom, 1947-—Political and social views.   5. Clancy, Tom, 1947-—Characters—
Jack Ryan.   6. Ryan, Jack (Fictitious character)   7. Politics in literature.   I. Title.
II. Series.
PS3553.L245Z88   2005
813'.54—dc22

2004023170

First Edition: May 2005

Printed in the United States of America

0 9 8 7 6 5 4 3 2 1

To Talley Sue.

Putting up with this project was a sign of true love.

Thank you.

Contents

Acknowledgments

I'd like to thank Brian Thomsen for his work in shaping this project and editing the manuscript. I would also like to thank Frank Wyman, for drawing up a good contract; Josh Rubins, for his thoughtful review; Bonnie Sashin at the Boston Bar Association; and the New York Public Library.

Preface

September 11, 2001, started as a perfect day. New York City had just endured a lengthy August heat wave. This sunny day had a welcoming feeling. It was sunny and cloudless.

By mid-morning, terrorists had hijacked two airliners and crashed them into the Twin Towers. While the news stations covered the event, word came out that a third airliner had crashed into the Pentagon. Shortly thereafter, a fourth plane plunged to the ground in Pennsylvania.

Never did truth seem stranger than fiction.

It is an unwritten rule among writers of spy books and thrillers to "tone it down." Don't make the plot too far-fetched, or no one will believe it. Tom Clancy has written his share of far-fetched plots. Beneath the veneer of fiction, however, are many similarities to reality.

What fiction writer concocted a plot to put some funny powder in Fidel Castro's cigars that would make his beard fall out, destroying his charisma and ability to control Cuba?

This sounds stupid? Congressional hearings in the 1970s uncovered this plot receiving serious consideration by the CIA.

How about assassinating a pope who threatened the Soviet grip on Eastern Europe?

Sorry, that story made it as far as the shooting, followed by a twist ending in real life, as the pope forgave the man who shot him.

And did you hear the one about the Bulgarian dissident who was killed in London after being jabbed by an umbrella that shot a poisoned pellet into his leg? Ian Fleming didn't write that one up. The Bulgarian KGB did in real life.

And let's not forget how the Israelis killed a suspected Palestinian bomb maker with an exploding cell phone.

Crazy as all this sounds, it is not far removed from fiction.

As America's most successful author of techno-thrillers, Tom Clancy has fashioned a number of "tall stories." Start with his all-purpose hero, Jack Ryan, facilitating the defection of a Soviet nuclear missile submarine. The outgunned modest history professor thwarts Irish terrorists—twice in the same novel. The same hero plays a major role in getting a KGB chairman to defect, helps rescue a U.S. covert force from Colombia, contains runaway escalation with the USSR after a nuclear terrorist strike, manages a war against Japan, becomes an accidental president of the United States, and wins wars against a hostile Iran and later China.

Every U.S. president has to manage at least one crisis during his administration, but in Clancy's world, every book is a crisis—for a president, the CIA, the armed forces, the FBI, even the Coast Guard. Jack Ryan is always there (or to a lesser extent, Clancy's other all-purpose action hero, John Clark).

As the action proceeds, Jack Ryan becomes a vehicle for conveying the author's political views, used as a template to meet the challenges facing the United States. Not surprisingly, military force is the major tool used to fix fictional problems. In real life, force is harder to use. It's crude, imprecise, unpredictable, and capricious. It can cause as many problems as it solves. But in Clancy's fiction, force solves all problems.

Such a view finds its roots in "blue collar nationalism." How often has the working man viewed any challenge to American power as a matter of "going there and kicking butt"? How many times can you recall a friend or coworker saying "what we oughtta do is send over some commandos and take out that dictator"? It probably happens millions of times a day, usually during the lunch hour or over beer after work.

With a few keystrokes, the bad guy strikes first, the good guy comes back and wins, the bad guy loses, and America stands tall once again. Clancy can cheaply write a scene where a Japan Airlines Boeing 747 crashes into the Capitol during the State of the Union address. Wiping out the president, Senate, House of Representatives, U.S. Supreme Court, the Joint Chiefs of Staff, and the cabinet, Clancy clears out Washington's political gridlock and gives Jack Ryan a clean slate to write his own political agenda, focused less on politics and more on "good government" based on American strength and a sure sense of right and wrong. The beauty of fiction is that the author is free to shape the world any way he pleases.

In real life, the jetliners still crashed into the Pentagon and the World Trade Center. America swiftly went to war with Afghanistan, which was sheltering the terrorist group that perpetrated the attacks, with diplomacy playing a major role in shaping that strike. And while our forces fought halfway around the world at short notice, the bad guy still was not caught. At the time of this book's writing in the spring and summer of 2004, Al Qaeda founder and leader Osama bin Laden is still at large, despite America's military might and the superhuman efforts of Special Forces to capture or kill him.

If only we could capture or kill the bad guy as easily as in a Tom

Clancy novel. Where's Jack Ryan when you need him? He is always handy to save the world and set right all its wrongs—until the next book comes out.

This book looks at the fictional world Tom Clancy has crafted for Jack Ryan, and compares it to the real world that our elected and appointed officials have to deal with every day.

After this book introduces Jack Ryan to the reader, the focus will shift to the presidency. Whether Jack Ryan is on the periphery of power or wielding it in the Oval Office, any action or reaction by the United States must bear the approval of the president. The Constitution does not vest the majority of power in the presidency, dividing it instead between the executive branch, Congress, and the Supreme Court. But the president is an all-powerful demigod in Clancy's world, wielding his sword with little political interference.

The book then shifts its attention to the weapons and the way they are used to fight wars. Clancy is a shameless weapons buff, and an unabashed admirer of the U.S. military. The weapons always work. The army, navy, air force, and marines always win. And the war always gets wrapped up in a matter of weeks, not years. That has been true many times in recent years—except in Iraq.

The spotlight then shifts to the use of covert and Special Forces to "get the bad guys before they get us." Special Forces, commandos, terrorists, assassins, and spies—their work is dramatic, dangerous, adventurous, and exciting. But do they work as well as advertised? What happens in a novel may not always be so in real life.

Then there is the difference between the book and the movie. Clancy's worldview is conservative, but often gets rammed through a liberal filter when Hollywood turns text to film.

Finally, there is the path not taken. Clancy once collaborated with Larry Bond to produce *Red Storm Rising*. Jack Ryan is nowhere to be seen, but the elements of Clancy's fiction stand in fascinating contrast with his uncredited partner, who also went on to write a few techno-thrillers of his own.

Look through all of Clancy's novels, and one will see Jack Ryan as the embodiment of Clancy's worldview, making the changes that suit his conservative politics. Force works. Diplomacy does not. Kill the bad guys when you can find them. Congress should follow, not lead. Doers should head agencies and cabinet departments, not careerists or office politicians. Action counts for more than process. The difference between right and wrong is clear and never compromised. The United States is always right.

That is the Jack Ryan Agenda.

The Jack Ryan Agenda

ONE

Meet Jack Ryan

So who is Jack Ryan?

Ryan was born as the figment of Tom Clancy's imagination as the underestimated good guy who must always triumph over adversity. He can do whatever the author wants him to do. Ryan can prove any point, get the last word in, and make the right decision when the time to act is nigh.

And Ryan, as a result, suffers from the same problem affecting all fictional heroes . . . each daring deed must be outdone in the next book. By the time the reader gets to the fifth or tenth installment, the hero begins to look unbelievably superhuman.

If Jack Ryan were a real person, what would his biography look like?

Ryan's first appearance in print was in *Hunt for Red October*, set loosely in the early 1980s, sometime during Ronald Reagan's term in office. Ryan is in his early thirties, which places his birthday somewhere around 1950 or so. He is a baby boomer, coming to adulthood too late to have been directly affected by the Vietnam War. Son of a Baltimore detective and brought up a good Catholic, Jack Ryan is imbued with a sense of right and wrong that is certain and doubtless. Attending Boston College, a Jesuit school, Ryan kept his hair short, never tried smoking a joint, didn't protest, probably didn't get laid, and opted for Marine Corps ROTC. Commissioned, he served briefly in the corps as a platoon leader, his career cut short by a helicopter accident over Crete that caused a major back injury in the JFK tradition. (Though, for some strange reason, no matter what physical exertion Ryan makes in later books, his "bad" back never acts up.)

Ryan marries rich, but still goes on to make his own fortune. Cathy Muller is the daughter of a successful executive at Merrill Lynch. She goes to medical school, becoming an outstanding eye surgeon. (She has been driving a Porsche since her sixteenth birthday.)

Along the way, Ryan also picks up his doctorate, albeit in history, and does the good son-in-law bit. He goes to work at Merrill Lynch, where he makes the right investments early in the high-tech boom, becoming independently wealthy. Safely ensconced at his estate overlooking Chesapeake Bay, Ryan writes history books and teaches young midshipmen at the nearby Naval Academy at Annapolis. His wife, Cathy, is also doing well at Johns Hopkins in Baltimore. No matter what Jack Ryan chooses to do for a living, there will be no financial shortcomings suffered by the family given the existing fortune and a surgeon's salary. Ryan could even stay home and be a househusband with no visible impact on the family income or assets.

Even though Clancy starts writing about Ryan in *Hunt for Red October*, the Ryan story really begins with *Patriot Games*, the third Clancy book to make print. Ryan is in London, doing some tangential research in British naval archives as it dovetails with his main project on Admiral William Halsey.

Ryan's upbringing, steeped in law-and-order and service, would not permit him to stand aside as armed Irish terrorists try to kidnap the prince and princess of Wales. He tackles one suspect and uses the loose gun to shoot the other assailants. (As the British would say, typical American.) His choice, made in a split second, will dictate the course of his life, though he does not know it yet.

One terrorist vows to avenge the death of his brother in the attack Ryan foiled. Ryan finds out the hard way that men with guns are now out to kill him and his family. After one failed attack, Ryan swears to fight back. His previous contract work as a freelance analyst at the CIA put him in the good graces of Admiral James Greer, deputy director of intelligence. (The other half of CIA is focused on operations.) With access to raw intelligence, Ryan pieces together the whereabouts of the Ulster Liberation Army. Partially in revenge, they crash Ryan's dinner party for the prince and princess of Wales at the Ryans' Peregrine Cliff estate.

Ryan thus becomes a man of action again, and the evil plot is foiled. But the real change is at the job level. Ryan is now an analyst at the CIA. Like joining the IRA, it's "once in, never out."

Ryan is then sent to the CIA station in London, where he focuses on the Soviet navy in *Hunt for Red October*. He accidentally becomes a man of action again! Ryan's queries on the SSBN *Red October*'s superquiet propulsion system, coupled with information coming from a CIA spy with access to the Soviet Politburo (code-named CARDINAL) set into motion an elaborate operation to take delivery of the defecting sub while covering up its absence. The Russian experts the navy was flying in die in a tragic helicopter crash. Ryan and a British colleague must handle taking custody of the sub, amid a gunfight and a harrowing game of cat and mouse against a Soviet attack sub.

Ryan's second London adventure becomes a vain attempt to thwart the assassination attempt on the pope, outlined in *Red Rabbit* (written out of sequence only a couple of years ago), jamming the event into the continuum of Ryan's cold war adventures.

In *Cardinal of the Kremlin* (Clancy's fourth book, but third in the Ryan series), Ryan interferes with KGB chief Gerasimov's ploy to seize power. Ryan makes it known that the missile sub *Red October* was stolen on Gerasimov's watch, and that if word got out, Gerasimov would be discredited, thus simply ending the power play. Ryan instead offers the KGB chief a chance to defect, which he accepts.

Ryan emerges as an in-demand analyst who still gets into "trouble" outside of his department. But he never shirks responsibility when a chance appears to protect or advance the interests of the United States.

Reagan's term ended in 1989.

In *Clear and Present Danger*, the succeeding president is code-named WRANGLER by the secret service.

He is never named.

James Greer, Ryan's mentor, dies from pancreatic cancer, resulting in Ryan becoming the acting deputy director for intelligence. He uncovers the illegal insertion of U.S. light infantry in Colombia, as well as the plot to abandon them to maintain deniability. As Greer is laid to rest in Arlington National Cemetery, Ryan flies off to Panama to improvise the helicopter rescue effort, and winds up manning one of the door guns on the MH-53, taking fire and firing back.

Ryan also has to deliver the weekly intelligence briefing to WRANGLER's challenger, J. Robert Fowler. That places the action in 1992 (or 1996, depending how you count the years in later books).

They do not hit it off.

Fowler becomes president in *Sum of All Fears*, and Ryan becomes the full-time deputy director of intelligence, officially replacing James Greer. Fowler achieves the high point of his presidency—a resolution of the old, ongoing Arab-Israeli crisis. The downside is Fowler's crisis mismanagement when terrorists set off a rebuilt nuclear bomb in Denver during the Super Bowl. Fowler accepts the official misinterpretation that the Russians detonated the bomb, and subsequent confrontations between U.S. and Russian forces elsewhere in the world (some of them provoked by other terrorists) reinforce that judgment. As Ryan sees Fowler rapidly climbing up the escalation ladder, his intelligence work uncovers data that the bomb was set off by non-Soviet terrorists, and he cuts into the hotline conversation between the White House and the Kremlin to bring this information to light. Both sides undertake a phased stand-down of forces.

Once Fowler is briefed that Iranian-sponsored terrorists committed the nuclear bombing, he orders a nuclear counterstrike on Qom, Iran's holy city. Ryan refuses to concur, thus negating the launch order. In a matter of plot convenience, there were no other authorized cabinet officers or appointees with the necessary confirmation clearance. Ryan will not countenance the slaughter of innocent bystanders just to kill one person (Iranian leader Ayatollah Daryaei), in an act of retribution. After failing to order the strike, Fowler has a nervous breakdown, resigns, and passes the presidency to his vice president, Roger Durling.

Ryan's career now rebounds into the White House in *Debt of Honor*. Durling has a poor grasp of foreign policy. He needs a new national security advisor, and Ryan is right for the job. Despite having a background more on the analytical side of the CIA rather than the operational side, Ryan takes action, planning and executing covert operations to reassert American power abroad.

Durling reaches the high point of his presidency when he signs a treaty with Russia to dismantle the ICBM arsenals of both nations. This is marred by a trade deficit with Japan that is causing many U.S. factories to close down. Eventually, the U.S. finds itself at war with Japan again, with Japan firing the opening shots. Ryan helps craft the war-winning strategy. Durling is smart enough not to interfere.

The presidential election is just around the corner (placing the action in either 1996 or 2000), and Durling looks likely to win. He asks Ryan to fill in as vice president to replace the recently resigned VP, Ed Kealty. The president promises Ryan that he only has to serve out the remainder of the current term, focusing on national security and foreign policy.

Durling intends to tap a real running mate for the election, who will take over the vice presidency come January. Ryan's sense of duty does not allow him to decline. While politically he would be serving a president, an appointment to any post in Washington also means one serves his country and the American people. Ryan clearly perceives those responsibilities.

But January never comes for Durling. As he is about to deliver the State of the Union address, he is killed (along with most of the cabinet, Congress, and Supreme Court) when a crazed pilot dives a Japan Airlines Boeing 747 into the Capitol. (The pilot is striking back after the loss of his brother and son in the war.)

Ryan is now president, and he never wanted the damn job. There is nothing in Ryan's life that even hinted at this outcome. All offices he held before were by appointment. Ryan never once ran for office, not even for class president.

In *Executive Orders*, Ryan has to rebuild the U.S. government, a grave domestic challenge, and has to face down Iran, which recently "annexed" Iraq following the fictional assassination of Saddam Hussein. The combined might of two tyrannies now faces Saudi Arabia. A robust American response like Desert Shield/Desert Storm is out of the question, as Iranian terrorists launch a far-reaching biological attack on the U.S. that immobilizes most of the units before they can intervene. Ryan orders intervention anyway, believing that the U.S. never deserts its allies. What few U.S. forces that are sent into the theater win the war, and Ryan then orders the assassination of Daryaei.

The world for Jack Ryan has suddenly changed.

In *The Bear and the Dragon*, Ryan now sits in the Oval Office as an elected president. This places the action in 1997 or 2001, depending how the reader marks the years. Shoehorned into the time stream is *Rainbow Six*, where a multinational commando team defeats an effort by U.S. environmental extremists to launch a worldwide epidemic using a genetically modified strain of the Ebola virus, to be let lose at the 2000 Summer Olympics in Sydney.

Returning to the plot of *The Bear and the Dragon*, Russia has made major discoveries of gold and oil deep in eastern Siberia, and President Ryan must now find a way to protect Russia from a Chinese invasion to seize the resources. Diplomatic efforts are for naught, so the U.S. must dispatch whatever forces it can muster to support the Russians.

The U.S. helps win the war, providing a major assist to the Russians, who provided the bulk of the ground forces. Ryan once again shows that the U.S. stands by its allies. He even engineers Russian admission to NATO to deter China from attacking. Ryan's refusal to leave Washington, D.C., during a nuclear attack also underscores his sense of leadership, which is a willingness to face the same challenges as those faced by servicemen who must obey his orders.

Ryan is out of the White House in *Teeth of the Tiger*, which takes place some time after 2004. His role in this book is minimal. He has resigned the presidency. Robby Jackson, his vice president, becomes the first black president of the United States, a position he holds until gunned down by a radical Ku Klux Klan member who was not pleased by this reality. Ed Kealty manages to get elected president. (And Kealty's scandals did not come to light?)

Prior to leaving office, Ryan has set up a self-funded intelligence service in the guise of a private investment firm, with access to all CIA and National Security Agency (NSA) files and zero oversight by Congress or the White House. The firm, Hendley Associates, is staffed by analysts and operatives forwarded from a number of government agencies and services. Analysts develop information on terrorists abroad. Operatives are then dispatched to kill them. If anyone gets into legal trouble, a stack of undated presidential pardons signed by Jack Ryan sits in the Hendley safe, ready to be dispensed like they were "get out of jail free" cards in a deadly game of Monopoly.

By this time, Ryan is about fifty-plus years old, which is on the young side to be a retired ex-president. Clancy may not know what to do with his old superhero, especially now that Jack Ryan Jr. is an analyst at Hendley who seems to share his father's penchant for getting involved on the operational side.

•   •   •

Jack Ryan has no love for American politics, treating it more as a shabby process to be endured. Typically, politics sidelines or overlooks those who try to do the right thing in the name of the common good. Ryan made sure that politics ceased during his brief tenure in the Oval Office to make sure that good people were appointed to the top jobs at the FBI, CIA, and the various cabinet departments. Occasionally, Ryan complains vehemently in private about the direction Kealty is taking the country, but like a good ex-president, he maintains his public silence about actions taken by his successor. Left unmentioned are any plans for a Jack Ryan presidential library or even a brief word about the ex-president's office, small staff, or Secret Service detail.

What Ryan does from here is entirely up to Clancy. It is not unreasonable to hope that Jack Ryan (senior) will return to his first love, studying and teaching history, as well as writing history books. Having an ex-president teach a seminar on government to a bunch of graduate students would truly be a singular experience.

Jack Ryan will probably also make a pretty good grandfather.

Clancy's Presidents

I do solemnly swear that I will faithfully execute the office of President of the United States, and will, to the best of my ability, preserve, protect and defend the Constitution of the United States.

With these words, power is peacefully transferred at twelve noon on January 20, following a quadrennial election. Sometimes the man taking the oath is coming back for a second term. Sometimes it goes to a newcomer after a tired incumbent ends his two-term rule. Or it is transferred from the election's loser to its winner. And in the worst case, the vice president takes the oath after the president is killed, dies, or resigns.

Now that the United States stands as the world's only remaining superpower, the presidency is the most powerful job in the world. The pressure and long hours can age a man beyond his years.

The President Is the Most Powerful Man in the World?

The presidency casts a large shadow over the plotlines in many of Clancy's novels, even when the president is a bit player. Sometimes the president is unnamed, but known to the reader wise enough to read between the lines.

In *Hunt for Red October*, the unnamed chief executive is Ronald Reagan. In *Without Remorse*, it's Richard Nixon. Even Jack Ryan goes nameless in *Rainbow Six*.

While Jack Ryan or John Clark ride the spear point of action in the story, the events that instigated that action started in the Oval Office.

So what can a president really do?

Article II of the Constitution is pretty concise. The president is the commander in chief of the armed forces. He can make appointments, with the advice and consent of the Senate. He must report on the State of the Union to Congress. He can recommend a course of action for Congress to adopt.

In actual practice, the presidency has become far more than that. Even though on paper the budget begins in Congress, in truth it starts in the Office of Management and Budget, an office of the executive branch. Even though Congress retains the power to declare war, presidents have long wielded force where it was needed to extend or protect American interests. The president looks to have his agenda enacted, with the State of the Union address much akin to the presentation of the budget message for the year.

In Clancy's vision of the world, it is the president as commander in chief that gets the most play. He is the man at the helm directing the ship of state, regardless of whether he is gifted or flawed. In every book, there is a crisis in need of resolution. It may require action at a covert level, or it may take a war. The president acts, or his agents and appointees act in accordance with his bidding.

As for Congress?

Go to the previous article, Article I. The Constitution grants Congress the power to tax, impeach, make laws, borrow money, regulate commerce among the states and other nations, establish rules of naturalization, coin money, fix weights and measures, establish a postal service, regulate patent and copyright, establish courts, declare war, finance the military, and regulate the militia.

Historically, there has always been a tug-of-war between Congress and president. How much power a president has at his disposal depends largely on the character of the officeholder. Abraham Lincoln, driven by the necessity of the Civil War, made it very clear in his policies that the Constitution was not a suicide pact.

There was no declaration of war.

Lincoln did not wait for Congress to appropriate funds to raise armies.

He suspended habeas corpus and put military tribunals in place to try civilians accused of treason.

He even freed the slaves by signing an executive order.

Now look at his successor, Andrew Johnson. He used the power of the presidency to water down congressional edicts regarding reconstruction, and immediately ran afoul of the body when he tried to fire Secretary of War Stanton. This earned Johnson an impeachment and trial in the Senate, but no conviction.

Between the terms of Andrew Johnson and Theodore Roosevelt, Congress pretty much ran the United States. The presidents during this stretch were pretty weak and forgettable. Rutherford B. Hayes? Benjamin Harrison? Chester A. Arthur? Can anyone recall any major accomplishment?

In the real world, president and Congress compete for power. The balance shifts back and forth, depending on which parties are in control of which branch of government, and where the president stands in time relative to reelection. A president is strongest in his first two years in office, and again in the first year of his second term. Domestic power slackens in the third year of the first term, the time when presidents traditionally show a greater interest in foreign policy—something he can control without the need for congressional approval. A presidency goes into stasis during reelection, and is truly weary by its seventh and eighth years, assuming the officeholder merited a second term.

Things sometime get more complicated when government is divided between the two parties. A president will be more likely to compromise to get some of his measures enacted. He may rely on executive orders to implement some policies. Or he may use his veto and depend on his congressional allies to sustain the veto when Congress votes to override.

Perhaps the most important power the presidency has acquired is over the budget. Starting with Warren Harding's presidency in 1921, Congress shifted the power of the budget to the Treasury's Office of Budget. This power was further amended under Richard Nixon's presidency, when the Office of Management and Budget was created, shifting the initial budget power directly to the White House.

Now, the budget power sounds boring, but it is profound. Money is the fuel of all action, and no matter what your political beliefs are like, nothing on your wish list will see enactment into policy without funding.

That is real life.

Fiction, however, is free from such annoying constraints.

In all of Tom Clancy's novels, the president is supreme, be he a real American or a real dunderhead, and Jack Ryan must serve every president before accidentally becoming one himself.

Clancy sticks to the commander-in-chief role of the presidency, paying lip service to Congress and the courts. Congress is a mere afterthought, informed as a courtesy but better left out of the loop.

Another Crisis, Another President

The actual timeline of presidents and crises is a pretty busy one from 1980 to 2004. Each president had to deal with at least one crisis while in office. Throughout the 1980s, Reagan had the ongoing cold war against the Soviet Union to worry about, but he also funded counterinsurgency in El Salvador as well as covertly supporting insurgencies against Communist governments in Angola, Afghanistan, and Nicaragua. There were "shooting deployments," like the interventions in Lebanon and Grenada in 1983, plus several aerial dogfights and an air strike against Libya. (Lebanon was marred by retreat following the suicide bombing of the U.S. Marine Corps barracks in Beirut, killing 241 Marines. U.S. citizens in Lebanon were also taken hostage by terrorists repeatedly throughout Reagan's presidency, and most were lucky enough to make it home alive.)

George H.W. Bush was even busier, with an invasion of Panama in 1989 to oust dictator Manuel Noriega, a war against Iraq to free Kuwait in 1990–91, and the initial intervention in Somalia in late 1992 to forestall a famine in the midst of an anarchic civil war.

Bill Clinton's two terms saw no respite. The Somalia intervention came to a bitter end in 1993, when U.S. Rangers, trying to apprehend warlord Mohammed Farah Aideed, suffered eighteen dead and over eighty wounded (an event so well chronicled in *Black Hawk Down*). U.S. troops were pulled out after that defeat, much as they were from Beirut in 1983. Clinton also deployed two carrier battle groups to deter Chinese war moves in 1996, following Taiwan's presidential election.

Cruise missiles became Clinton's favored tool when using force, using them to strike Baghdad in revenge for Iraq's planned assassination of ex-president George H.W. Bush. Again in late 1998, cruise missiles struck training camps belonging to the terrorist group Al Qaeda in Afghanistan and a pharmaceutical plant in Khartoum, Sudan, suspected of making chemical weapons for Al Qaeda as well.

Clinton ordered air strikes against Baghdad in Operation Desert Fox in 1998, retaliating for the expulsion of UN weapons inspectors in Iraq. Air strikes were used in Bosnia against Serb ground units around Sarajevo, forcing Serbia to the negotiating table at Dayton to settle that war. In 1999, U.S. air units fought the bulk of the Kosovo war from the air, forcing Serbia to retreat and relinquish its political hold on this ethnically Albanian province. Despite much criticism, Clinton had the distinction of presiding over the only war that did not see a single U.S. combat fatality.

Clinton was followed by George W. Bush, who presided over a war in Afghanistan, ousting the Taliban regime and Osama bin Laden's Al Qaeda terrorist group in 2001–02. A second war was fought to rid Iraq of dictator Saddam Hussein in the spring of 2003. After both wars were "won," U.S. units still had to fight counterinsurgencies against disgruntled and stubborn remnants that would not admit defeat.[1]

These crises can be divided into two categories: smaller events requiring brief combat operations, well-handled by the president alone as commander in chief; or larger events requiring deployment of U.S. troops abroad and major combat operations over a period of time running from months to years. In the latter category, a president must go before Congress to outline his reasons for fighting and obtain a congressional resolution authorizing the war. The resolution is a cheap substitute for a declaration of war, a power rarely exercised by Congress. A president will also have to address the nation, making his case to the people to cultivate the public support needed to fight.

Where Truth and Fiction Part Company

The fictional and actual timelines start in the same place. Clancy can't undo history previous to Ronald Reagan's presidency. Reagan is the unnamed president in *Hunt for Red October*. The unnamed president is an "implied Republican." (*Patriot Games* makes no mention of the president.) Ryan is way down in the pecking order as an analyst and protégé of his boss, Rear Admiral James Greer, deputy director for intelligence at the CIA. The main caper is trying to find a way to bring in a defecting Soviet missile sub (*Red October*, Typhoon class) that has been taken over by renegade captain, Marko Ramius, and his handpicked officers. This results in the U.S. Navy mustering much of the Atlantic fleet to run interference against a major Soviet naval deployment in the North Atlantic, whose sole purpose is to find and sink *Red October*.

In Clancy's timeline, the unnamed Reagan is still in office for *Cardinal of the Kremlin* (fitting, given Reagan's advocacy for space-based antimissile defense—the high-tech centerpiece of the book). Here the action is more covert. Soviet KGB agents try to kidnap one of the leading U.S. experts on space-based weapons systems. U.S.-backed Afghan rebels try storming a Soviet test facility in central Asia, near the Afghan border.

Next is *Clear and Present Danger*.

In real life, Vice President George Bush succeeded Ronald Reagan in 1989.

In Clancy's fiction, that honor goes to another unnamed POTUS, whose secret service code name is WRANGLER. Here WRANGLER's intervention is the covert use of U.S. light infantry to search for and destroy illegal drug processing labs belonging to Colombia's drug cartels. (The Colombian government is not informed of this U.S. deployment, making it a pretty gross violation of that nation's sovereignty.)

The U.S. has tried using some military means to staunch the smuggling of illegal drugs. The E-3A AWACS has been used to identify drug flights for interception by law enforcement. The 1989 invasion of Panama, while prompted by the need to protect the Canal Zone, also was needed to oust dictator Noriega once he became suspected of aiding the Colombian drug trade.

Currently, the U.S. is supporting Colombian president Alvaro Uribe to the tune of $700 million a year, mostly in military aid, to actively combat a left-wing insurgency financed by the cocaine trade. Note that it is the Colombian Army and national police force that is doing the fighting, not covert teams of American troops.[2]

In Clancy's world, the election was a close one in 1992 (not so in real life), and J. Robert Fowler, the implied Democrat, beats WRANGLER by two points. (The elder Bush also ran a lackluster campaign for his reelection, a mildly prophetic call by Clancy.)

The presidency becomes more central to Clancy's storytelling the farther up the chain of command Ryan goes. Now our hero is the acting deputy director of intelligence at the CIA. He has to deal with Fowler and his national security advisor, Elizabeth Elliot, on a regular basis, and the relationship is pretty tense. Much of what Fowler wanted could not be enacted in his first term due to a recession, budget cutting (peace dividend), and revenue shortfalls. The midterm elections were coming up, which places Clancy's tale around 1994 on the alternative timeline.

Clancy über-hero Jack Ryan plays a role in Fowler's masterstroke to solve the vexing and persistent Middle East crisis, which would become the high point of his brief presidency. Jerusalem becomes an open city policed by a neutral Swiss army detachment while the U.S. guarantees Israel's security with serious commitments—one armored cavalry regiment, a carrier battle group based in Haifa, and one wing of F-16 fighter planes.

Here Clancy reintroduces the reader to Middle Eastern terrorism.

Palestinian extremists acquire an Israeli nuke accidentally lost during the 1973 October war, and hire an East German nuclear expert to rebuild the bomb. The nuke is shipped to Denver, where the terrorists hope to set it off in the stadium where the Super Bowl will be played. A concurrent plot by an allied West German terrorist group (reminiscent of the Baader-Meinhof Gang) is underway to stage a provocation between the U.S. Berlin brigade and Soviet forces around the divided city.[3]

Fowler quickly reaches the low point of his presidency once the terrorists set off their nuclear bomb, which does not completely detonate . . . but U.S. early warning satellites detect its flash. Based on that data, the size of the blast is misinterpreted to be ten times greater—too big to be a device planted by terrorists.

Fowler does several things. As a precaution, U.S. forces go to DEFCON 2. (Defense condition 2. DEFCON 1 is highest alert, while DEFCON 5 is lowest.) Fowler is stuck at Camp David during a snowstorm, with his helicopter out of action due to a mechanical difficulty. He orders Vice President Durling aboard the National Emergency Airborne Command Post (NEACP—pronounced *kneecap*). And he dispatches the FBI to all media outlets to squelch any effort to report the attack to forestall national panic.

Fowler next exchanges messages with his Russian counterpart Narmanov via the hotline. As the impact of unexpected events is compounded by incomplete information, Fowler and Narmanov stumble toward nuclear exchange. Soviet and Libyan MiG 29s and U.S. Navy F-14 Tomcats dogfight over the eastern Mediterranean. An overaggressive commander of a U.S. missile sub tangles with a Russian attack sub in the Pacific. The German terrorists, disguised as Russian soldiers, open fire on the U.S. soldiers of the Berlin brigade. The firefight escalates into full-blown combat between American and Russian troops. Shots are being exchanged just beyond the threshold of control exercised by both national leaders.

Each event escalates the crisis.

Ryan is cut out of the loop during the confrontation. When he obtains the true information about what happened in Denver, he rushes over to the Pentagon and cuts into the hotline to post it. Deus ex machina! The crisis subsides as U.S. and Russian forces undertake a phased stand-down.

Once information surfaces that the terrorist strike on Denver was sponsored by Iran, Fowler redirects the escalation by ordering a nuclear strike on Qom (Qum), Iran's main religious city and home of its unelected holy leader, Ayatollah Mohammed Daryaei, a fictional successor to Ayatollah Ruhollah Khomeini. Ryan's refusal to confirm the launch order (no other designated cabinet secretaries are handy), results in Fowler suffering a nervous breakdown. His presidential power preempted, Fowler resigns a few days later. Durling becomes president.

Not once did the president inform the congressional leadership, which is probably the best that can be done during a fast-moving crisis. Moreover, during the crisis, Fowler orders the FBI to stop any broadcast by any outlet of what was happening in Denver at the moment, arguably to prevent nationwide panic, as well as to "control the story." This is also counterintuitive, as presidents are very quick to inform the public when a crisis is underway. A nuclear strike would also trigger the emergency broadcast system, which government uses to inform citizens about what is expected of them during an emergency or disaster. Even this does not come into play in Clancy's fictional plot.

Now the adversary changes with the administration.

In *Debt of Honor*, Durling guides the U.S. through a trade war and a shooting war with Japan. The book came out in 1994, well after Japan's growing economic competition with the U.S. was ended by a lengthy recession that began in the early 1990s, though the public's perception of a powerful Japan may have still been fresh.

Today, Japan is very reluctant to assert power. The country was militaristic and very expansionist from the 1890s to the 1940s, receiving a very hard comeuppance primarily at the hands of the United States and to lesser degrees by Britain, Russia, and China. Total destruction of Japan's cities by U.S. firebombing, climaxing with the atomic bomb attacks on Hiroshima and Nagasaki, killed Japanese civilians by the hundreds of thousands. With a past marked by severe defeat and immense human suffering, Japan today is very reluctant to deploy its forces outside of the home islands. Only recently has Japan sent peacekeeping forces abroad, in this instance to Iraq in 2003–04. Neighboring states are also very reluctant to see Japan do more than defend itself, and the lack of apologies for brutal occupations of the past still mar Japanese relations with China, South Korea, and many other states in east Asia.

In Clancy's geopolitical world, Japan will use its military to assert its place on the world stage. The government is but a puppet in the hands of the *zaibatsu*, Japan's informal clique of company executives and industrialists. Prime among them is Yamata, who wants to reoccupy the Marianas, acquire nuclear weapons, and take control of Russia's resource-rich eastern Siberian territories.

The U.S.-Japanese trade tensions of the 1980s were already in decline when Clancy resurrected them for his plotline. The World Trade Organization, which adjudicates trade disputes, was not in existence when the book was written, and the trade imbalance with Japan weighs heavily on the U.S., as factories here close in defeat to Japanese manufacturing prowess. When a Japanese carmaker ships a new auto with a defective gas tank to the U.S., resulting in some fiery fatalities, the U.S.

retaliates by imposing the same crazy importation rules on Japanese goods that Japan imposes on its imports.

Durling's presidency is not exactly popular, as tough economic times undercut his agenda. While pretty good on domestic matters, Durling's foreign policy is in need of aid. He has already fired his national security advisor Tom Loch (who followed Fowler's Elizabeth Elliot) and has tapped Jack Ryan for the job.[4]

Traditionally, there is some tension between the National Security Council and the State Department. When the job of national security advisor is done properly, the president is informed of all foreign threats and problems facing the United States and his options for dealing with them. The national security advisor can be likened to an orchestra conductor, who manages the inputs on policy from the secretaries of state and defense, the service chiefs, the CIA, and other actors in foreign policy. Brent Scowcroft, who held this office for Gerald Ford and George H.W. Bush, is looked upon as the best practitioner in the history of this office.

But more often than not, the national security advisor can run the president's own mini–State Department from the White House. Again, there are good and bad examples of this. Henry Kissinger did well here, brokering the U.S. rapprochement with Communist China during the Nixon presidency. This was a nice stroke of realpolitik, as the U.S. made up for its decline following the Vietnam War by picking up an informal ally to maintain the balance of power with the Soviet Union.

On the downside, national security advisor Robert "Bud" McFarlane engineered the working parts of the Iran-Contra scandal, the byzantine attempt to bypass a congressional ban on aid to the Nicaraguan counterrevolutionaries by using funds from arms sales to Iran. The expected return favor was the release of U.S. hostages held in Lebanon by Iranian-backed Shiite terrorists. McFarlane opened up the Reagan presidency to a politically crippling scandal that risked Reagan's impeachment.

As national security advisor, Ryan is no Scowcroft.

Not-so-nice operations are crafted in Ryan's office, with Durling's approval, to reassert American power wherever it has been checked.

Clancy's other focal hero, John Clark, in partnership with Ding Chavez (another hero from *Clear and Present Danger*), successfully kidnap Somali warlord Mohamed Abdul Corp. (Corp is the stand-in for Mohammed Farah Aideed, the Mogadishu warlord who inflicted the defeat on U.S. Rangers detailed in *Black Hawk Down*.)

Durling's political high point is a disarmament treaty signed with the Russians, dismantling all intercontinental ballistic missiles (ICBMs). Traditionally, a president leans on foreign policy in the latter half of his term because that is where he can exert some power and control, as the domestic agenda falls prey to politics and turf wars.

But Durling's moment of statesmanship is cut short by Japan's covert and overt attack on the U.S. Yamata uses his influence as part-owner of the Wall Street fund management firm Columbus Group to trigger a false meltdown of the stock market. Two U.S. aircraft carriers are crippled in an "accidental" firing of torpedoes from a Japanese destroyer. Two U.S. nuclear attack submarines are also sunk by Japanese subs during the same naval exercise. And Japan air-lands several divisions to seize Saipan and Guam.

Durling has his hands full, and knows he must act.

The "big meeting" takes place in the Oval Office, as Durling, Ryan, the secretary of defense (unnamed), Hanson (state), Fiedler (treasury), and Chief of Staff van Damm start mulling the options.

In wartime, an inner "war cabinet" gets formed to craft options and share information. Usually, it will be the president, vice president, national security advisor, secretaries of state and defense, chairman of the Joint Chiefs of Staff, and others as needed. The second Gulf War is a good example of this. Bush's inner war cabinet included Vice President Dick Cheney, Secretary of State Colin Powell, Secretary of Defense Donald Rumsfeld, Central Command Commander in Chief Gen. Tommy Franks, CIA Director George Tenet, and National Security Advisor

Condoleezza Rice. Chief of Staff Andy Card and press secretary Ari Fleischer provided links to the press.

In Clancy's Japan war scenario, Durling's "inner cabinet" analyzes the chaotic situation. Something must be done to reopen the markets after Friday's big meltdown. Ed Kealty, the vice president and Ted Kennedy stand-in, will be resigning after being embroiled in a sex scandal that resulted in an ex-paramour's suicide, and a possible criminal rape charge (suppressed to allow for a quiet resignation). The Indian situation regarding Sri Lanka must be taken into account while also focusing on the other big crisis, the Japanese invasion of Guam and Saipan.

Durling commits the U.S. to war. News of the Japanese invasion is slow to leak, thanks to a news blackout and the media's preoccupation with the meltdown of financial markets. Durling takes a lot of political heat once the damage becomes known, but stays the course as Ryan sets into motion the machinery to craft the winning strategy.

Clancy's depiction of the U.S. order of battle is not far removed from reality. It really was cut down by half after the cold war ended. It is with the depleted arsenal and a few high-tech weapons in prototype that the U.S. counterattacks.

The war is fast, furious, and high-tech, with Durling absent from planning the finer details. Rather, the president is informed of events after they happen.

Durling, a Vietnam veteran, understands how war works at the front and how the mission comes first. He is willing to delegate the fighting of the war to his generals and admirals. He is the president.

And the war goes well. The U.S. wins.

Durling's reelection prospects are much improved.

Contrast this with the rough political fortunes of presidents George H.W. Bush (father) and George W. Bush (son), for whom "victory in war" did not add much to their political fortunes when facing reelection.

In real life, if the economy tanks and people lose their jobs, a resounding victory in a splendid little war counts for less.

The Leap from Veep

Durling taps Ryan to be the next vice president, replacing Kealty. He makes it clear to Ryan that the job is to run only through January. As VP, Ryan will oversee all aspects of national security and foreign policy, making up for Durling's lack of depth in these areas.

Ryan is willing to do his duty, even though he is an "implied Republican," serving an "implied Democrat."

The process of making Ryan vice president takes place during the president's State of the Union address, which traditionally is given some time in late January or early February. The Senate conveniently confirms Ryan's nomination by voice vote. (Ryan has yet to be brought into the chamber to be sworn in.) In real life, House Minority Leader Gerald Ford (R-Michigan) and former New York governor Nelson Rockefeller both faced Senate committees to confirm their nominations to be vice president. The hearings played out over days instead of several pages of storytelling.

Durling's proposed role for Ryan's vice presidency fits in nicely with the concept of the modern vice president, born during the actual Carter administration. Carter had vowed that his vice president would play a meaningful role in his administration instead of being the dummy kept out of the loop, waiting to step in if the president died. Vice President Walter Mondale was very much a partner in Carter's administration, which unfortunately worked against him in his failed bid for the presidency in 1984 against incumbent Ronald Reagan. The Carter-Mondale administration was a popular barb hurled by many Republicans against Mondale, but truthful in that the veep was politically joined at the hip with the president.

George H.W. Bush, Dan Quayle, Al Gore, and Dick Cheney all served as vice presidents in the Mondale mold. Bush may have had a questionable portfolio given possible involvement in the Iran-Contra scandal, but his numerous diplomatic trips built powerful contacts that overcame many problems organizing Desert Shield/Desert Storm.

Quayle, despite his lightweight image, was kept in the loop throughout Desert Shield/Desert Storm, attending all inner-cabinet meetings guiding war strategy. Gore was given the environmental portfolio, as well as the regular duty of meeting his Russian counterpart, Viktor Chernomirdin, on a semiannual basis to keep U.S.-Russian relations on track.

Had Clancy's timeline proceeded without the fiery ending of *Debt of Honor*, Ryan's vice presidency would have borne a startling resemblance to that of Dick Cheney, the current vice president under George W. Bush. Cheney was given the energy portfolio, but found his brief expanding quickly in the months leading up to the second Gulf War (March–April 2003) to take in operational guidance and political strategy for that conflict. In effect, Ryan would have been exercising power in the same way as Cheney.

Fictional worlds, however, provide more fortuitous opportunities for heroes.

Keeping in the spirit of the thriller, with its sudden plot turns and twists, Clancy has an embittered minor character crash a JAL Boeing 747 into the south end of the Capitol during the State of the Union address, thus killing most of the U.S. government. While Clancy did this to wipe the slate clean for a Ryan presidency, he could not have foreseen the resemblance between his fictional event and September 11, 2001, when two hijacked airliners leveled New York's World Trade Center while a third slammed into the Pentagon.

George W. Bush was out of Washington when the U.S. was attacked that day. A practical problem then emerges, typical of any crisis: What is happening?

When in doubt, protect the president.

Bush spent much of the day airborne, first touching down at Barksdale AFB in Louisiana before flying to the old Strategic Air Command center at Offutt Air Force Base outside Omaha, Nebraska, then returning to Washington around in the early evening. He addressed the nation promptly to provide reassurance.

In the fictional world, Ryan and his family are in one of the Capitol's underground tunnels on their way to the House chamber when the plane hits. A trio of secret service agents hustle him out. At Ryan's request, they head straight to the marine barracks in downtown Washington (street location—Eighth and I). After being sworn in by a federal judge, Ryan makes a stirring impromptu address to the nation to a live TV crew on the street corner, assuring all that the U.S. will not be defeated by the disaster.

In truth, the U.S. political structure is quite sound. Eliminating a dictator can trigger a civil war in other countries as competing cliques vie for power in a game with no rules. Here, the system works on autopilot—no matter what crisis evolves, the Constitution has some mechanism to make sure there is always a president.

The Ryan presidency marks a sharp break point in Clancy's fiction, to be fleshed out in greater detail in *Executive Orders*. The author's political views and judgments now fill more space in the book, running alongside the story. Despite this, Clancy's fictional president is still bound by the same rules as his real-life counterparts and the manner of Ryan's accession, while by the rules, is awkward. Like Gerald Ford, Jack Ryan was not elected at all. Ford was House minority leader when an embattled President Nixon tapped him to be vice president following Spiro Agnew's resignation in 1973. Upon Nixon's resignation in August 1974, Ford became the first unelected president in American history, and when he ran for election in his own right in 1976, he lost to former Georgia governor Jimmy Carter. (Ironically, Ford's political ambition was to become speaker of the House—third in line of succession, not president.)

Any similarity between Ford and Ryan, however, ends there.

(In all fairness, Ford was dealt a pretty bad set of cards when he placed his right hand on the Bible and solemnly swore to do his best. In the cruel balance of the cold war, the United States lost Vietnam, Cambodia, Angola, Mozambique, and Ethiopia to communism during Ford's watch, and the Cambodian seizure of the U.S. freighter *Mayaguez* prompted a rescue that turned into a deadly ambush, killing

over forty marines. Moreover, Ford pardoned Richard Nixon, which after all the political ill will generated by the Watergate scandal did not
endear Ford to the masses.)

The wreckage Ryan confronts is quite different—reassuring the nation in the wake of the kamikaze attack, rebuilding the U.S. government, surviving a constitutional challenge from recently resigned vice
president Ed Kealty, and fighting a war against a recently unified Iran-
Iraq . . . and don't forget the terrorist strike with the Ebola virus.

All this happens less than ten months before Election Day.

Crisis Management

Crises rarely pile on so quickly in real life. Looking at some past "worst
case" scenarios, we find Eisenhower facing the Suez crisis and the Hungarian revolution at the same time in 1956. Ike opted for settling the
Suez crisis, which got the French, British, and Israelis to knock off their
war against Egypt to recover the recently nationalized canal. But Eisenhower chose not to confront the Soviets over their bloody reoccupation
of Hungary. U.S. aid was limited to accepting refugees fleeing over the
border into Austria.

The current administration of George W. Bush is also quite busy,
handling a low-level counterinsurgency campaign in occupied Iraq, another counterinsurgency against Taliban and Al Qaeda remnants in
Afghanistan, and yet another American intervention in Haiti. All these
balls had to be juggled in March 2004, with a reelection campaign getting underway.[5]

A more massive headache could only be imagined, but in fiction
that is doable.

Ryan has to restore the government, now bereft of most of its senators, representatives, Supreme Court justices, service chiefs, and cabinet secretaries. Many characters that made regular appearances in past
Clancy novels as "doers" are finding themselves promoted into top slots
to head the agencies they work for. Dan Murray becomes FBI director.
Scott Adler is now secretary of state. Ed and Mary Pat Foley become

head of CIA and CIA's directorate of operations, respectively. Robby Jackson is made J-3 (head of operations) for the Joint Chiefs of Staff (and later will become vice president). Tony Bretano leaves TRW, Inc. for Defense. George Winston, head of Columbus Group, a Wall Street fund management firm, goes to Treasury.

Many of these appointments are technically recess appointments, as the characters must exercise power without being first confirmed by the Senate. In more normal times, the recess appointment is a tool rarely used by the president, as it can be politically offensive to the Senate. Bill Clinton once used a recess appointment to fill the post of assistant attorney general for civil rights. George W. Bush likewise used the same power to appoint several federal appeals court judges after seeing those nominations stymied by Democratic filibusters in the Senate.

Filling Senate vacancies is a power exercised by governors, usually picking someone of their own party. The implied Democratic majority went up in flames when the JAL 747 hit the Capitol. They are replaced by an implied Republican majority as more than half the states in Clancy's storyline have governors belonging to "the other party."

House elections are slated for later in the year. (Clancy is not very specific about the timeline.) In one of many speeches to the nation, Ryan asks voters to elect new representatives who are not professional politicians or lawyers. In Clancy's worldview, lawyers and politicians only gum up the works, playing for points rather than doing a good job on behalf of constituents.

The standing of Congress in the public eye was quite low in the mid-1990s, when Clancy penned his most massive missive of the Ryan saga. *Gridlock* was the term used to describe how little got done by a Democratic president and a Republican Congress, though the proper term for this is *divided government*. Making the situation worse in Congress was the lack of comity and an abundance of political attacks, which all substituted for debate.

The Clinton impeachment was no more than a bitter climax of a foul trend. Lucky for the free world that Ryan was not so badly hobbled.

Where Is History?

Ryan's first presidential crisis occurs early in the book, shortly after Durling's presidential funeral. Iran had planted a sleeper agent who managed to infiltrate the security detail of Iraqi dictator Saddam Hussein. At the appointed moment, the sleeper agent pulls out his pistol and guns down the Iraqi strongman during a mass rally carried live on Iraqi TV.

Saddam should have been so lucky to die in 1996!

In December 2003, he was captured by troops of the Fourth Infantry Division on occupation duty in Iraq. He now faces trial for crimes against humanity in a newly re-formed Iraqi court. Hussein had been toppled from power in April 2003, by a controversial U.S. invasion that is still the subject of bitter debate by those on the left and right.

Hussein's sons Uday and Qusay, as we recall, were not so lucky, dying in a gangland-style shootout with troopers from the 101st Airborne in July 2003. Uday Hussein was the designated successor until his dad deemed him too violent and unstable. Succession was given to Qusay. Neither was present in Clancy's story to take the reins in a headless Iraq.

Leaving the realm of fact for fiction, the Republican Guard generals and Baath Party officials are at a loss for what to do next. Normally in many dictatorships, a strongman emerges to take over and eliminate rivals. This can be done gently, as in the Soviet Union where Khrushchev shelved Malenkov, or when Brezhnev sent Khrushchev to an early retirement . . . or it can be bloodier, like Laurent Kabila taking over Zaire with the help of foreign troops after kleptocrat-in-chief Mobutu dies in exile. No such luck in Iraq.

Here Iran's chief bad guy Daryaei, a protégé of the late Ayatollah Khomeini, sends word that he will facilitate the flight to exile of any army general who wants it. In the novel, we are only talking about dozens of generals, their families, bodyguards, and mistresses, and Sudan is willing to accept the lot. If this had to happen in reality, the numbers would have been far more daunting. The Iraqi Army, after the first

Gulf War of 1990–91 saw its strength cut from over one million to about five hundred thousand. But it was still run by eleven thousand generals and fourteen thousand colonels. The U.S. Army, which is similar in size today, only has three hundred generals and 3,500 colonels.[6]

You do the math.

Now, to be fair, Iran did not have to provide transit for the whole star-ridden command horde in Clancy's novel. The top tier was enough. The offer did not extend to the Republican Guard, nor did it go down to the brigadiers and colonels that ran the divisions and brigades. The offer was not extended to the Iraqi Baath Party.

Daryaei's overall political ambition is to rebuild the caliphate—the political realm of Islam that once extended from Morocco to central Asia. This is a very tall order, since this geographic span is divided between twenty-three different countries (twenty-four if you count Palestine; go for twenty-five if Kashmir ever is detached from India). There are significant ethnic differences that draw the borders. True, it is an Arab world, until you get to the Iran-Iraq border. Once crossed, the language changes to Farsi and the ethnicity is Persian, not Arab. Faith changes slightly with language and accent, as Iran is Shia while the bulk of the Arab world is Sunni. The difference sounds as casual as Protestant and Catholic—still Christian, but, in fact, the difference is quite profound, dating back to Islam's early days, when a successor to Muhammad had to be found following his ascension as Allah's last prophet. Go further east and the fractures get worse. Central Asia is divided between Turkic- and Persian-speaking peoples—so much for Kazakhstan, Turkmenistan, Tajikistan, Uzbekistan, and Kyrgyzstan. Cross into Afghanistan, and you have Tajiks, Uzbeks, and Shiite Hazaras vying for power with Sunni Pashtuns. Cross the Pakistani border and the same Pashtuns are again intertwined with other tribes and ethnic groups before reaching the Urdu-speaking city folk in Punjab, and don't forget that Pakistan is 20 percent Shiite. These differences of ethnicity, faith, and language cannot be easily dismissed.

If there was ever a time when Persia/Iran could have stretched beyond its natural borders, it was in the early 1500s. Persia was then a vassal of the dying Mongol empire. Ismail al Safawi took Persia out of the Mongol orbit and forced the masses at swordpoint to convert from Sunni to Shia Islam. Safawi's grand strategy was to extend his rule into central Asia, then turn his attention to his western borders with the Ottoman empire. But plans miscarried when the Shiites raised their rebellion along the Ottoman border while Safawi's forces were enmeshed in central Asia. Ottoman Sultan Suleiman (the Magnificent) crushed the uprising and invaded Persia, but his troops refused to march farther east than Tabriz. Empowering the Caucasian but Sunni Muslim Kurds to police the border, Suleiman rushed his forces to pluck a declining Egypt before Safawi could. The spiritual prize was the caliph of Cairo, then the chief spokesman and interpreter of the Muslim faith—the closest thing then to an "Islamic pope."

Fast-forward five hundred years. Focusing on Iraq exclusively, it is hard to see how Iran could pull off an annexation, given the difficulties the United States has had over the past year occupying the same country. Granted, many of these vexing issues only came to light to the general public because the American media was there to report about the hassles of governance on a daily basis.

Long ruled by a Sunni Muslim minority, Iraq only stayed together through sheer repression of the Shiite majority (60 percent of the population) and the Kurdish minority (20 percent). The Kurds are divided between two clans (Talabani and Barzani) who for now work together because they have materially gained by such an alliance under American oversight. (No pun intended here, since the Kurdish region thrived with de facto autonomy under the northern no-fly zone policed by the U.S. Air Force.)

The issue of Shia rule becomes more complex as the center of this faith is found in Iraq, not Iran. Najaf is the burial place of Imam Ali, the Prophet Muhammad's son-in-law, in whom Shia argue the line of descent should have been traced following Muhammad's Ascension. Karbala was the site of a battle where the Shiite cause lost out to what became the

Sunni branch of the faith. Iran's holy city of Qom is a place where many Shiite imams attended seminaries, but following Hussein's overthrow by the U.S., Shia's theological center of gravity has returned to Najaf.

If Najaf is Shia's Vatican City, then Grand Ayatollah Ali Sistani is the first among four equals who can issue teachings, or fatwas, on questions of faith and practice. His influence is deep, profound, and direct. The four grand ayatollahs form the Hawza, or governing body that oversees the network of Shia seminaries in and around Najaf. The U.S. suffered some embarrassment and had to change its plans for developing interim self-government in Iraq owing to Sistani's objections over the plan's details. Yet the fictional Iranian Ayatollah Daryaei suffers no such friction from the Hawza while imposing a theocratic union on Iraq. One may argue that Shiites stick together. But the reality belies the claim. Many Iraqi Shia imams who ducked out in Iran during the Saddam years have no desire to let Iran call the shots in their own country. Currently, Shiite politics is split among several parties and leaders. Sistani can move the greatest number, but Dawa, SCIRI, and the street movement coalescing around junior Ayatollah Moqtadeh Al Sadr are also competitive. As a cleric, Sistani will not involve himself in politics. That does not stop others from trying.

Now return to Jack Ryan's situation. Saudi Arabian Prince Ali expresses his concern to President Ryan that the United Islamic Republic (Iran plus Iraq) will make a move south to seize the oil fields as well as the Islamic holy places of Mecca and Medina. Again, the same occupation worries that hobble the U.S. in Iraq would also become evident if Iran (UIR) moved on Saudi Arabia. On the plus side, most of Saudi Arabia's Shiites are concentrated in the northeastern corner of the country, where most of the kingdom's oil fields are found, theoretically making the takeover that much easier to keep. But the larger minus is the Wahhabi variant of Sunni Islam that is practiced in Saudi Arabia, which regards the Shiites as apostates. (This alone makes Saudi Shiites second-class citizens in their own country.) Such strongly held convictions would not make an Iranian occupation easy in real life.

In fiction, these little technicalities are quietly overlooked and made to disappear.

Too bad they count for so much in the real world.

Domestic Headaches

As if the growing UIR problem was not enough for President Ryan, things also heat up on the home front. Recently resigned vice president Kealty claims his resignation never went through, as the recently killed Secretary of State Hanson sent the note back asking for some revisions. (Kealty had one of his loyalists at State purloin the letter from the dead Hanson's desk.) Resignation has only happened three times in American history: in the 1830s, when Vice President John Calhoun resigned, again in 1973 with the resignation of Vice President Spiro Agnew, and finally in August 1974, with the resignation of President Richard Nixon.

Ryan is a novice at presidential politics, a point that is held against him by a chorus of regular politicians, lobbyists, and foreign leaders ill-disposed to the United States. He founders in several press conferences as reporters take issue and question him about conservative Supreme Court appointments and less than precise language over the relationship of Taiwan to China (despite the fact that the U.S. is officially ambiguous about this). These distractions are small, but vexing enough to throw the Ryan administration "off message."

The presidency is a bully pulpit. Used well, a president can dictate his agenda and force his opponents to the defense in reply or criticism. But when a president is tripped off message, he loses the initiative and must play defense. This robs him of the momentum he needs to drive his points home and enact his agenda. Ryan finds himself repeatedly wrong-footed because he has not mastered this process. A novice president, he is even less qualified as a politician.

To cut through such clutter, a president has to restate his case in a friendlier, more controlled venue. A commonly used tool is a presidential speech given to a friendly audience at a planned event. This makes for good television and limits press coverage to the president's words.

Any criticism is contradicted by the image of the president looking presidential.

It comes down to controlling the message.

Ronald Reagan was a master at this, and his example has been followed by all of his successors. Avoid press conferences, as they are too unpredictable and can make a president look bad. Stick to public appearances and speeches, giving the press nothing more than the event to cover, without opportunity to ask questions. Go with a winning script and avoid improvisation—two classic Hollywood formulas.

Here Clancy writes about Ryan getting out of the White House to make speeches before friendly audiences in friendly states. Enthusiastic crowds and warm applause bathe Ryan's ego, reassuring him that the nation is with him even if the players inside the Washington, D.C. beltway are not.

Absent from the story is the fact that it is a presidential election year. With all potential challengers killed off by the kamikaze attack on the Capitol, Ryan is pretty much unopposed. But Clancy ignores how the presidential campaign plays out against the backdrop of rebuilding a stricken government or dealing with a myriad of foreign crises, as this is not where the concerns of his plot lie.

In the real world, wartime presidents don't get a free pass on elections. Abraham Lincoln, Franklin Roosevelt, William McKinley, Harry Truman, Richard Nixon, and George W. Bush all had to face the voters while bullets were flying elsewhere.

A president has to be judged by his results. The Union Army taking Atlanta helped Lincoln's reelection in 1864. FDR eagerly pushed the invasion of North Africa in November 1942 to show the electorate that he was doing something about the war—even if the timing was too close to midterm elections. In 1944, FDR was not shy about hitting his Republican opponents over the head with their prewar isolationism to drive the point home that voting Democratic was the patriotic choice.[7]

McKinley and later Theodore Roosevelt presided over a dirty little counterinsurgency in the Philippines, which did not rankle the public as badly as Korea or Vietnam, thanks to the absence of a twenty-four-hour news cycle. Lack of results in Korea resulted in Truman losing the New Hampshire primary in 1952 to Democratic challenger Estes Kefauver, and this convinced Truman it was time to hang it up. The Vietnam War drove Lyndon Johnson out of office, making his reelection dubious after seeing challenger Senator Eugene McCarthy pick up 40 percent of the vote in the 1968 New Hampshire primary. The Vietnam War dragged on throughout Nixon's first term in office, but the prospect of peace was very close come election day, 1972. That didn't hurt Nixon at the polls. The problematic Iraq war did not help George W. Bush's standing in the polls, but he managed to get re-elected despite the body count.[8]

As for what the imaginary voters would have said about the Ryan presidency in the alternate world of 1996/2000, we have scant idea. Clancy passes over this point, writing few words to serve as clues. Clancy is not interested in examining the details of drafting policy, which can be likened to making sausages, even though this is how things get done in Washington. He skips over the dreary daily repetition of the presidential campaign. Action, not process, is at the core of the Jack Ryan agenda. Even when Ryan makes policy, it is still action, and very brief.

Scandal: The Skeleton in the Closet

The Ryan administration is not exactly scandal-free, either, but scandal here is a loose term, at best.

Ryan's secret CIA past becomes public while he is president. Ex-KGB chief Gerasimov surfaces in Virginia. Ryan induced Gerasimov to "defect" while he was plotting to overthrow Narmanov by revealing the truth behind the loss of the *Red October*. (This was a key event in *Cardinal of the Kremlin*.)

Also coming to light is the U.S. secret war in Colombia, which was the centerpiece of *Clear and Present Danger*. Ryan's role in the after-the-fact scandal is peripheral, being one who cleaned up the mess rather than make it. After uncovering the secret deployment of light infantry teams to eliminate Colombian cocaine processing labs, Ryan goes in country to get the teams out, following a move made by then National Security Advisor James Cutter to leave them there to be eliminated by the Colombian drug lords while maintaining deniability.

At one point, fictional NBC anchorman Tom Donner uses this information to sandbag Ryan during a live interview (to make up for a taped interview that was allegedly "ruined" when the videotape passed through the White House metal detectors). The interview produces more heat than light as Ryan steadfastly refuses to discuss any intelligence matters in public. The fictional interview is reminiscent of a similar conflict between CBS anchorman Dan Rather and then Vice President George H.W. Bush, who in January 1988 was again seeking the presidency. Rather spent over ten live minutes of the *CBS Evening News* trying to pin Bush on some disturbing points in the Iran-Contra scandal. Bush got fed up and questioned Rather's professionalism in a previous incident when he had walked off the set of the *CBS Evening News* because it was being preempted by the U.S. Open tennis match. It was not the finest hour for broadcast journalism, or the institution of the presidency.

The information used to play "gotcha" with Ryan was leaked to Donner by Kealty. Okay, such melodrama is the necessary stuff of over-the-top thriller fiction, and this can be easily given a pass. Donner's coanchor, John Plumber, finds out the subterfuge from *Washington Post* reporter Dan Holtzman. (Holtzman researched a deep article on Ryan's past that was more favorable, but not in print yet.) Principled to the end, Plumber gives his last commentary for NBC news. His unscripted piece details the lie told by Donner and his unfair advantage interviewing the president.

This part of the story line finds Clancy focusing some skepticism on whether the press can be fair, objective, and unbiased when dealing with the White House. Public trust of the press is pretty low, given the steady stream of scandals that afflicted this institution throughout the 1990s. While the press helped uncover the truth about Vietnam and Watergate, earning it enormous public trust, that goodwill was blown away as a number of journalists falsified or fabricated sensational stories, in effect placing fame and fortune above the ethics that govern the profession. Start with Janet Cooke winning a Pulitzer Prize for the *Washington Post*, writing about a fictional eight-year-old heroin addict in the 1980s. The *Wall Street Journal* also suffered in the mid-1980s, when R. Foster Winans made available drafts of his "Heard It On the Street" column to a rich investor before seeing it in the paper the next day. CNN's Peter Arnett blew away his credibility when presenting a badly researched story on U.S. covert operations in Laos that involved the possible use of nerve gas. The *New York Times* foundered on the shoals of untruth when it could not block the repeated fictions and mistakes made by its reporter Jayson Blair. *USA Today* also fired senior reporter Jack Kelley for fabricating a number of sensational stories aboard.

Most of the working press does an honest day's work, telling the news as best as it can be told by deadline. But today it is more common for news to be sold, not told, now that TV news shows and newspapers must place profits above news. Even without the previously mentioned scandals, much of the media's credibility has been compromised by the business of journalism, which places higher ratings and circulation above fairness and accuracy. Even this reality gets a passing nod from Clancy, as he places the profession's scanty virtue on the print side rather than with television. Nevertheless, Clancy's criticism of the press pales in comparison to those leveled by media critics and pundits.

The Vultures Come Home to Roost

As the plot continues, an alliance of convenience takes shape between India, Iran, and the People's Republic of China. India wants a free hand to take Australia for its open spaces and resources. Iran wants to take over the Arabian Peninsula, central Asia, and Pakistan. China wants to move north into Siberia.

Growing states with territorial ambitions were a reality of the nineteenth century, not the twenty-first. Clancy's fiction reflects a worldview more familiar to a Victorian Englishman than a post–cold war American. Again, a tall tale worth reading can't be told without a bit of exaggeration, so its time to once again issue the author another pass from criticism, but the point must be compared to modern times, and the comparison is still found wanting.

Australia may be resource rich, but it is water poor. The majority of the nation's population of twenty-five million is concentrated in the southeastern quarter, as well as that continent's limited number of rivers carrying freshwater. Already many rivers fail to reach the sea, as much of the water has already been drawn to support farms and cities. How likely is it that India can park any fraction of its population of one billion in a continent that is mostly desert and barely has enough water to support twenty-five million? Tall tales are fun, but they can be brought up short by facts.

Revisit Iran's desire to control Arabia, central Asia, and Pakistan. The points made previously illuminate what an administrative headache such a challenge would be, given the dizzying array of ethnic groups, languages, and religious disparities. They may be all Muslims, but not all are Shia or Sunni and the difference matters.

Now consider China's ambition to expand northward. Far-fetched? Russia's far-eastern maritime province, best known for its port of Vladivostok, was wrested from China's control in 1861. The claim is not forgotten, but has not been pressed by China as it has been with Taiwan. Currently, twenty-five million Russians out of a national population of one hundred and fifty million populate Siberia. The harsh climate is not attracting any new Russian migration, though four million Chinese have gone north of the border in search of work, and Russo-Chinese relations right now seem to be stable. China wants modern warships, subs, and fighters, and Russia provides these for a good price. The purchases are meant to provide a capability to project power into the Taiwan Straits to reacquire "the renegade province" by force if need be, and invading Siberia is not an acknowledged war aim of the PRC to date.

That's the situation in the real world.

Now, back to Jack Ryan's situation.

As the plot thickens, the war aim of the anti-U.S. unholy alliance is to go one step further than Japan and India did in *Debt of Honor*. The U.S. may be the sole superpower, but its forces are half of what they were at the height of the cold war, and they can't be everywhere at once. During the Clinton administration, the Pentagon still espoused the two-war standard—the ability to fight two major regional conflicts at the same time.

The expected worst-case scenario was another war with Iraq coupled with renewed conflict with North Korea at the same time, with plans and projected allocations set to meet those needs.

The truth falls far short of doctrine.

The air force had to give short shrift to its policing of the no-fly zones in northern and southern Iraq during the Kosovo crisis in 1999. (It fell outside of the simultaneous Iraq/North Korean War scenario.) With the same force structure, America is very hard-pressed to fight an active counterinsurgency in Iraq while doing the same in Afghanistan and keeping an eye on North Korea. A major effort on one front deprives resources from the other, and in this case it was Afghanistan that had to be placed on the strategic back burner while Iraq was brought down from a hot war to a simmering occupation, plus nation building thrown in for good measure.

To stretch American commitments beyond the breaking point, Clancy crafts the following scenario: First, Chinese exercises in the Taiwan Straits conflict with Taiwanese forces. A dogfight between PRC and Taiwanese warplanes results in the downing of a nearby jetliner, which later is found to be a deliberate shoot down by the PRC. Acting Secretary of State Scott Adler is dispatched to mediate while a U.S. carrier battle group is shifted from the Indian Ocean to waters east of Taiwan.[9]

The second act is the growing threat of the UIR to Saudi Arabia. Joint exercises between paired Iraqi and Iranian divisions point to impending action. This would be pretty tough to do given differences in language and culture. Differences in training and doctrine would also have to be resolved. In Clancy's timeline, that resolution takes a few weeks, not a few years.

The forces on hand to block such a move are limited.

The U.S. does pre-position tanks, infantry fighting vehicles, and trucks in places where it expects to fight a war. Flying in troops who then man this equipment can yield a division-sized deployment in a couple of days, rather than a month if all that equipment had to move by ship. In this fictional scenario, there are pre-positioned stocks that can field a brigade each in Kuwait and Saudi Arabia, followed by four maritime prepositioning ships based at Diego Garcia that can equip a third brigade.

The third act is the deployment of the Indian Navy, with its two pint-sized aircraft carriers, taking a blocking line between the entrance of the Persian Gulf and the U.S. base in Diego Garcia Island. This is a problem for the U.S., which in the scenario has shifted its only available carrier battle group to Taiwan, and running the Indian gauntlet will be the problem of any cruisers, destroyers, and frigates on hand.

The next act is a bioweapons strike on the U.S. by Iranian-sponsored terrorists. The terrorists visit ten cities, dropping off aerosol cans (disguised as cans of shaving cream) that will spray a variant of the deadly and contagious airborne Ebola virus. While the original aim is to spread terror and distract the U.S., it has the inadvertent effect of pinning down many American units as a few Ebola cases crop up in every division—except units training at Ft. Irwin and a third based in Israel.

The fifth act is a squad-sized attack on the day care center where President Ryan's youngest daughter spends her day. This results in an action-packed firefight, but distracts from the larger plot. (The kid lives, the bad guys die.) It makes for a good read, but is relatively inconsequential to Clancy's overall scenario.

The sixth act is the presence of a sleeper agent on the president's secret service detail who will kill Ryan at an opportune moment, which of course fails.

The unlikely scenario shows the U.S. being stretched on the rack of its obligations. The U.S. still manages to improvise a response by relying on units that are not affected by the plague. Sent to Saudi Arabia are North Carolina National Guard mechanized brigade training with an armored cavalry regiment at Ft. Irwin, a second armored cavalry regiment deployed in Israel, two squadrons of F-16s also in Israel, and an air force fighter wing based in Idaho.

(The operational details of the fictional deployment will be dealt with in a later chapter.)

The action is quick and bloody, as the troops from these units are airlifted to the theater of operations, marry up with their pre-positioned equipment, and trounce the UIR forces in a few days. Even though the U.S. is strapped for sufficient forces, the French and the British are not asked to provide troops, as they did in the first Gulf War of 1990–91. Saudis and Kuwaitis fight for their countries with their limited armies, but no other states pitch in.

Note that during the entire crisis, the U.S. does not go before the UN to ask for a Security Council resolution approving the action or condemning the UIR invasion. The U.S. is attacked by the Ebola bioweapon, and while a NATO member, makes no invocation of the NATO alliance (an attack on one member is an attack on all). There is literally no diplomacy exercised before the shooting starts, save an assurance to Saudi Arabia and Kuwait that America will defend its allies. Clancy is not concerned with these details—they detract from the action and can be dropped from the Jack Ryan Agenda.

Diplomacy for Ryan means issuing a direct threat to India not to interfere with U.S. naval movements from Diego Garcia to Dhahran. Saudi and Kuwaiti diplomacy fails to open up any dialogue with the UIR to prevent the crisis. Likewise, acting Secretary of State Scott Adler makes no headway with the UIR—or the People's Republic of China over the downing of the jetliner.

In short, diplomacy does not work in Clancy's geopolitics, but it is a necessary step that must be exercised before the shooting starts. It is also useful for conveying threats.

Finally, once it is ascertained that Iran was behind the Ebola strike,

Ryan orders Daryaei's residence bombed in a precision strike by a pair of F-117 stealth fighters. (This necessitates Ryan overturning Ford's executive order prohibiting the U.S. from assassinating rival heads of state.)

The U.S. has a well-earned grudge against the fictional Daryaei, who was the indirect backer of the nuclear strike on Denver as well as the direct perpetrator who orders the Ebola strike. Ryan will not countenance a retaliatory strike against a nation, with its inevitable "collateral damage" and certain injury and death to nearby civilians. (Nuking Qum certainly would have done that!)

The air strike is carried live on TV, as Daryaei's residence is blown to bits at a time when he is known to be home. As Americans watch the house explode, Ryan delivers his ultimatum to Iran: allow allied Russian technicians to inspect and secure Iran's bioweapons lab within twelve hours or suffer a low-yield nuclear strike. There will be no repatriation of all UIR prisoners of war until all participants in the Ebola strike are surrendered to the U.S. If this is not done, the U.S. will wage unlimited war on the UIR, particularly Iran.

In Clancy's statecraft, killing the guilty party is the solution, and it is easily done. With surgical precision and certain aim, the U.S. kills the dictator Daryaei in his lair. Finding him is difficult, but not impossible—a matter of days. Contrast this with the months it took to find Saddam Hussein and the years it has taken to try to find Osama bin Laden (more on this in a later chapter).

If Only It Were as Easy as the Book

There is no residual friction in fiction.

In reality, nothing ever moves this smoothly.

The U.S. Senate has been targeted twice by bioweapons attacks. In the fall of 2001, finely powdered anthrax made its way to the office of then Senate majority leader Tom Daschle (D-South Dakota), as well as to the office of NBC anchorman Tom Brokaw and the offices of the American Media Inc., a supermarket tabloid publisher. Postal sorting centers in several states were shut down when postal workers came down with the disease. Other mail was also contaminated, infecting and killing several unintended recipients but increasing the terror quotient.

It was not known at the time if the anthrax attack was an adjunct to the 9/11 attacks on the World Trade Center and the Pentagon. A second bio-attack on the Senate occurred in February 2004, this time involving ricin, which is derived from castor beans. No one was infected or killed, but this did force yet another shutdown of the Senate Office Building. The person or persons behind both attacks have not been caught yet, either.

But in *Executive Orders*, Clancy's heroes manage to identify the series of clues that point back to Iran's state-sponsored terror attack, doing in a matter of days what hundreds of FBI, CDC, and law enforcement agents could not do in several years, thus allowing Ryan to take action.

As for suffering a direct terror attack on the United States, the results were plainly seen in the aftermath of 9/11. Al Qaeda, a stateless terrorist network, was operating out of Afghanistan under the protection of Mullah Mohammed Omar and his governing Taliban movement. Within six weeks of the September attacks, the U.S. infiltrated Special Forces into Afghanistan to contact the forces of the anti-Taliban Northern Alliance. Fluent in the local languages and capable of calling in accurate air strikes, U.S. Special Forces helped rout the Taliban and Al Qaeda in the field, reclaiming Afghanistan in a matter of weeks. Air support was provided by three U.S. navy carriers operating in the Arabian Sea, able to reach Afghanistan with overflight rights granted by neighboring Pakistan. (A fourth carrier supported Special Forces operations.) U.S. Air Force tankers and bombers staged from bases farther away to maintain air power on call.

The bottom line in Ryan's first months in office is "don't mess with the U.S."

The post–cold war sensibility of multilateral diplomacy, the primacy of the United Nations to help resolve international differences, the boundaries of international law, and the civilized reluctance to use force are nowhere evident, even though they delineate the acceptable boundaries of action for many smaller nations. The U.S. is a unilateral actor on the world stage. Even the European public is not staging peace marches against U.S. policy in Clancy's fiction, although that was plainly seen during the duration of America's war and occupation of Iraq (or at least Clancy sees no need to mention such events). An author can shape an ideal world with a few bold strokes on the keyboard. Heads of state are lucky if they can shape one part of the world with a bold stroke of their own. More often than not, political reality shapes the approach to any crisis, with compromise and fear of consequence limiting action to half-measures, sometimes halfheartedly taken.

The Reelection: Calm Between the Storms

The Ryan presidency, phase II, can be found in *The Bear and the Dragon*. Written in 2000, the book places the action roughly the year after Ryan's reelection. That can either be 1997 or 2001, depending how you count the years in Clancy's timeline.

Not much is said about the campaign. Clancy makes no mention of an opponent, his policies, and his platform, how many states he carried or how many votes he got. The campaign only lasted ten weeks, with Ryan making eight to nine campaign appearances a day, reciting pretty much the same stump speech (with minor changes to suit locality or current events).

In the realm of presidential campaigning, a ten-week rush is mercifully short. Campaigns have ballooned to fill all available time in the election year. For challengers, the campaign leading to the first primary or caucus may last anywhere from six months to a year. For the front-runner as well as the incumbent, the campaign consumes the election year.[10]

The plotline in this book is a shaggy dog that wags a big tail. Russian intelligence chief Golovko is nearly assassinated when a nearby identical white armored Mercedes is blown to pieces by an assassin firing a rocket-propelled grenade, who then gets away. Golovko is shaken by the event, and stirs himself to get to the bottom of the attack. The victim turns out to be a Moscow pimp with many ties to the city's underworld. Was the rubout done by a bunch of crooks bent on revenge or was there an assassination attempt that got the wrong car?

As this plotline progresses, Clancy introduces his main bad guy, Zhang Han Sen, senior minister without portfolio in the Politburo of the People's Republic of China.[11] He now stars in his own effort to guide a Chinese takeover of Siberia, which would mean waging war against a much-weakened Russia.[12]

Given Clancy's nineteenth-century worldview of mercantilist states conquering distant lands to control strategic resources, a Chinese invasion of Siberia makes sense. The Chinese would gain valuable empty space to park its excess tens of millions of people. In real life, there are about four million Chinese emigrants there now, holding jobs they could not hope to find in China.

Clancy adds major oil and gold strikes to the pot and stirs. Such abundant resources would help finance Russia's restructuring and modernization. For a resource-hungry China, the area is worth stealing. That is Zhang's plan.

But the plan does not stay secret. Operating without diplomatic cover, CIA agent Chet Nomuri (working for Japanese electronics giant NEC) manages to install some spyware on the PC belonging to the secretary of another Politburo member, minister without portfolio Fang Gan. (It helps that Nomuri seduces the secretary and gets her to do this for him, under the guise of installing a software upgrade.) The spyware e-mails a copy of those notes to Nomuri's boss, Mary Pat Foley, director of operations at the CIA. Two things stand out in this plot element. First, it highlights the ongoing trend at the CIA to rebuild the human intelligence side of its mission, and the agency is currently building a corps of spies who can operate covertly and without diplomatic cover. Second, a piece of software plays the insider role that was performed by an operative like CARDINAL, long the U.S. source of Soviet Politburo intelligence in earlier Clancy books.

Concurrent with this is continuing U.S.-China trade tension. China is running a trade surplus of about $85 billion in its favor with the U.S. Copyright and trademark practices are flouted as China copies whatever it wishes without compensating U.S. companies. And they have the gall to ask for most favored nation status and membership in the World Trade Organization.

This does not go over well with Ryan and Treasury Secretary Winston. They threaten to apply the Trade Reform Act, which automatically mirrors the offending nation's import rules to reduce any trade imbalances. A diplomatic mission sent to Beijing to argue this point founders as the Chinese foreign minister takes the U.S. to task for recognizing Taiwan as an independent nation.

Trading Pains

A little history and current events are in order here. Historically, China's friction with the West has its roots in trade. In the late 1790s, Britain dispatched an ambassador to petition the Chinese emperor for access to Chinese markets. Britain was already a leading trading state at the forefront of the Industrial Revolution. But there was nothing that Britain made that China wanted, and the request was turned down with a measure of Chinese cultural arrogance and disdain for "barbarian" goods. China will export, but not import.

Keep in mind that gold was used for currency in those days. For a nation to suffer a trade deficit meant seeing its money supply drain away in favor of the nation running the trade surplus. Such a gold drain bankrupted the Roman Empire over a thousand years previous to the British overture. The only foreign good that would sell in the Chinese market was opium. By smuggling the stuff into China, Britain and France managed to recover gold currency spent on acquiring Chinese silks and porcelains for their home markets.

Sadly, this trade was creating a massive drug problem in China, as a significant minority became addicts and turned to crime to support their habits. Chinese attempts to cut off the trade led to two wars with Britain and France in the mid-nineteenth century. After suffering defeat, China was forced by treaty to open its domestic markets to foreign goods and cede territory to the victors so they could set up their trading houses.

Humiliation at the hands of foreigners was pretty galling for China. Worse, the Manchu Dynasty then in power was too corrupt and inept to deal with its problems, fostering further defeat and humiliation. The Taiping Rebellion of the 1850s–60s undermined the legitimacy of the ruling dynasty. Germany, Russia, and Japan also demanded slivers of Chinese territory. Japan wrested control of Formosa (as Taiwan was called then) after winning a war against China in 1894. As the last imperialist power with designs on China, Japan invaded in 1937, taking the eastern third of the country, which it held until the end of World War II.

Since them, China has pursued a policy of reacquiring all the lost bits. Sometimes that involved using force, as it happened with the invasion of Tibet in 1959. Or it could be through more peaceful diplomatic means, as with Hong Kong in 1997. Taiwan, however, remains elusive.

Shortly after the end of World War II, China suffered a civil war, as the Communists under Mao Zedong vanquished the U.S.-supported Kuomintang under Chiang-Kai-shek. The KMT fled to Taiwan, where it set up the Republic of China, which the U.S. recognized as the real government of China while diplomatically ignoring Mao's People's Republic of China. Chiang ran a one-party dictatorship in Taiwan until his death in the 1970s. His successors maintained an authoritarian government until implementing democratic reforms in the 1980s, leading up to Taiwan's first presidential election in 1996.

The U.S. withdrew recognition of Taiwan when President Richard Nixon staged his famous rapprochement with China in 1971. Nixon undertook the move to counter the growing power of Soviet Russia while U.S. power was diminished owing to the loss of the Vietnam War. (Russia and China ended their own alliance in the early 1960s—a divorce fueled by historical incompatible differences.) However, the U.S. Congress passed a law pledging U.S. aid in the event Taiwan is ever attacked.

Since the late 1970s, the U.S. policy on Taiwan and China is one of studied ambiguity. The U.S. pressures Taiwan not to declare independence from China, but will not tolerate the use of force by China to recapture Taiwan.

One such test came in 1996, when Taiwan held its presidential election, only to see China conduct missile tests with splashdown points in sea-lanes surrounding the island. President Bill Clinton dispatched two carrier battle groups to waters east of Taiwan to show U.S. concern.

U.S.-China relations received another shock in 1999, when China's embassy in Belgrade took a bomb hit from U.S. aircraft bombing Serbia during the Kosovo War. Apologies were made and compensation paid to the families of the dead, but the incident rankled deeply with the Chinese people. Another shock was suffered in April 2001, when a U.S. Navy surveillance plane was accidentally downed in a collision with a Chinese fighter plane. The navy pilot successfully landed the stricken plane at a Chinese base in Hainan, but the crew did not have sufficient time to completely destroy secret documents, manuals, and electronic surveillance gear.

These incidents illustrate the differences between the American and Chinese styles of crisis management. In the U.S., a president relies on his National Security Council to pull together all relevant information while coordinating action among the armed services, Defense, and State departments. There is a practiced organization to respond to crisis, support the president, and implement his decisions after consultation and exchange of information. This allows a range of options to be developed for the president to consider, and ensures timely response to an emergency. But in China, no such organization exists. Crisis management is improvised and the lines of authority are unclear. While the armed services and cabinet departments are by law subordinate to the president here in the U.S., the same is not entirely so in China, where the services and departments operate as factions that do not always take direction from the office of the premier. In fact, then president Jiang Zemin played off two factions against each other—the economic development faction under Zhu Rongji and the military faction under Li Peng. Getting a response from the Chinese took time as Jiang had to resolve office politics in his government before getting back to the U.S.

Until September 2004, Jiang Zemin retained his title as head of the Central Military Commission. That made him a player in institutional politics even though he has passed the presidency to Hu Jintao. While heading the military committee, Jiang did not have to answer to Hu.

Let's Pretend

Returning to Clancy's narrative, we find a reflection that is not quite representative of the real world scenario. Yes, there is a faction-ridden Chinese Politburo and the hawks are outvoting the doves. A hard-line policy is being pursued against the U.S. on trade and Taiwan while an invasion of Russia is being readied. That project requires China to spend massive amounts of its foreign reserves to equip a modern mechanized army that can advance from the Russian border north to the Arctic coast to seize the fictional oil and gold fields.

In real life, China is keeping its military focus on Taiwan. Purchases of modern warships, subs, and planes are aimed at establishing air and naval superiority in the Taiwan Straits, while backing this with four hundred short-range missiles aimed at the "errant province." But China under the current president, Hu Jintao, has accorded a higher priority on economic development. China is keeping relations with the U.S. on an even keel, avoiding confrontation while securing needed investment capital to maintain economic growth and shut down inefficient state-owned industries. Russia is still selling advanced arms to China, but the country is not even trying to go broke financing its rearmament. The problems China faces are different: closing down inefficient state-owned industries, ameliorating rural poverty, grappling with democracy at the local level. All this has to be done without stirring the people into rebellion as great changes upset many livelihoods, not always for the better.

China's cyclical history should be noted here. Since 200 B.C., a procession of dynasties has governed the country. So long as the basic needs of the people are met and the nation suffers no disasters, emperors had the legitimacy to rule (i.e., they "enjoy the mandate of heaven"). But when the economy goes into a tailspin because of flooding, famine, war, or political corruption, then the dynasty would fall, China would fragment, and local warlords fought each other until one triumphed to start a new dynasty. This cycle repeated itself through the Han, Tang, Sung, Yuan, Ming, and Manchu dynasties, finally culminating in the present Communist "dynasty," which is just as sensitive to popular uprisings as its imperial predecessors.

So it was no surprise in 1989 that the Communist Politburo, answering to behind-the-scenes boss Deng Xiaoping, brutally put down the student protests in Tiananmen Square. China's premier from that time, Zhao Zhiyang, is still under house arrest for failure to crush the uprising. Since then, the democracy movement has been stifled and replaced by an increased nationalism under Zhao's successor, Jiang Zemin.

Jiang was very quick to suppress the Falun Gong movement in the 1990s, following that group's peaceful protest where it mustered ten thousand followers to briefly surround the government compound in April 1999. Falun Gong is a spiritual movement that turns back to older Chinese meditation and dietary practices for inspiration. It is very ironic that it is being suppressed by a ruling clique whose ideology—Marxism—is a western import.

In Clancy's narrative, the same problems of economic failure, domestic unrest, and legitimacy are very much in play. If China is hit with retaliatory nontariff trade barriers by the United States (China's largest export customer), then the economy will collapse, domestic rebellion ensues, and the ruling regime will be cast out.

The CNN Effect

The unpredictable spark that triggers unrest is a parallel plotline that Clancy introduces early in the book.

A papal nuncio arrives in Beijing at a time when China is repressing Christian churches that operate without the government's blessing, of which the Catholic Church is one. Religious beliefs come into conflict with China's one-child policy, a holdover from the 1980s when China used coercion to limit family size owing to population pressure. (The policy is not vigorously enforced anymore). An evangelical protestant Chinese pastor tries to disrupt the delivery-room killing of a second child being born by one of his congregants. He has the papal nuncio and his assistant in the room with him. This was being televised live by CNN when several Chinese police officers intervene, resulting in the shooting deaths of the nuncio and the pastor. Police also break up a subsequent prayer meeting in front of the home of the slain Chinese pastor, again live on CNN.

American political reaction comes from the grassroots, as consumers close their wallets to any goods carrying the "made in China" label. Zhang does not see the need to ameliorate the situation through diplomacy, much less apologize. Instead, he sees a greater need for China to punch north with its army and seize Siberian gold mines and oil fields. After presenting the U.S. with a fait accompli, Zhang figures it would only be a matter of time before business returned to normal. Zhang is making this decision within a Marxist context, reading true the Red aphorism that the capitalist will sell the very rope used to hang him.

At a Politburo meeting, the decision is made to invade Siberia and assassinate Russian president Grushavoy, using the same covert network that failed to kill Golovko. The gamble is that if the war can be won quickly enough, the world will acquiesce to the fait accompli and go back to doing business as usual with a stronger China. Again, this is a very nineteenth-century worldview (that carried over to World War II), using war as a policy tool. True, every war must have a political objective that can be called a victory once it is attained. But war is a capricious tool, unreliable since it develops its own dynamic of action and reaction that can slip beyond the control of national leaders. Zhang's Siberian invasion can best be described as a gamble. There will be no political recovery for the present regime if things go wrong.

The U.S. finds out promptly via the well-placed spyware that forwards the notes on these meetings from the desktop PC of Fang's secretary. This information is forwarded to the Russians, of course.

Now it is time for the U.S. to make some hard decisions.

The American military arsenal is still pretty thin, not having grown much since the war with Japan in *Debt of Honor*. The Russians are in worse shape. Gennady Bondarenko, a perennial "good Russian" in the Clancy universe, is given command of the Far Eastern Military District. He finds himself commanding a paper army of one armored division, six motorized rifle divisions, and an artillery division. In actuality, it is more like one MRD at 85 percent readiness and the rest of his units at cadre or regimental strength. Only fifty serviceable aircraft are available.

On a visit to Warsaw for a NATO summit, Ryan dispatches Secretary of State Adler to Moscow to pay a discreet call upon Grushavoy and Golovko, offering Russia membership in NATO to counter the expected Chinese invasion. The NATO alliance will treat any attack on a single member as an attack on all, thus mobilizing all members to come to the defense of the stricken member. NATO came into being in the early 1950s to defend Europe from a possible Soviet invasion. The irony here is that Clancy is bringing Russia in as a member of the very alliance that was formed to thwart it. In real life, post–cold war Russia has a nonvoting presence in the NATO council, basically exercising a right to be informed. During the cold war, NATO's main front was the border between East and West Germany. Following Germany reunification in 1989, NATO membership has expanded to include the Baltic States and former members of the Warsaw Pact, Soviet Russia's counteralliance to NATO that took in its Communist client states of

Eastern Europe. (The NATO alliance has been invoked only once by its members in the past fifty years, shortly after the terrorist attacks of September 11, 2001 on the U.S.)

The announcement does not go over well in Beijing, but Zhang interprets it as window dressing. The invasion goes forward. The Russians trade space for time, rushing a few available divisions eastward. The U.S. responds with what it has, sending an armored division eastward from Germany and flying in an assortment of air force squadrons to establish defensive air superiority. The U.S. counterstroke, coupled with a successful Russian defensive battle, guts the Chinese offensive. The gamble has been lost.

Now the Beijing Politburo meets again. The shelling of the coast by the U.S. Navy is misinterpreted as preparation for an amphibious assault, even though the U.S. capability here is weak. China's loss of its only missile sub, plus defeat on the Siberian front, leaves China with two options. Fang and Qian Kun favor negotiated settlement. Zhang wants to use the ICBMs to threaten the U.S.

Meanwhile, Ryan is cognizant of the PRC missile threat. Lacking the right weapons at the right place, Ryan asks Golovko to aid a joint RAINBOW/SPETZNATZ commando assault on the PRC missile site. (RAINBOW was in Russia conducting joint training exercises with its spetznatz colleagues.)

During the raid, the general in charge of the missile field informs the PRC defense minister that his base is under attack, and is ordered to launch (use them or lose them). Only one missile gets off.

Once NORAD (North American Air Defense Command) ascertains the missile is inbound for Washington, D.C., emergency evacuation of the government is ordered. Bound for the National Emergency Airborne Command Post, Ryan orders his helicopter to land on the helipad of an AEGIS cruiser tied up at the Washington naval yard. True to the call for a tense ending, Clancy has the USS *Gettysburg* down the incoming missile with its last SMR-2 Standard missile.

The potboiler does not end yet.

Chinese college students get the real news over the Internet on what is happening to the People's Liberation Army and its Siberian invasion. No news was made public about this to the Chinese people. The students gather in Tiananmen Square (where else?) and rush the Politburo building during a meeting. Okay, this is deus ex machina in less than twenty pages, but Clancy ends his tale by having Fang order the arrest of Zhang, the premier and defense minister, for dragging China into an unwanted war. He also orders Foreign Minister Shen to open up negotiations with the U.S.

Might Makes Right?

The Ryan administration has thus weathered its second major war in less than eighteen months, yet in both wars, President Ryan executed his actions pretty much the same way. Nary a word is said about the need for massive supplemental appropriations to pay for military operations in time of war—always more expensive than training in peacetime. Congress was never consulted to pass a resolution or declaration of war against China or Iran (United Islamic Republic). Neither time was a UN Security Council resolution against the offending belligerent ever sought. Other Western allies made no major contributions in either war, though RAINBOW does draw some manpower from Britain, Germany, and Italy. (Clancy mentions a British brigade making ready to ship to Siberia from Germany in *The Bear and the Dragon*.)

Two more high points of the Ryan administration deserve mention. The first is depicted in detail in *Rainbow Six*, where a special multinational commando team is formed to combat terrorism. Ryan is not mentioned by name, though Ed Foley is still director of Central Intelligence. Rainbow Six takes place in the months leading up to the 2000 Summer Olympics in Sydney, Australia, but before the Russo-Chinese War.

The other more explicit touchstone of the Ryan presidency is the establishment of Hendley Associates, as outlined in *Teeth of the Tiger*. A privately held trading firm, Hendley is a front for a secret government organization that is not financed by public funds, nor does any congressional committee oversee it. Given its ideal location halfway between CIA headquarters in Langley, Virginia, and the Ft. Meade, Maryland home of the National Security Agency, Hendley draws intelligence from both agencies for use by its own analysts to track and target terrorists abroad.

Here Clancy has Ryan treading on very dangerous legal and constitutional grounds by setting up an ersatz government agency with no budget, no oversight, and no subordination to any government official, elected or appointed. A stack of signed but undated presidential pardons sit in a Hendley vault, waiting for the insertion of names and dates in the event a Hendley "employee" lands into any legal trouble.

Hendley Associates is worth mentioning here because it touches on the power of the president to issue pardons. It's a tool usually exercised right before a president leaves office. But there are times when the pardon power has a political purpose, and the consequences can be huge.

Shortly after assuming the presidency in August 1974, Gerald Ford issued a pardon to his predecessor, Richard Nixon, who was taking a lot of legal heat as an unindicted coconspirator in the Watergate scandal. There was a very real possibility that Nixon would be indicted and tried on criminal charges, continuing the political agony of Watergate. Ford made a courageous but controversial decision to pardon Nixon for any crimes he might have committed. But the act of statesmanship hurt Ford's own chances of getting elected two years later.

Ronald Reagan was also quick on the draw here. After the destruction of the Marine Corps barracks in Beirut by a suicide bomber in 1983, Reagan issued pardons to the two marine officers in command there. The pardon may have saved the two officers from facing a court-martial, but is also removed any chance for them to be exonerated. The pardons also buried the fact that the White House crafted rules of engagement that forbade the marines guarding the barracks from carrying loaded weapons.

Bush also demonstrated good timing in 1992 by issuing a pardon to Reagan defense secretary Caspar Weinberger, as well as other individuals who played a role in the Iran-Contra scandal, thus shutting down another lengthy and politically damaging investigation.

Not to be outdone, President Bill Clinton also issued a bevy of pardons before leaving office in 2001, though none were as pragmatically political as the Nixon or Weinberger pardons. (One such pardon was granted to Marc Rich, a campaign contributor who was hiding out from the law in Switzerland to avoid prosecution for financial misdeeds here.)

Ryan does not serve out his full term after getting elected in 1996/2000, depending on which branch of the timeline is correct. (Clancy does not practice detailed multivolume plotting like J.K. Rowling.) In *Teeth of the Tiger*, Clancy alludes to Ryan's resignation from the presidency, having become bored with the job he never sought. His vice president and close friend Robby Jackson becomes the first black president of the U.S., only to be gunned down by a Ku Klux Klan fanatic. Ed Kealty finally got elected, with Ryan quite displeased in private but holding his public tongue.

Kealty is Clancy's fictional stand-in for Senator Ted Kennedy of Massachusetts. Ted Kennedy took his best shot at the presidency in 1980, challenging President Jimmy Carter for the Democratic nomination. While Kennedy went the distance in the primary campaign, he unsuccessfully tried to use the convention's political process to undo the lock Carter had on the nomination. Since then, Kennedy has focused his energies on being a senator and becoming the so-called liberal lion of the Democratic Party.

Stick to Real Life Over Fiction

If one were to compare the presidency in Clancy's timeline with the actual record, the U.S. has a really rough time in fiction. After Reagan's departure, not a single president serves two terms.

WRANGLER is defeated after serving one term.

Fowler resigns after cracking up.

Durling is killed in office.

Ryan serves out Durling's term, gets elected, and resigns.

Jackson is killed in office.

Kealty is elected.

In the span of twelve to sixteen years, the U.S. goes through five presidents—a very chaotic tempo.

For a similar trip, look at 1961–80, when we went through five presidents during a stretch of war, domestic upheaval, and economic chaos. Kennedy's first term is cut short by assassination. Johnson declines reelection, his popularity shredded by the Vietnam War. Nixon gets reelected but resigns in disgrace as the House proceeds with impeachment. Ford serves out the remaining term only to lose to Carter, also a one-term president.

Compare this with the real timeline from 1980 to the present, and we only go through four presidents. Reagan and Clinton served two terms, interspersed by the single term of George H.W. Bush while the son, George W. Bush, succeeded Clinton and managed to win his own reelection this year (2004). For a better example of continuity in crisis, look at 1933–60. Only three presidents served during that long stretch—Franklin Roosevelt, elected four times; Harry Truman, who served the remainder of FDR's fourth term and got elected; and two-term president Dwight Eisenhower. The Depression, World War II, and the beginning of the cold war is a lot to deal with.

A two-term presidency is a desired norm with mixed blessings. The U.S. gains continuity in policy and a measure of stability. The downside is that presidents don't age well politically. They become scandal-prone sometime during the second term.

Eisenhower had some problems with his chief of staff, Sherman Adams, who left office after accepting some politically questionable gifts from parties with business before the government. Toward the end of his second term, Eisenhower lied out of necessity about the U-2 flights over Russia, which damaged the public trust in the office of the presidency.

Likewise, Reagan's second term was mired in the Iran-Contra scandal, which conveniently did not lead to impeachment . . . but it was a major distraction.

Clinton's second term was to see his agenda torpedoed by his fling with White House intern Monica Lewinsky. Lying about the affair during a deposition being taken for a similar lawsuit was enough to target Clinton for impeachment. While the Republicans had the votes to bring charges in the House, they lacked the numbers in the Senate needed for conviction and removal. The substance of the charges against Clinton were far less than the balance-of-power issues that fueled the Andrew Johnson impeachment, the impending impeachment of Nixon, and the Iran-Contra scandal.

Ryan suffered some of these problems as his CIA past twice enmeshed him in scandals that did not result in his removal once the facts came out. But for someone who did not seek the presidency, but served out of duty, it is very odd that he should leave before completing a full term.

The fiction belongs to the author, who has the power to tell the story any way he pleases.

History has written a different book.

Only three presidents in the past sixty years ever served "out of duty"—Truman, Eisenhower, and Ford. None of these men needed to be president. More commonplace is the rule: those who become president want the job badly enough to campaign ceaselessly for it. Not an election cycle goes by without some pundit or journalist pointing out a name or two of someone who is better qualified. Yet every alternate candidate lacked the persuasiveness to get the votes, or the ambition needed to work for the election.

The fictional Ryan presidency is an adrenaline-fueled takeoff, to some degree, of that old Frank Capra movie *Mr. Smith Goes to Washington*. Put a common person in high office, let him try to do good as best as he can, and watch how he is tripped and fouled by the more cynical forces that are common inside Washington, D.C. But Capra was dealing with small change compared to the Ryan presidency. All Mr.

Smith wanted to do was to set up a patriotic boy's camp on some land coveted by an evil political boss back in Smith's home state. Heading the lone superpower, Ryan had to fend off an evil alliance between Japan, India, Iran, and China to forcibly expand at the expense of neighboring countries and take the U.S. down a few notches.

The challenges the U.S. faces are no less grave in real life. They are not as neatly resolved in the realm of make-believe. We enjoy the fiction of the president as a man of action, since action speaks louder than words. Yet even in real life, when a president does take action, it is after a problem has festered for months or years. The military option is usually the last one chosen, not the first, and the policy reviews and closed meetings leading up to the decisive moment are many and lengthy. If Clancy told a story using the real-life measure of a crisis, there would be more words than action.

In Clancy's world, the results matter more than the process. There is no connection between the office politics of the presidency and the duties of that office. That disconnection speeds the story, dwelling on the peaks of action and conflict without wasting too much time in the valleys of deliberation, negotiation, and diplomacy. The end result should always be the safety and primacy of the United States, a goal that must never be compromised by politics.

In real life, politics and war are intertwined. There is no such thing as a war without a political objective, and it is the president's responsibility to define that desired outcome when he sends the armed forces into harm's way. Lack of a clear objective can turn a war into an ambiguous morass with no end in sight.

One never sees a president in Clancy's fiction do this. All three fictional major wars—with Japan, Iran, and China—all result in a return to the status quo before the war started, after a change in the enemy nation's government. This type of outcome seems to be good enough for Ryan. How ironic that the man of action merely reacts to world events, rather than dictating them.

THREE
Weapons
The Right Tools for the Right Plot

It all started with a Russian submarine. . . .

Tom Clancy is credited as the chief practitioner of the techno-thriller, where the technological weaponry counts for as much as the characters. Throughout Clancy's fiction, detailed explanations abound on how various weapons systems work and fight. Aside from being a "blue collar nationalist," Clancy is a shameless weapons buff.

Many armchair generals begin their study of national security by focusing on the tanks, ships, and planes.

For some people, this is as far as they go.

The topic is rich with detail, amazing technology, and lots of action . . . and the numbers matter.

Having more weapons is good—having better weapons is best.

How much a weapons system costs, what is the doctrine for its use, how it will dovetail with other weapons and tactics, and how servicemen will be trained to use them, is all boring to the weapons buff. Yet those issues are all very real to the unit commander, his service chief, the various theater commanders in chief, and to a lesser extent, the congress and the president.

The United States military is only half the size it was during the height of the cold war, when many of its current weapons were initially purchased. Replacements are needed soon, as various tanks, planes, and ships become too costly to maintain after twenty or thirty years of usage and upgrades . . . but what shall be picked as a replacement? Maybe an unmanned aerial vehicle (UAV) makes more sense than another manned fighter or a new reconnaissance helicopter. Perhaps a refitted Ohio-class SSBN firing cruise missiles will be a better buy than an arsenal ship. Maybe peacekeeping makes a light armored car a better choice than a new main battle tank. These are very real choices confronting the United States that will cost billions of dollars.

Democrats and Republicans have long argued over weapons and their price tags, and the inflationary 1970s saw some ineffective purchasing. Once the price of a weapons system went up, fewer weapons would be purchased per year in the name of economy. But this economy would prove false, as weapons purchased in later years cost more per unit.

The debate became very heated during the Reagan years, when a five-year $1 trillion rearmament plan[1] went into effect. The U.S. was going on a massive shopping spree, but it was not certain that all the tanks, planes, and ships being purchased would perform as promised. Sometimes a new plane or tank needed a "teething period" where adjustments are made to ensure operational reliability. The F-18 came through this and eventually compiled an exemplary combat record. The B-1 bomber did not, and has been a dog in the arsenal for several decades. The F-16 was a dream come true, and cost less than its predecessor, the F-15. The A-12 never came to be, getting the ax as the program spun into a costly morass of mismanagement.

Critics also rightfully complained about some industry pricing practices, where program costs were shifted to tool kits and spare parts. This was the source for all those wonderful horror stories about $100 hammers, $600 toilet seats, and $1,200 coffeemakers—items any American could buy off the shelf for a fraction of their inflated costs, and they would perform just as well. Today the military will buy equipment off the shelf if the component meets military specification, or *mil-spec.*

The blank check of the Reagan years has given way to some pretty stiff budgetary pressure.

You will see none of this in a Clancy novel.

The price tag of a tank, sub, or plane is never mentioned. Every weapon performs as it should: flawlessly, and the exceptions are too few. Our stuff always works better than the enemy's stuff. Yes, Americans do get killed from time to time in combat, but it is never due to any shortcoming in the weapon system. The defense budget is never mentioned except when it doesn't buy as much as America needs to defend its interests, and post–cold war America never has enough to cover all its security needs.

Weapons systems play at three levels in Clancy novels: strategic, operational, and tactical. At the strategic level, we are talking about nuclear weapons and their delivery systems, or countermeasures to nuclear attack. At the operational level, units above battalions, squadrons, and carrier battle groups use high-tech weapons to fight battles and win wars. At the tactical level, small units like squads or Special Forces teams will engage in firefights for local terrain against other small units or terrorists (this segment will get special focus in the next chapter).

Strategic Warfare

Hunt for Red October has a political beginning.

Captain Marko Ramius has become disenchanted with the Soviet system. He has handpicked a group of officers willing to defect to the West—and deliver his ballistic missile submarine (equipped with a prototype advanced propulsion system) to the U.S. Ramius makes good his head start, after sending a letter to the fleet's political chief, announcing his intention to defect. The Soviet fleet musters and deploys very quickly to the mid-Atlantic, only to be met in a tense standoff with U.S. and British naval forces. Ramius's clique fakes a nuclear accident, offloading the Russian crew on a nearby U.S. support vessel.

To add to the necessary excitement, Ryan boards the *Red October*, where he has to fight and kill the undercover GRU agent, who has instructions to scuttle the boat. One final tangle takes place in the waters near Norfolk as a Soviet Alfa-class attack sub tries to sink the *Red October*, only to be outmaneuvered, rammed, and sunk. The story ends with *Red October* pulling into a submarine dry dock in Norfolk, ready to be stripped for its intelligence value.

The story is an anti-Soviet, pro-American cold war tale, but the real star is the weapon.

The *Red October* is a Typhoon-class ballistic missile submarine, but with a new propulsion system that makes it much harder to detect. During the cold war, the flashing red "clear and present danger" sticker was slapped onto any weapon the Soviets made that was the least bit better than our stuff. Could the new improved *Red October* have been such a threat if it existed in real life?

To answer that we have to return to the theory of nuclear war, as it was understood during the cold war. Nuclear weapons were only used twice in military history—both times in August 1945, when the U.S. destroyed Hiroshima and Nagasaki. The two bombings forced Japan to surrender unconditionally, thus ending World War II. Military strategy is based on past experience, modified by the understanding of current technology. There is little history to base a strategy when it comes to nuclear weapons. Technology became the predominant determinant, and any capability acquired by the USSR was indicative of its intent.

Back before the global positioning system (GPS) became commonplace, the land-based missile was the most accurate delivery vehicle for a nuclear warhead. You knew the exact location of the launch site and the precise coordinates of the target. Add to this the missile's guidance system, which gave the warhead accuracy measured in hundreds of meters, termed the *circular error probability* (CEP). Because of their greater accuracy, land-based ICBMs were best targeted against the enemy's massively reinforced land-based missile silos, where you need to score a direct hit (or very close to it) to get a kill. Such weapons were known as "counterforce weapons" in the parlance of nuclear strategy.

If the U.S. chose to ride out a first strike, then it must have something left to strike back with. This move was called a second strike. Sub-based missiles were ideal for this mission since they were most likely to survive a first strike. Subs could never know their launch location with the same exact precision as the land-based missiles, given the technology of the time, so their missiles had larger CEPs. Despite this, the sub-launched ballistic missile (SLBM) could still hit a larger target, like a city. (Hence the term *counter city weapon*.) Today, given the capability of GPS, a U.S. Ohio-class submarine can fire its Trident D-4 missiles and hit nuclear targets with the same accuracy as land-based ICBMs—with close to zero CEP.

But back in the 1980s, that figure was more like one-third of a mile for the older Poseidon- and Polaris-class boats, which is a significant factor.

With its huge landmass and poor outlets to all seas save the Arctic Ocean, the Soviet Union played to its strengths by choosing land-based missiles. The Soviets also had a bomber force as part of their strategic triad, but it was too minimal to contribute much to deterrence. Bombers take a long time to fly to target and drop their bombs or launch their cruise missiles. (On the plus side, they can be recalled.) That left the Soviet Navy, which still had some minimal sub-based deterrent at sea to make the U.S. think twice about nuking Russia. The U.S. Navy made it standard practice to shadow every Soviet missile sub putting to sea, and in the event of a nuclear war, sink the Soviet SSBNs before they could launch their missiles. The Soviet nuclear subs were also noisier, and thus more easily tracked by the American subs, which have better sonar systems.

But that U.S. advantage would be nullified once Clancy endowed the *Red October* with the science-fictional "caterpillar drive," a tube-based propulsion system much quieter than a propeller-driven system. Clancy's invention would make it possible for a Soviet sub to give the slip to a pursuing American attack sub and be ready to launch missiles in the event of nuclear war.

It is this massive advantage that Ramius would be surrendering to the U.S. if his defection scheme goes through.

Star Wars and Arms Control

The nuclear issue gets no rest in Clancy's fictional series.

The Cardinal of the Kremlin is a spy story about a U.S. asset with Politburo access, but the football the plot passes around is antimissile defense. In the theoretical scheme of nuclear war planning, strategists argued over whether missile defense might indeed be destabilizing to deterrence. A nation could use its missile defense as a shield to protect itself from retaliatory strike while launching a devastating first strike against the enemy nation.

During the 1960s, the U.S. and USSR developed antiballistic missile systems (ABM) that would be used to defend their home countries from nuclear strikes. The Soviets built a sixty-four-missile system ringing Moscow. The U.S. was deploying a 100-missile system in North Dakota to defend the Grand Forks Minuteman missile base. ABM required huge targeting radars to identify and fix incoming warheads, which the nuclear-tipped ABM missiles would kill, assuming that interception was achieved at a prudent distance.

ABM, which was started under the presidency of Lyndon Johnson, was eventually scrapped by his successor, Richard Nixon, as part of the SALT I Treaty. SALT, which stood for *strategic arms limitation talks*, set predictable ceilings on the number and category of nuclear weapons that could be verified by the spy satellites of both sides. SALT I specifically limited ABM systems to two hundred missiles.

The Soviets kept their Moscow installation.

The U.S. scrapped its partially deployed ABM system, Safeguard.[2]

But the Soviet missile force took on a different complexion afterward. The Russians were not adept at miniaturization, so they tended to design massive boosters that used brute force to lob huge warheads. This design philosophy paid a threatening dividend when advances in technology (first made by the U.S.) yielded the MIRV—multiple independently targeted reentry vehicles. Now a single missile could carry multiple warheads that could hit many targets at once. The inefficient big boosters in the Red arsenal became highly efficient bomb trucks. With 80 percent of the Soviet nuclear force made up of land-based missiles, this translated into an immense capability for launching a massive and accurate first strike that could conceivably eliminate the U.S. land-based missile force.

One proposed solution to counter this was the MX missile. MX—which stood for *missile experimental*—was a ten-warhead ICBM that would be housed in one of many missile shelters. The last plan was for two hundred missiles (with two thousand warheads) to be shuttled to about 4,600 shelters in the American west. The Soviets would have to expend 9,200 warheads (two per target, just to be sure) to kill two hundred missiles. (This did not take into account the 1,052 other land-based missiles in the U.S. arsenal, Titan II, Minuteman I, II, and III, all housed in hardened underground missile silos.) The Soviets only had 5,302 warheads mounted on 1,398 land-based missiles. Under the collar of weapons ceilings negotiated in the SALT II treaty, the MX shell game would destroy the first-strike math of the Soviet nuclear war plan. MX, however, never came to pass. The multiple shelter scheme was scrapped as too costly by the Reagan administration, which deployed the MX as the Peacekeeper in missile silos.[3]

Reagan's strategic counterstroke was "Star Wars," also known as the Strategic Defense Initiative.

SDI was a huge funding umbrella for basic research into the technology of missile defense. The Reagan administration expended billions of dollars in basic research, but did not come up with even a prototype of a defensive antimissile system. Like the ABM system before it, SDI did raise the specter of the U.S. possessing an effective missile shield that would protect the nation should it conduct a first strike against the USSR, which is what the Soviets feared. As neither side could trust the other on the basis of good faith, cautious planners always assumed the worst of their enemy. Capability equals intent.

It is within this context that *Cardinal of the Kremlin* takes place.

Clancy portrays U.S. and Soviet researchers trying to develop new systems that could shoot down incoming missiles, within the balance of power worries that were typical of nuclear war planning in the cold war. Any breakthrough in research that could be turned into a deployable system would give the winner in this arms race a huge advantage.

Here Clancy resorts to using covert operations as a means to gain the strategic outcome by hobbling the SDI research of the opposing side. The KGB dispatches four agents to the U.S. to kidnap one of the SDI program's leading scientists. U.S.-funded Afghan rebels stage their own attack against a Soviet research facility just over the Soviet-Afghan border. The Afghan rebels come close to destroying the Soviet facility, thus giving the U.S. a lead in this arms race that lengthens further when the U.S. makes a research breakthrough.

In real life, SDI was mooted by real events rather than gripping plotlines in a pulp novel. The strategic arms reduction talks (START) begun by the Reagan administration drastically cut the number of nuclear warheads deployed by both sides. The end of the cold war and the dissolution of the Soviet Union in 1991 also removed an able peer rival that gave the U.S. much grief for half a century. While research continued on SDI, it was at a reduced tempo.

Two unexpected events renewed the Star Wars debate in the 1990s. The first Gulf War is where it starts, when the U.S. deployed Patriot antiaircraft missile batteries to intercept incoming SS-1 "Scud" missiles fired by Iraq.

The Scud was a late-1950s vintage surface-to-surface missile fired from a mobile launcher. Scud A had a 75–100-mile range while the later model Scud B was good for about 100–175 miles. Iraq had figured out how to build its own Scuds with extended range and had used them for conventional city bombardment during the Iran-Iraq War of 1980–88. Yes, it was a replay of the Nazi V-2 bombardment of London, which also had a serious political impact in that it could have driven war-weary England to make a separate peace as it lost more civilians at home than on the battlefields of Europe. The difference is that Iraq's missile bombardment succeeded. When Iranian civilians found out their political leaders were ducking out in the suburbs of Tehran to avoid the Scud bombardment, it became politically impossible to continue the war. (Leaders not of the Jack Ryan mode, who skipped sharing the risks faced by their citizens, quickly lose the right to lead.) It was better for the Iranian theocracy to make peace with Iraq than lose power at the hands of an angry mob, especially since Iraqi offensives in the field were taking back ground that was grudgingly won by Iran in earlier years.[4]

When Iraqi dictator Saddam Hussein fired his Scuds at Israel in 1990–01, it was with the hope that Israel would declare war on Iraq. Should this have come to pass, the Gulf War would no longer be a common Arab-western defense against a regional bully. Egypt, Syria, and most importantly Saudi Arabia would not side with the U.S. against Iraq if Israel were going to be on the same side. To make sure Israel stayed out of the war, the U.S. deployed its Patriot antiaircraft missile batteries to defend Israel. Politically, this was a lot for Israel to swallow, as this country's strategic bottom line was to depend on no nation to guarantee its survival.

It was here that Scud and Patriot became the props of political theater while renewing the SDI debate. CNN showed dramatic footage of Patriots being fired in twos against each incoming Scud.

Detonations were clearly seen.

Conclusion: the incoming missiles were successfully intercepted.

Israel was saved.

But appearances can be deceiving.

First, Scud missiles had terrible accuracy, so firing them at a target as big as Tel Aviv was the only way to guarantee a "hit." Second, Patriots may have hit incoming Scuds forty-five times out of forty-seven tries, but the wreckage still rained down on Israel, unavoidably inflicting some collateral damage. Patriots successfully hit Scud missiles, but not Scud warheads, which fell on Israel just the same.[5,6]

Patriot's antimissile capability came about thanks to a software improvement that allowed for the increased accuracy despite short intercept times. That has been improved since the first Gulf War, so the question is rightfully asked: Why can't a missile intercept an incoming missile?

The second part of the issue focuses on North Korea, which spends a fearful proportion of its meager economy on maintaining a large army and an aggressive missile and nuclear weapon development program.

North Korea successfully tested short-range missiles, which crashed into the Sea of Japan. But in 1998, the hermit kingdom successfully test-flew a missile over Japan, which landed about 3,350 miles away in the western Pacific.[7] U.S. intelligence expected North Korea to eventually acquire the ability to hit Alaska, Hawaii, and the western edge of the continental U.S. in the near future. This would provide the impetus for the U.S. to develop its own strategic antimissile defense system, now referred to as national missile defense (NMD). While research and testing continued, President George W. Bush undertook the development of a twenty-missile battery to take into account the possibility of a North Korean strike against the U.S., but would also prove capable of blunting a Chinese missile strike as well. This program necessitated the U.S. abrogation of a portion of the SALT I treaty with Russia that banned ABM systems.

Testing of NMD has been controversial, as technical data suggests that the system, which costs about $1 billion per war shot, was not capable of distinguishing between dummy warheads and the real things, and not always capable of hitting their targets head-on. (Already a system is being deployed in Shemya, Alaska.) At best, NMD is a weapon of political theater, since we can't be sure the system will work every time. Neither can North Korea. Still, spending $15 billion in the real world is an awfully high price for "maybe."

Returning to Clancy's fictional timeline, ICBMs disappear from the U.S. lineup after the near-war with the USSR following the Denver terrorist nuke attack. Japan and China both have ICBM arsenals. Even though they are minimal, they loom in importance because the U.S. has none. The U.S. has to solve the problem of how to de-fang a foreign nuclear threat to prevent escalation in case the enemy is losing the war.

In the case of Japan, the silo-based twenty-missile arsenal sits at the bottom of a gorge. A strike made by B-2 bombers dropping GPS-guided bombs hits the silos. And for good measure, a few bombs are targeted on the dam at the top of the gorge. The dam breaks, flooding the stricken silos, thus ensuring a sure kill of the Japanese nuclear arsenal.

China proves to be a tougher nut to crack. That nation's twenty-missile silo field sits in the far west, close to Russia. A joint RAINBOW-SPETZNATZ raid backed by attack helicopters of the First Armored Division wipes out the missile base security perimeter. Commandos are getting into the silos and dropping satchel charges to blow up the missiles when the launch order is transmitted. Only one missile gets away clear, which is, of course, bound for Washington, D.C.

As a precaution during the Sino-Russian War, President Ryan orders several AEGIS-class cruisers to dock at various U.S. cities on the East and West coasts, where they can use their Standard missiles in ABM mode thanks to software updates similar to Patriot. The AEGIS-class cruisers come equipped with the powerful SPY-1 radar system linked to a multitargeting computer system, enabling the duo to track about 120 targets in the air, on the surface, and below the waves. The USS *Gettysburg* has been tasked with defending Washington, D.C., and about half its missiles received the crucial software upgrade.

President Ryan and his vice president, Robby Jackson, are evacuated to NEACP, but Ryan orders his helicopter to land on the *Gettysburg*, where he will make his "last stand." As the lone Chinese nuclear warhead reenters the atmosphere, the *Gettysburg* begins firing its missiles. All the modified ones miss, as their reprogramming orders their warheads to detonate too late by a fraction of a second. The last of the unmodified missiles hits the nuke, triggering a massive explosion well above the doomed city, saving the day. There was no collateral damage—not even blown-out windows—and the interception happened in the nick of time. It is a novel, after all.

One hopes that national leaders have not forgotten how terribly destructive nuclear weapons are. Yet hopes have been dashed before. The world once recoiled from chemical weapons after seeing their horror in World War I. This past experience is a big reason why many belligerents in World War II shunned the use of poison gases . . . yet Iraq had no such memory, and Saddam Hussein's army freely gassed its Iranian enemies with mustard and chlorine gas—essentially World War I technology. Iraq saved its nerve gas for use on the rebellious Kurds! Horrible weapons, once forgotten, have a way of being remembered by the power hungry and the unscrupulous.

Ships

Clancy's first love is the United States Navy.

His homework in naval affairs shows well in his earlier works, replete with detail about how subs work, as well as their antisubmarine opponents. Yet modern naval warfare is a big question mark. The British and the Argentines had a go at each other during the Falklands War, but other than that, the world has not seen a decent fleet-sized engagement since World War II. Examples of modern naval combat are few, but that does leave Clancy a pretty large canvas to fill, and he does so with a mix of imagination and clichés.

The U.S. has never taken delivery of a defecting Soviet submarine, which makes *Hunt for Red October* a tall tale well worth telling. The U.S. and the Soviets never fought a fleet action against each other, either, and *Hunt for Red October* is probably as good as it gets in this department.

The U.S. Navy operated with a geographic advantage during the cold war, as the main mission was to secure the sea-lanes between the United States and Europe in time of war to resupply and reinforce U.S. forces in Europe. All Russian subs making for the North Atlantic have to pass between Greenland and Iceland, or Iceland and Britain. This sea region is termed the GIUK Gap. Deployed along the sea bottom here is the SOSUS line—large arrays of sonar microphones placed on the sea floor to detect passing submarines. So long as all Russian subs can be detected, they can be sunk to protect the sea-lanes.

Looking at a map of the old USSR, one can't help but notice that every route to an open ocean must pass through some easily monitored narrow strait, or "chokepoint," except one. Russia does have a long coast facing the Arctic Ocean—it is the U.S. that must pass through chokepoints to reach the waters at the top of the world, either through the Bering Strait, the GIUK Gap, or the myriad straits between Greenland and Canada.

The main tool the U.S. had for killing Soviet subs was the attack sub. Starring in that role was the "688 class," also known as the Los Angeles class submarine. Still in use today, the 688 class sub has four torpedo tubes mounted amidships and a vertical launch array for fifteen cruise missiles. Speed and diving depth are classified, though publicly the listed top speed is 30-plus knots. U.S. subs are generally thought to be able to reach a two-thousand-foot depth, though that may be deeper. Calling the sub a "boat" is a bit of a misnomer, as a 688-class SSN is 360 feet long and displaces six thousand tons when surfaced.

Just as the cold war was ending, the larger Seawolf class was coming on line, but only three were built before the program was terminated. The *Seawolf* and *Connecticut* entered service as attack subs, while the *Jimmy Carter* was sent back to dry dock for extensive modifications to turn it into a test bed for future technologies. The newest Virginia-class subs will be replacing the 688-class boats as they are retired throughout this decade. But the tempo of acquisition is in flux owing to budget politics.

Another asset getting major play is the carrier battle group. The U.S. concept is the naval equivalent of combined arms. The carrier has eighty to ninety aircraft to provide the air cover that protects the entire group and projects the striking power against hostile air, surface, sub, and land targets. Destroyers and frigates provide much of the antisubmarine protection, supported by their own helicopters and the carrier's antisubmarine warfare aircraft. Cruisers provide close- and area-air defense. An attached sub or two also provides protection against enemy subs.

The British Navy replicates this on a smaller scale. Its carriers are smaller than the Essex-class flattops the U.S. operated in World War II. They were originally built to operate helicopters for antisubmarine warfare, but were refitted with a sloping ramp nicknamed a "ski jump" on the forward end of the flight deck to help launch the naval version of the Hawker Harrier V/STOL jet fighter. The Invincible-class carriers can carry about twenty-two aircraft—a mix of Sea King helicopters and Harriers. During the Falklands War, two British carriers plus escorts provided the barest naval air superiority needed to pull off an intervention that had no margin for error. Even so, there were significant destroyer and frigate losses, given the need for these escorts to perform radar picket duty away from the protective air cover the carrier provided. In Clancy's novel, *Invincible* will be a useful transit point for Ryan as the effort gets underway to contact and escort *Red October* to the U.S.

As the chase unfolds, we find the *Red October* also pursued by a Soviet Alfa-class attack sub. Instead of being made of steel, the Alfa has a hull made entirely of titanium, one of the lightest and strongest metals known to man. Titanium is difficult to work, as it can only be welded in a vacuum. The Soviets had a cavernous sealed building made solely to construct Alfa subs, with yard workers clad in space suits entering the airless building to weld the hull plates. Alfas are reputed to be faster and deeper-diving than U.S. subs, but suffer from a noisier nuclear power plant. Theoretically, they were easier to detect, but harder to catch. Also, the titanium hull is nonferrous, so it cannot be detected by the magnetic anomaly detector (MAD), a sensor that juts out like a nasty spike out of the tail of the USN's P-3 Orion maritime surveillance plane.

The Soviet surface navy also gets a supporting role in Clancy's sea story, as three Soviet task forces make for the mid-Atlantic. The first is based on the aircraft carrier *Kiev*, which operates a limited number of the YAK-36, a roughly lesser plane compared to the British Sea Harrier, as well as ASW helicopters. The helicopter carrier *Moskva* commands a second group, but cannot operate fixed-wing aircraft. The third group is built on the super-cruiser *Kirov*, displacing close to thirty thousand tons and bristling with a mix of over two hundred SAM and antiship missiles. All three ships operate with an array of cruisers, destroyers, and frigates as escorts. All together, there are twenty-nine surface warships looking for *Red October*, and their antiship missile punch is considerable.

Another counterforce puts to sea west of HMS *Invincible*'s group. This is a surface action group based on the battleship USS *New Jersey*, plus escorts and the helicopter carrier USS *Tarawa*. This last ship is not optimized for ASW work, but is really designed to carry marines for amphibious invasion. Nevertheless, a squadron of ASW helicopters has been crammed onboard to aid the hunt.

During the cold war, the U.S. pulled all four of its Iowa-class battleships out of mothballs to become the basis for four surface action groups (SAGs). The last battleships ever built—*Iowa, Missouri, New Jersey*, and *Wisconsin*—kept their main fifteen-inch main gun armament. The real punch would be in the thirty-two Tomahawk cruise missiles and sixteen Harpoon antiship missiles. Each battleship was also accompanied by the usual escorts, a mix of cruisers, destroyers, and frigates to provide antisubmarine and antiaircraft protection. Conventional wisdom, however, puts surface ships at a combat disadvantage whenever facing airpower. In Clancy's story, the *New Jersey* SAG will get some support from land-based aviation, as the USS *Saratoga*'s air group will be operating from bases in the northeastern U.S. All this will be supported by an E-3 AWACS to track any inbound enemy aircraft or missiles.

As the narrative unfurls, the Soviets lose one of their Alfas about three hundred miles northeast of Norfolk to a freak nuclear reactor accident. Losing a sub is a grim tragedy. The U.S. suffered two sub losses the 1960s. (The USS *Thresher* went down in a training accident, while USS *Scorpion* may have sunk owing to the accidental explosion of an onboard torpedo.)

Russia also had its share of hard-luck sub accidents. The best known is the *Kursk*, which went down in October 2000, again owing to a probable torpedo explosion. Another famous sinking was in the Pacific, when a Golf-class SSBN exploded and sank. In the mid-1970s, the U.S. government paid $500 million to equip an underwater mining ship, the *Glomar Explorer*, which really was equipped to recover the sunken Soviet sub. It was hoped that the sub's code equipment could be recovered intact, but the sub broke up while being recovered and the portion with the desired gear sank.[8] At least that was the story that was public. In Clancy's fiction, the sunken *Alfa* so close to the U.S. would be vulnerable to recovery, just like the old Golf-class vessel.

While the massive Soviet naval deployment is being done under the cover of an air-sea rescue effort, everything becomes too real. Punctuating the confrontation between the U.S. and Soviet fleets are repeated "incidents," where U.S. and Soviet aircraft try repeatedly to penetrate the air space of each other's battle groups as friendly reminders of unfriendly consequences if anyone gets trigger-happy. A YAK-36 is successfully intercepted and escorted away by four F-15s. A flight of four F-14s is intercepted by a flight of YAK-36s, and one of the Tomcats is damaged in an accidental firing of air-to-air missiles by one of the YAKs. A flight of four A-10s successfully buzz the *Kirov* as it is paying more attention to an inbound flight of F-4 Phantoms and A-7 Corsairs.

Incidents like these were commonplace during the cold war, as ships and planes oftentimes tested the boundaries of escort in international waters and airspace. The U.S. and USSR once had to negotiate a code of accepted behavior dictating how ships, subs, and planes would approach each other to prevent accidental collisions and/or war shots being fired, lest these incidents escalate into a real conflict . . . and that risk will go up. By the last quarter in *Hunt for Red October*, the *New Jersey* SAG is just twenty miles away from the *Kirov* battle group, with three more carrier battle groups converging on this patch of the Atlantic.

During the Reagan buildup of the 1980s, one oft-heard complaint was that the navy was too small, with four hundred and fifty ships. Twelve carrier battle groups was the best the U.S. could muster, and two of those flattops were the *Midway* and *Coral Sea*, the largest holdovers from World War II that became the smallest carriers in the fleet as the huge *Nimitz*-class carriers were being delivered. The buildup of forces took the navy up to six hundred ships by the end of the 1980s, with sixteen carrier battle groups and four SAGs based on the battleships.

While these numbers sound impressive, they are not available for deployment at all times. Typically, one-third of the carrier force is down at any time for major refit and maintenance, while another third of the force would be training to relieve the remaining third on deployment. The U.S. could surge carrier deployments where needed in time of crisis, as it did during the first Gulf War of 1990–91, when it operated six carriers in the Persian Gulf. During the Afghan war of 2001–02, four carriers were deployed in the Arabian Sea south of Pakistan, with three flattops providing air power and the fourth supporting Special Forces by helicopter. Even during the intervention in Haiti in 1994, the navy improvised by stripping a carrier of its air wing and replacing it with a gaggle of army helicopters that would be used to support troops on the ground.

Today, the navy is down to about three hundred and fifty ships, with no more than twelve carrier battle groups. The rigid three-year refit, training, and deployment cycle has been scrapped, as Secretary of Defense Donald Rumsfeld does not see the wisdom in giving any potential adversary a useful schedule to predict carrier operations. Rather, the navy will do surge deployments to trouble spots as needed.

The carrier still offers a tremendous strategic and political utility. It is sovereign U.S. territory wherever it sails, acting as a portable air base to be sent wherever trouble beckons. This gets around many political difficulties that can arise, as nations adjacent to any trouble spot cannot be depended upon to offer air bases and overflight rights.

The United States got a good taste of this during the Afghan war of 2001–02, when Saudi Arabia refused to let U.S. aircraft operate from its soil to support the ouster of the Taliban regime in Afghanistan, along with elements of the terrorist group Al Qaeda. Being able to park four carriers in the Arabian Sea got around that difficulty. Likewise, carrier-based sorties were vital in supporting the U.S. ground war in Iraq in 2003, as basing capacity in the Persian Gulf became pretty limited thanks to Saudi nonparticipation.

The role of the navy waxes and wanes throughout the Clancy timeline. In *Cardinal of the Kremlin*, USS *Dallas* plays a smaller role landing John Clark, Clancy's other über-hero, into the USSR to extract the wife and daughter of renegade KGB chief Gerasimov. Supporting espionage and covert operations has long been a strong suit of the submarine, given that it spends most of its time unseen underwater.[9] While the Clark job was the stuff of suspense novels, a more mundane task is tapping underwater cables or sticking an antenna above the surface to see what can be obtained by electronic eavesdropping.[10]

Moving on to *Clear and Present Danger*, the naval role is minimal in the plot. The navy does support some operations against antidrug smuggling flights, shooting down drug-laden cargo planes inbound to the U.S. In real life, the Peruvian Air Force did this during the Fujimori regime.

In *Sum of All Fears*, the navy's profile is much higher, centered on the nuclear missile sub USS *Maine*.[11] Captains of nuclear subs have to be even-tempered and reliable, as well as being leaders in their own right. *Dallas*'s captain Bart Mancuso in *Hunt for Red October* is the archetype. The fictional captain of the Ohio-class SSBN USS *Maine*, Harry Ricks, doesn't quite fit the mold. Too well-schooled in the engineering of his boat, Ricks is not a "people person," and does not command with the welfare of his crew somewhere in his mind. After a while, his abusive command style alienates the crew of the *Maine*, who seek transfers off the boat. Ricks is too aggressive pursuing a Russian nuclear sub when he should have been true to the boomer's first mission: stay quiet and disappear on station, until the missiles need to be launched.

As Clancy's potboiler simmers, the U.S. is sucked into a nuclear confrontation with the USSR (as described in the preceding chapter). The *Maine*'s propeller fouls itself on three submerged wooden beams linked by a chain that got swept off the deck of a container ship hundreds of pages before. This happens in the Pacific, an ocean so vast it spans twelve time zones. Okay, this is a pretty flaky plot development, but the accident makes the *Maine* noisy and the shadowing Russian attack sub has no trouble dispatching the stricken boomer. Harry Ricks goes down with his ship.

Ricks, a fictional character appearing in a 1991 book, bears an eerie and unintended resemblance to Commander Michael Alfonso, skipper of the USS *Florida*, also a Trident-class SSBN. In 1997, Alfonso was relieved of his command, despite achieving the highest certification and inspection grades for any post-overhaul Trident sub. In the military "culture," commanding officers praise in public, but penalize in private. Alfonso preferred to berate crew members in front of their shipmates. This scared the crew to the point where they would not tell their skipper when something went wrong, a factor noted by Rear Admiral Paul Sullivan, commander of Sub Group 9, when he relieved Alfonso of command.[12]

The carrier battle group returns to center stage in *Debt of Honor*, and so do the subs. The fictional war with Japan sees two U.S. carriers, the *John Stennis* and the *Enterprise*, crippled by "accidental" torpedo firings. With their screws damaged, they cannot make sufficient speed to launch aircraft. And therein lies the heart of the carrier's symbiosis with the aircraft.

Launching a plane is not done by magic, even though it may seem so. Most airports boast runways one to two miles long to allow a plane to get to a takeoff speed of around 120 mph. The aircraft carrier has to get the same job done in less than five hundred feet. How? By cheating the laws of aerodynamics. The fastest a carrier can travel is about 30–33 knots—that's about 35 mph. By steering into a headwind, a carrier can add another 10–15 mph to a plane's takeoff speed. But that is still not fast enough. It takes the plane taking off at full power, with a little assistance in the form of a steam-powered catapult, to get aloft.

American subs also get off to an inauspicious start. The attack boats *Charlotte* and *Asheville* are sunk in similar training exercises with Japanese subs. With only four attack subs left in the Pacific Fleet, the U.S. turns to its Ohio-class boomers to fill in. Irony makes an appearance here, as Clancy chooses this force of SSBNs named after the battleships sunk or damaged at Pearl Harbor in 1941: *Maryland, Tennessee, West Virginia, Nevada*, and *Pennsylvania*.[13]

Clancy's fictional Japan war ends with an epic air-sea battle over Guam and Saipan. The *Stennis* is renovated quickly in dry dock, removing two of its four damaged drive shafts. (This is reminiscent of the damaged *Yorktown*'s forty-eight-hour turnaround in Pearl prior to Midway in May 1941). Now running on two screws, *Stennis* returns with an air attack wing heavy on fighters and light on ASW assets. *Stennis*'s fighters have no trouble besting their Japanese rivals,[14] while cruise missiles fired by U.S. subs litter the runways in Guam and Saipan with cluster munitions that blow up returning Japanese fighters. (The tactic is very reminiscent of what went on in *Red Storm Rising*, which gets its own treatment in a later chapter.)

As for the subplot placing the two U.S. carrier battle groups in the Indian Ocean? After spending the bulk of their time sparring with their diminutive Indian flattops, the threat to back off is driven home by a flight of B-1s operating out of Diego Garcia Island. Coming in very low at Mach 1+, the B-1s' sonic booms cause minor damage to the Indian battle group, mostly shattering glass. The Indian Navy turns away and makes for port to repair the damage.

In *Executive Orders*, the navy returns in a key supporting role: making sure that one brigade's worth of equipment based aboard four maritime pre-positioning ships sitting at Diego Garcia Island makes it to the Persian Gulf to equip arriving troops. (One brigade's worth of equipment is already prepositioned in the Persian Gulf region. The Tenth ACR, based in Israel, is close enough to bring its own stuff.) The navy's lone carrier battle group, based on the USS *Eisenhower*, shifts from the Indian Ocean to the western Pacific when Chinese military exercises threaten Taiwan. That leaves the U.S. in a desperate fix, as two smaller Indian carrier battle groups can block entrance to the Persian Gulf, thus stopping U.S. resupply.

The AEGIS-class cruiser *Anzio*, with destroyers *Kidd* and *O'Bannon*, must escort the four MPS ships northward from Diego Garcia to Dhahran, Saudi Arabia. Transiting from the eastern Mediterranean via the Suez Canal and Red Sea is a second surface group based on AEGIS-class cruisers *Normandy* and *Yorktown*, escorted by the Burke-class AEGIS destroyer *John Paul Jones* and the frigates *Underwood, Doyle,* and *Nicholas*. This second group will rendezvous with the Anzio group to become Task Force 61.1.

Some aggressive American diplomacy is used to "persuade" India not to interfere with the task force.[15] Normally, surface ships without air cover are at a disadvantage in the face of air attack, even though the AEGIS-class cruisers are optimized for air defense. But that still leaves the hard part—getting into the Persian Gulf without getting hit by the Iranians from air and sea.

A calculated risk is taken to run Task Force 61.1 under the nose of the Iranians. The AEGIS-capable ships escort the four MPS ships, hugging the Arabian coast to get lost amid the clutter of offshore oil rigs and tanker traffic. The second group made up of the remaining destroyers and frigates, led by the *O'Bannon*, guard two replenishment ships, hoping to appear on radar as the first group, thus acting as a decoy. Without a visual sighting (which can also be misleading), the Iranians may have to settle for firing their radar-guided antiship missiles at the biggest blips they can see on their radar screens.

In real life, "firing at the biggest blip" is what the Iraqis did, accidentally hitting the USS *Stark* back in the 1980s. The Argentines did little better, hitting the container ship *Atlantic Conveyer* when they were looking to score a hit with their Exocet missile against one of the British carriers in the Falklands War.

Back to the novel. Combat is brief, as a helicopter from *Normandy* sinks one Iranian motorboat that manages to fire two missiles at the second group. A flight of four Iranian F-14s spots the *Anzio* and *O'Bannon* groups, but *Anzio* vectors a flight of four USAF F-16s out of Saudi Arabia that splash in the inbound Tomcats. *Jones* separates from the *Anzio* group, keeping its radar dark while the other ships light up the sky to track any inbound Iranian aircraft or missiles. Detected are about a dozen inbound Iranian aircraft, four of them carrying Chinese-made 802 "Silkworm" antiship cruise missiles. The *Jones* gets a lock on the hostile flight and fires its Standard SMR-2 antiaircraft missiles while the Silkworms are fired at the ships. The cruisers go on automatic, letting their computers control antimissile fire. The *Yorktown* takes two hits from the Silkworms. Eventually the MPS ships make it to Dhahran, where they successfully deliver their cargo.

In the real world, the U.S. Navy is no stranger to the Persian Gulf. During the Iran-Iraq War, the U.S. Navy provided escorts for U.S. flagged tankers, basically daring the Iranians to take their best shot. At one point the navy captured an Iranian landing barge loaded with sea mines. At another point, the Iraqis pumped two Exocet missiles into the USS *Stark*, nearly sinking the ship.[16] The frigate *Samuel G. Roberts* also did not fare well, hitting a mine. Perhaps the saddest of the incidents was on July 4, 1988, when the AEGIS-class cruiser *Vincennes* accidentally downed an Iranair Airbus jetliner that was mistaken for an incoming Iranian F-14. The mistake occurred as the *Vincennes* was fighting off an attack by Iranian speedboats. Such ups and downs of misfortune eluded Task Force 61.1 in *Executive Orders*.

In *Bear and the Dragon*, the navy's role again diminishes. Simultaneous with the destruction of the Chinese "B" Army and the rail bridge nexuses at Harbin and Bei'An, the U.S. Navy strikes every Chinese naval base with a combination of air strikes and cruise missiles. One action Clancy singles out is a dogfight between two squadrons of F-14s and about 100 Chinese fighters. Firing the AIM-54 Phoenix missile, the F-14 can engage targets up to 120 miles away. The first volley of Phoenix missiles down many PRC fighters, depleting their numbers before the close-in dogfight takes place with heat-seeking missiles. This effort covers an inbound strike force of F/A-18 Hornets to take out a nearby sub base. The Americans shoot down tens of PRC aircraft for every single loss—a lopsided margin of victory. The navy also has no trouble dispatching the lone Chinese SSBN with its nuclear attack sub escort. The naval war shifts back to the Chinese coast, where an American surface action group centered on AEGIS-class cruisers *Mobile Bay* and *Princeton* shell Chinese shore gun and missile batteries. This last attack is mistaken by the Chinese Politburo as a prelude to an amphibious invasion by the U.S. The order is given to launch a first strike against the U.S. with China's minuscule force of ICBMs.

But don't blame the navy for that.

Planes (and Helicopters, Too)

Air power is the trump card of modern warfare.

Armies can take the land.

Fleets control the seas.

Neither can happen if the enemy has air superiority.

Thirty years ago, the U.S. refocused fighter design to emphasize dogfighting. Couple this with a doctrine that long stressed pilot initiative and you have a peerless air force. (Count the navy and marines here as well—they fly fighters and do air support, too.) Aircraft design integrates many branches of technology, and they must add up to a machine that can win any fight.

The U.S. has strived to maintain its technical edge in air power, even though it lacks an enemy worthy of the effort. In *Debt of Honor*, the second fictional war with Japan finds the U.S. responding with limited numbers of its next-generation weapons: RAH-66 Comanche, F-22 Raptor, B-1 and B-2 bombers.

The war Clancy cobbles together is a mix of conventional and unconventional action. A covert Special Forces team is inserted into Japan to support a small flight of RAH-66s that infiltrates Japanese airspace from ally Russia. The U.S. also has several CIA agents in Japan operating without diplomatic cover, among them Clancy's other pair of überheros, John Clark and Ding Chavez, masquerading as Russian journalists. The RAH-66s are used to shoot down a Japanese version of the AWACS, while Chavez and Clark take out the other two (see section on "Killing" for details). The Commanches are even used for several aerial assassinations of various *zaibatsu*—the Ford order only bars the U.S. from killing hostile heads of state. Of stealthy construction, the RAH-66s were very difficult to pick up on radar, allowing them to operate in Japanese airspace as if they were invisible. The choppers eventually leave Japan, refueling off the deck of the Ohio-class SSBN *Tennessee* before proceeding to an aircraft carrier for final recovery.

Using helicopters to assassinate unwanted opponents is actually a pretty old tactic, one well practiced by Israel in real life. Over the past three years, Israel has "rubbed out" a number of mid-level and high-level leaders of Islamic Jihad and Hamas, two Islamic-based Palestinian resistance groups, using an AH-1 Huey Cobra firing a TOW missile to do the dirty work. Perhaps the most notable recent hit was in March-April 2004, when a helicopter was used to dispatch Hamas head Sheik Ahmed Yassin as he was leaving a mosque in Gaza.

As for the RAH-66? It achieved the rare distinction of being one of the few weapons programs ever canceled by the Pentagon. While it performed flawlessly in fiction, in fact the program could never field a working prototype that performed to spec after a decade of development.[17] The RAH-66s mission was aerial reconnaissance for target-hungry attack helicopters, but that was made redundant by equally stealthy unmanned aerial vehicles, most notably Predator and to a lesser extent Global Hawk.

Another weapons system getting star billing in *Debt of Honor* is the F-22 Raptor. The F-22 is supposed to be the replacement for the F-15 Eagle. Again, the specifications are impressive. The F-22 is stealthy, with no right angles that can present a decent radar reflection. It has "super cruise"—the ability to go to Mach 1 without using its afterburner. Missiles are carried in recessed weapons bays that open and close rapidly to permit firing. And it has an advanced avionics suite, of course.

The F-22s play a key role in penetrating the Japanese AWACS screen. A previous attempt to penetrate with a flight of four B-1 bombers ended in bloody failure, as the AWACS could obtain high-powered radar lock-ons from hundreds of miles away that vectored in air-to-air missiles fired by nearby F-15Js on combat air patrol. The Japanese fighters and the AWACS go down in flames as F-22s flying close formation with more radar-visible F-15s manage to invisibly slip in as their older escorts turn away.

So, are there squadrons of F-22s in flight today?

Well, not quite.

The F-22 was intended to have a long development cycle, as the Pentagon recognized that the 1990s were going to be short of budget dollars for new weapons purchases, unlike the cash-rich 1980s. Yet, try as they might, the plane's advocates in Congress and the air force could not undo the plane's huge price tag. The program cost has now reached $72 billion, and 381 F-22s will be built between now and the beginning of the next decade. If the numbers remain unchanged, that should work out to about $188 million per plane.[18] Transition training to form the first F-22 squadrons began in 2004. The first wing of seventy-two aircraft should be completely formed by 2007. In real life, the F-22 is becoming operational about five to ten years *after* Clancy has used them to fight his fictional war with Japan.

The third star in *Debt of Honor* is the B-2 Spirit. In the book, the B-2 flies a precision bombing mission against a narrow gorge where Japan has based about twenty ICBMs to provide a nuclear deterrent against the U.S., now recently disarmed of this weapon in Clancy's fiction. "Operation Tibbets"[19] wipes out the missile silos, and hits a dam at the head of the canyon to flood the silos for good measure.

The B-2 Stealth bomber has compiled a brief but impressive combat record. First used during the Kosovo War in 1999, the B-2 flew straight from Whiteman Air Force Base in Missouri to bomb selected targets in Belgrade. Each bomber carried twenty-four GPS-guided bombs that can literally be "addressed" to hit a target. The B-2 can accurately hit the wrong address as well, like the embassy for Communist China, which had just relocated to a new building in Belgrade. Other nations took notice of this capability. In March 2003, as the U.S. was preparing to fight Iraq for a second time, the State Department was peppered with faxes from various nations listing the correct addresses for their embassies in Baghdad, coupled with pleas not to bomb them by mistake.

The B-2 was already under development during the Carter administration, which canceled the 1970s-vintage B-1 in anticipation of the Stealth bomber. Made by Northrop, the B-2 was the first military plane to take flight without a prototype. Using computerized design techniques, Northrop stamped out the first production model in the $25 billion program. There were supposed to be about 272 B-2s purchased, but the fleet stands at only twenty aircraft.[20] Spread the development cost over the small size of the fleet and you will end up with a bomber that costs over $3 billion each.

The B-1 was revived by the Reagan administration to be a stopgap until the B-2 could go into production, and the full run of 100 planes was purchased at the cost of about $200 million per bomber. Yet the plane was problem-plagued and was not deployed during the first Gulf War in 1990–91. It was used—finally—during Operation Desert Fox against Iraq in 1998, and again during the Kosovo War in 1999. The B-1 got a further workout in the Afghan war of 2001–02 and the second Gulf War in 2003.[21]

The B-1 never got decent billing in Clancy's universe, either failing in battle or relegated to playing low-level supersonic pranks in *Debt of Honor*. Currently, the U.S. has over ninety of the planes, planned to drop the fleet down to around sixty but faced opposition from senators and congressmen from states where the planes were based. The B-1 is not stealthy and makes do with outmoded cold war technology to cover its electronic tracks, which does not always work as well as advertised. However, it has an eighty-thousand-pound bomb load. With the advent of GPS-guided bombs and a long loitering time, the B-1 has been used to provide bombs on target when needed. It was a B-1 dropping a quartet of two-thousand-pound bombs that leveled a Baghdad restaurant where Saddam Hussein was thought to be hiding, and the mission was executed forty-five minutes after receipt of the information.[22] (Saddam was not there.)

The air force maintains a high profile in *Bear and the Dragon*. In the fictional war between Russia and China, as in real life, the first units showing up belong to the U.S. Air Force, which can be anywhere in the world in twenty-four hours and ready to fly first missions within twelve hours of arrival. The first U.S. air units begin basing along the Lena River, about one thousand miles west of the Chinese area of operations.

Between F-15 fighters and E-3A AWACS, the U.S. is confident that it can establish defensive air superiority. The problem is going to come with ground attack and bombing, as it will take three days' worth of cargo flights to deliver one day's worth of bombs. To support the air force deployment, President Ryan activates the civil reserve air fleet (CRAF). In real life, this was done for the first Gulf War. U.S. airlines are requested to furnish a number of wide-body airliners and pilots to fly air cargo and passengers to rear areas near the war zone.

Perhaps the most important air assets flown in are the unmanned aerial vehicles. Clancy names this system Dark Star, which is a remotely piloted drone aircraft capable of flying at sixty thousand feet. The U.S. has three of these aircraft, each armed with nothing more than high-powered television cameras that can wirelessly deliver crisp, clear pictures back to Bondarenko's HQ in Charbarosovil, somewhere east of Chita.

In true life, the U.S. has two UAV systems. The smaller one, called Predator, is a propeller-driven aircraft with a TV camera and the ability to fire the Hellfire antitank missile. It is useful for gathering tactical intelligence. Global Hawk, the larger of the two, is powered by a single jet engine and can reach the sixty-thousand-foot altitude of Clancy's fictional Dark Star. One of Global Hawk's first operational flights was a nonstop from California to Australia, done mostly on autopilot.

Global Hawk and Predator are designed to have long loiter times over the battlefield, providing continuous TV coverage, not much different from a helicopter for a TV news program. The weak point for both systems, however, is electronic bandwidth. Orders and images are relayed via satellite to on-ground controllers hundreds or thousands of miles away, and the satellites only have so many wireless channels to carry that information.[23]

In the Afghan war and second Gulf War, Predator and Global Hawk played significant roles identifying ground targets for U.S. airpower and artillery. In *Bear and the Dragon*, Dark Star would do pretty much the same, finding and fixing major Chinese HQs, artillery units, and armor for destruction from above, as well as identifying important targets in the Chinese rear areas.

The opening shots of the air war are fired during a four-on-four dogfight between Russian and Chinese SU-27 interceptors. The Russians win, four kills for one loss. The SU-27 is a twin-engine, twin-rudder jet fighter very similar in appearance to the F-15. It is by far the most successful Russian design of the late cold war period and has found new life in several variants, including a ground attack version similar to the F-15E Strike Eagle.

Cash-strapped after the fall of the Soviet Union, Russia has sold seventy-two SU-27s to China, which has formed the modern core of the Chinese air force. These arms purchases, along with four Kilo-class subs and two Soveremeny-class destroyers, also form the foundation for any Chinese air and sea effort to seize control of the Taiwan Straits, a necessary precondition to invading Taiwan.[24]

Next, the U.S. gets to mess with the PRC Air Force, as four F-15s tangle with sixteen inbound SU-27s. Even though the aircraft are comparable in performance, tactics and training mark the difference in outcome. Nine SU-27s go down in flames, while the U.S. suffers no losses. After the passage of several days, the U.S.-Russian team has knocked down thirty Chinese aircraft, suffering only four losses.

Why such a grotesque outcome, aside from the author wanting it that way? There have been many instances of U.S. and Russian aircraft fighting each other, albeit under different flags. Bear in mind that the nation that sells the planes also trains the pilots, so tactics and doctrine are transmitted with the hardware sale. Soviet doctrine places more initiative and command burden on the ground commander who is vectoring the flight to the enemy. U.S. doctrine places the initiative on the commanding pilot on the scene, while AWACS provides guidance. The serial Arab-Israeli wars provide much background here. Egypt and Syria flew better or comparable aircraft, yet lost decisively against Israel, which took Western tactics and training to new heights. Perhaps the most lopsided outcome was in the 1982 Israeli invasion of Lebanon, when the Israeli air force shot down ninety Syrian fighters while suffering no losses. This was the first time the F-15 and F-16 got their workouts against Russian-made MiG 21s, 23s, and 25s. But it should also be noted that the Israelis were applying the lessons learned the hard way about electronic warfare in the 1973 war, when losses to SAMs were quite grievous.[25]

The first air battles ensure that the Chinese cannot penetrate north of the border with Russia, so air reconnaissance is not possible. The Chinese estimate they are facing two Russian motorized rifle divisions on the ground, and are claiming twenty-five American planes shot down in exchange for one hundred of their own. The Russians and Americans have limited means to strike ground targets, given the lack of Russian planes and American bombs. The ordnance used by both countries is not interchangeable. While the U.S. First Armored has not arrived, the division's aviation brigade has been airlifted in four days by C-5 Galaxy air freighters and is forming up at Charbosovil, where the Russian HQ is located. Already, about one hundred F-16s have arrived to perform ground strike missions once enough ordnance has been stockpiled.

As the Chinese ground offensive grinds northward, its air force tries to redress the imbalance in the skies over Siberia. About thirty J-7s—a Chinese-made copy of the obsolete MiG 21—try rushing past a CAP flight of four F-15s to nail one of the U.S. E-3 AWACS. The Chinese fighters come in on full afterburner and probably don't have enough fuel to get back to base—in effect becoming sacrificial pawns gunning for a chance to take out the AWACS "queen." While the effort fails, thanks to a second CAP flight rushing in to protect the E-3, the Chinese do manage to slip a recon aircraft north through an uncovered sector. The effort does not yield much more usable information.

As the Chinese offensive closes in on its first objective, the U.S. stages coordinated air strikes deep in China with about twenty-four F-117 Stealth fighters, targeting the railway bridges at Bei'an and Harbin. Both cities are railway centers, where more than one line meet, and form bottlenecks through which reinforcements and supplies must pass.

The F-117 is a Carter-era weapon, whose designation as "fighter" is a misnomer. The plane is really a strike aircraft, with an internal bomb bay that can carry a pair of two thousand-pound laser-guided bombs. If it was called a bomber, funding would have been jeopardized for the B-2 Stealth bomber, a strategic weapon that carries a far heavier bomb load. The principle behind Stealth design is to lower the plane's radar signature through a combination of features—radar absorbent materials, underlying structure that dissipates rather than reflects the radar beam, and the presentation of no right-angled surfaces that can reflect radar. Optimizing for Stealth has meant trading off speed and maneuverability to achieve the F-117 design. Already used in four wars, only one F-117 has ever been lost to enemy fire. That was in 1999, when a lucky Yugoslav SAM shot bagged an F-117 on the Belgrade run. (The U.S. deemed it a "lucky shot.") The F-117 is used only for high-value targets. About fifty were made—they were expensive for their day at about $50 million each. Since then, Stealth has been a standard design feature incorporated in two more fighters—the F-22 and the F-35.

Just before the climactic battle of the campaign, F-16 CGs are tasked with taking out Chinese SAM radars. Two squadrons of F-16s armed with JSOWs—joint standoff weapons—are inbound. They hit the three of the four divisions in the Thirty-fourth Shock Army, reducing their armored punch to little more than a brigade. Note that they draw no fire from ground-based antiaircraft guns or SAMs.

Airpower unchallenged over the battlefield can destroy anything it can see. One need not look at recent examples for proof. As far back as World War II, strike aircraft pretty much mauled ground units, whether it was the Luftwaffe in France or Russia in 1940–41 or the U.S. and British over Normandy in 1944. During the Korean War, World War II–vintage aircraft chewed up North Korean and Chinese forces as the USAF F-86s maintained air superiority with a 10:1 kill ratio against North Korean and Chinese MiG-15s. During Vietnam, U.S. airpower blunted and halted the 1972 Communist offensive, while air strikes on call were an abundant resource tapped in many ground operations.

But airpower proved to be underwhelming when it came to strategic bombing during the same period. In World War II, the German bombing of London in 1940 did not break the will of the British people to wage war. British nighttime bombing was so inaccurate that the RAF gave up on trying to hit factories, choosing instead to bomb entire cities. Each was a target too big to miss, and the strategy also called for breaking the will of the German people to wage war by wiping out their homes and workplaces, as well as their lives.

American daylight bombing promised to accurately hit industrial targets while sparing residential neighborhoods from excessive harm. The B-17s and B-24s were purpose-built for this mission. In practice, daylight bombing was sadly inaccurate, requiring one hundred bombs to score one to three hits per target. Even so, it still took the U.S. over two years of bombing to destroy German industry, and even then losses of planes and aircrews were horrendous until the advent of long-range fight escorts like the P-47 and P-51. And targets had to be hit repeatedly to be sure no factory could be rebuilt to resume production. Big raids on Schweinfurt (ball bearings) and Ploesti (oil) proved fruitless as production always resumed within a week or two of a singular big raid.

The A-bomb brought one-bomb-per-target capability, but on a very crude basis. Dropping one was sure to destroy the target city, as happened with Hiroshima and Nagasaki. Military targets would be obliterated—and outweighed in value by massive collateral damage.

The U.S. staged a more haphazard bombing campaign over North Vietnam. Political considerations limited target selection while losses mounted from flak, SAMs, and enemy fighters. It took one squadron to destroy one target—a notable improvement from World War II, but grievous losses were still suffered. Toward the end of the Vietnam War, laser-guided bombs made their first appearance. Now it was possible for one or two planes to destroy a target, and the hits were accurate enough to put it out of action for a while.

After refinement, the technology gained in usage during the first Gulf War, where about 10 percent of all bombs dropped were laser-guided. By the late 1990s the global positioning system was adapted to work with bombs. Now air planners talk about targets per plane, not planes per target, as each bomb can be dropped with an accuracy measured in a few meters. Reexamining history with technology in mind, if the USAF had to redo its World War II air campaign over Germany with the capability it had in the first Gulf War, it would wrap up the campaign in six weeks. Redoing the same campaign with today's technology, the same goal would be accomplished in a few days.[26]

Another weapons system caught in the throes of doctrinal change is the attack helicopter. The AH-64 Apache also does star turns in *Executive Orders* and *Bear and the Dragon*, but failed to live up to expectations in the Kosovo War, the Afghan war, and the second Gulf War.

The AH-64 Apache is the army's replacement for the AH-1 Cobra gunship. The AH-64 packs sixteen Hellfire antitank missiles as well as a 30mm chain gun. The Longbow version also sports a long-range radar unit.

The antitank role for the helicopter gunship was born in 1972, when the Huey Cobra was matched with the TOW antitank missile and used as a tank killer to stop the Easter offensive staged by North Vietnam. The AH-64 improves on the concept, and was used successfully in the first Gulf War. On the war's "opening night," AH-64s went deep into the desert, well ahead of ground units, to destroy SAM sites that would interfere with the air force's establishment of air superiority, the necessary prerequisite for all air missions.

In *Executive Orders* and in *Bear and the Dragon*, the AH-64 repeats the deep raid mission flawlessly, taking out tank concentrations, HQ units, and SAM sites. But the story was not the same in three real-life other wars. In 1999, an AH-64 battalion was moved from Germany to Albania to become the nucleus of Task Force Hawk. But it took several weeks to fly the twenty-six choppers down from Germany, and the unit lost two aircraft in training accidents. They were never used to attack Serb forces over the border in Kosovo.

The AH-64 played a major supporting role providing army air support in the Battle of Tora Bora in mid-December 2001, during the Afghan war. Unfortunately, the helicopters were badly riddled by ground fire and had to be withdrawn from the role. The air force and navy provided air support for the remainder of the battle.

Finally, the Eleventh Aviation Brigade was deployed to Kuwait to support ground units in the second Gulf War. All twenty-six Apaches were sent on a deep raid to take out Iraqi assets, much as they did in the first Gulf War. All twenty-six ships were hit by gunfire and damaged, with one helicopter crashing as a result. The Eleventh did not get a chance to do another deep raid for the remainder of the campaign.

Attack helicopters are not flying tanks. Offensively, they pack a lot of firepower. Defensively, they can be armored well enough to protect the aircrew. The engines are designed to run long enough when damaged to guarantee a safe landing well away from the fight. But helicopters can't take many hits. What once worked well in real life (and Tom Clancy novels) will have to be rethought if the AH-64 will continue in its air-support role.

The army adopted the helicopter in the 1950s to make up for the loss of its ground support aircraft to the air force, which does not take the ground support mission to heart. While the USAF reluctantly operates the A-10 Warthog, an aircraft built from the ground up to provide close air support, it has tried on numerous occasions to drop it from its roster. Every time this happens, the army offers to take the A-10, which then prompts the air force to keep them anyway.

The army lost its fixed-wing mission upon creation of the Defense Department in the late 1940s, combining the army and navy departments while creating an independent air force. The navy has kept the close air support mission within the Marine Corps, tapping the F/A 18 Hornet and the AV-8 Harrier, as well as a later variant of the AH-1 Cobra, to fulfill that mission.

Tanks and Troops

And the wars just keep coming.

In real life, the U.S. has gone to war six times between 1989 and 2004: Panama (1989), Somalia (1992–03), Haiti (1994), Kosovo (1999), Afghanistan (2001–02), and Iraq (2003–present). In Clancy's world, the U.S. fights Japan, Iraq/Iran, and China in a span of less than two years.

The war between the United States and Clancy's fictional United Islamic Republic, as depicted in *Executive Orders*, has a firm baseline for comparison: the first and second Gulf Wars. Clancy acknowledges the passage of the first Gulf War before getting down to real make-believe.

In the ensuing political chaos following the fictional assassination of Saddam Hussein, Iran facilitates the flight of various high-level Iraqi generals. Baathists are rounded up and shot, while the remaining Iraqi brigadiers and colonels acquiesce to the control of the new regime.

It's a given that the reader has to allow a certain amount of flexibility in the way real world events are portrayed to enjoy a Clancy novel; more than usual is needed at this point. The UIR cobbles together a combined army—three Republican Guard divisions with three Iranian armored and mechanized counterparts. Keep in mind that this is happening in the 1996–2000 time frame, less than a decade after the conclusion of the Iran-Iraq War of 1980–88. The fictional Iran's armored punch numbers several divisions, all Russian-equipped, even though the real Iran started out with a Western-equipped army following its 1979 revolution and has ever since had a hard time buying military equipment thanks to numerous U.S. economic sanctions. The fictional Iraq is also able to field several battle-ready Republican Guard divisions, even though in the second Gulf War these units were hobbled for lack of spare parts and replacements thanks to U.S.-UN economic sanctions. Both nations resorted to illicit purchase and trade to make up for shortfalls in their armies, but that strategy can only provide a fraction of what could be obtained within the good graces of the international system.

The Iraqi and Iranian armies fought each other with widely different doctrines during their eight-year war, and these differences would have to be surmounted to field a three-corps force with units from both nations. Iran played away from its weaknesses, namely a lack of tanks and APCs, stricken for lack of spare parts given the embargoes of the time. But Iran is three times more populous than Iraq, and naturally played to this strength by building a massive infantry army. By sheer numbers and heavy casualties, Iran successively breached the Iraqi lines, but each breakthrough never moved faster than walking speed. Offensives petered out after gaining three to five miles of ground, giving Iraqi armored reserves sufficient time to seal any breach.

Iraq's pre–Gulf War army was heavily armored and mechanized

along the Soviet model. It could stage limited offensives that rolled according to plan. Depart from that plan, however, and the battles would founder for lack of commanders experienced at improvisation. Saddam Hussein made things worse here, as he shifted many colonels and generals around the army so that no one could build up enough unit loyalty to stage a coup. By 1986, however, Hussein had to give his generals free rein to fight the battles as they saw fit. This allowed Iraq to regain lost ground and threaten Iran again, supplemented by an unending bombardment of Tehran with SCUD missiles, which the war-weary Iranian population had to endure until cracking. (The leaders didn't crack—they were safe and snug in the suburbs.)

In Clancy's UIR army, the Iraqi and Iranian armies are melded into a three-corps force of six divisions in a matter of weeks. Language barriers don't exist, even though the Iraqis speak Arabic and the Iranians speak Farsi. Differences in experience, tactical doctrine, and logistics hardly matter here, even though it would have taken several years to resolve. The combined army was readying for its big push south into Saudi Arabia.

So far how will they go?

In the first Gulf War, Saddam Hussein made sure his Republican Guard practiced for months before making a 125-mile push southward to take oil-rich Kuwait. The bulk of the Saudi oil fields were just south of Kuwait, and with a little more effort could have fallen into Saddam's grasp. In Clancy's fiction, the UIR war plan calls for a strike southward toward King Khalid Military City, located in the middle of the desert, nowhere near a single oil field. Okay, the author can write this up any way he wants—it's his book. As Clancy lays out his scenario, the Saudis refight the last war, stationing three of their five brigades south of Kuwait. The two remaining brigades would be facing at least one attacking corps three times their size.

Time to bring in the Americans.

After the first Gulf War, where it took thirty days to move a single armored or mechanized division, the U.S. sought to shorten this lag time by pre-positioning stocks of vehicles and equipment in the region. U.S. troops would be flown in, pick up their equipment, and re-form units in a fraction of the same deployment time.

Clancy keeps this doctrine in place, but puts further spin on his scenario by dropping a bioterrorism attack in the U.S. that immobilizes the bulk of the U.S. military and much of interstate commerce. Instead of sending the XVIII Airborne Corps to Saudi Arabia/Kuwait (101st Airmobile, Eighty-second Airborne, Twenty-fourth Mechanized Infantry Division), the U.S. has to settle for airlifting the troops of Tenth Armored Cavalry Regiment from Israel's Negev Desert, plus Eleventh ACR and a brigade of the North Carolina National Guard from the National Training Center at Fort Irwin, California.

Clancy is enthusiastic about the use of armored cavalry. The ACR is a mixed force of M1A1 Abrams tanks and M3 Bradley infantry fighting vehicles. The Abrams mounts a 120mm smoothbore main gun capable of first-round kills out to three kilometers (about two miles). The M-3 Bradley also mounts a TOW antitank missile launcher and its 25mm Bushmaster chain gun can penetrate older Soviet-era armor (T-54/55).

As the war progresses, the UIR offensive steamrollers southward, with a lead corps-sized element making contact with the Saudi Fourth Brigade. Two battalions are annihilated, while a third executes a fighting withdrawal toward King Khalid Military City. A downed U.S. pilot who was flying air support missions is now handy to call in four more air strikes to maul the UIR spearhead.

In these passages, Clancy shows the unnamed Saudi battalion commander practicing maneuver warfare against a plodding but massive enemy advance. Is this possible? The Saudi performance in the first Gulf War illustrates the gap between fact and fiction. Facing an attack from several battalion-sized Iraqi task forces at Ras al Khafji, Saudi units first fled south of the town before regrouping for a counterattack. Two Saudi battalions and a Qatari armored battalion were tasked with retaking the town, which they did in a slow and flat-footed fashion, supported by ample U.S. artillery and air power. A second Iraqi armored battalion that blundered into one of the Saudi battalions north of Khafji did get mauled, but the Saudis were fighting in a static defense mode. After three days of desultory operations, Khafji was retaken (though Iraqi demoralization after three days of getting shelled and bombed may have had something to do with it).[27]

Saudi brigades were core assets in Joint Task Force East and Joint Task Force North—the two principal Arab forces that advanced north into Kuwait. JTF East was hampered by a massive influx of Iraqi POWs and faced little to no organized resistance, yet it could not keep up with the marine division to its west that had to advance through combat. JTF North—which contained an Egyptian division—also moved slower than the battle-busy marines. It is kind of Clancy to give the Saudi military more ability than it has shown in real life.[28]

Meanwhile, the fictional UIR main line of advance is west of Kuwait, while Tenth ACR concentrates in Kuwait for a future counterstroke westward. The Eleventh's attack and recon helicopters fly into the desert to locate the UIR's main body, yet the choppers face no ground fire, flak, or SAM fire. The UIR II Corps, which led the breakthrough, wheels east to provide a flank guard facing Kuwait. UIR I corps now advances as the North Carolina NG brigade links up with the depleted Saudi battalion south of King Khalid Military City. The Eleventh ACR is located southeast of this position. The North Carolina NG unit fights a defensive battle, easily outranging the lead T-80s of UIR I Corps, while its towed artillery, divisional, and corps HQs are destroyed by U.S. artillery and air strikes. In short, two brigades face an enemy force three times as large and turn it into hash. North Carolina NG, supported by Eleventh ACR, now goes on the offensive, ripping into the remains of UIR I Corps. The NG unit is getting tank kills at four kilometers, whereas a kill at three kilometers is more the norm.

While this is going on, Tenth ACR goes on the offensive from Kuwait, driving north into Iraq, hooking west and driving into the rear-area elements of UIR II Corps and III Corps. The Eleventh ACR moves north of the North Carolina NG brigade, hooking into elements of III Corps. Eventually, the UIR "Army of God" HQ is wiped out. The mauled remnants can no longer put up a good fight.

In Clancy's war scenario, we see two coordinated outflanking moves, where smaller forces with near-perfect information on enemy dispositions wipe out forces much larger than themselves. How real is that compared to the two Gulf Wars the U.S. fought?

The first Gulf War was the largest deployment for the U.S. since Vietnam. Two marine divisions (with attached air assets), seven army divisions, and two armored cavalry regiments, six carriers with their air wings, and another 736 combat aircraft from the air force made up the predominant contribution to coalition forces. Egypt also spared two divisions, Syria sent one, Britain and France sent one each, with Saudi Arabia committing five brigades and Kuwait another three brigades (Gulf States contributed a few battalions, as befitting their size).

The doctrine governing the use of U.S. ground forces in the first Gulf War was called AirLand. Get past the catchy name and one finds a near-total integration of intelligence, communications, battle management, targeting, and damage assessment in near real-time. Combined arms operations is a given, and "jointness" of operations is stressed between the services. All this is combined to fight the war in any weather, day or night, striking as deeply as capability will permit, with an emphasis on maneuver.

Judging from the results obtained on the battlefield, the AirLand doctrine seemed like a smashing success. The U.S. Army managed maneuver warfare at the strategic level, shifting two corps to the west, into the same deep empty desert that became Clancy's battlefield in *Executive Orders*. The similarities end here. Even though coalition forces were outnumbered 3:2 theaterwide, the six-week aerial bombardment and overwhelming firepower at the opening of the ground war made quick work of the forward-deployed Iraqi infantry divisions. Iraqi armored units were shot up at long range, never having the chance to return fire. But the allied ground forces that moved forward were lined up flank-to-flank and moved in unison, while the Iraqi Army acted as a collapsing bag that masked the escape of a mauled Republican Guard.[29] This was not a war of deep dagger thrusts by nimble brigades against large, plodding corps, and the bad guys did get away to put down postwar Shiite uprisings that the U.S. encouraged but failed to support.

The second Gulf War was probably closer to Clancy's fictional equivalent. Here the array of forces was less than half of the previous engagement. The U.S. fielded three divisions, with a fourth that could not get to the war on time, plus several assorted airborne brigades. The Iraqi Army had five corps-sized deployments running south to north, with two corps of Republican Guard and one division of special Republican Guard concentrated on the approaches to Baghdad. Looking at the raw numbers, one would think that the U.S. was outnumbered in the theater by 6- or 7:1. But this was not so. First, much of the Iraqi Army chose not to fight and did not make its presence felt at all. Second, given the improvements in the integration of computerized networks and communications since the last Gulf War, battlefield information flowed faster and closer to real time than it did before. U.S. brigades equaled divisions as operational units of maneuver. The U.S. had to rely on maneuver given the smaller size of the force and the need to cover way more ground than the liberation of Kuwait. The war was over in two weeks, with U.S. units rolling into Baghdad as the Iraqi information minister appeared live on TV denying their existence.

Maneuver warfare as applied by the AirLand doctrine has demonstrated its effectiveness in large, set-piece battles. In the second Gulf War, greater reliance was placed on fewer units to deliver a greater outcome. But there is an unseen downside—if an individual battalion or brigade gets hit hard, it will not have the depth to absorb losses and continue its mission. This problem may become telling in the near future, as the army is reorganizing itself into two-battalion brigades, down from three or four battalions per brigade.

Another Clancy invention is the North Carolina National Guard brigade holding its own against a professional UIR army in a set-piece battle. During the first Gulf War, three round-out brigades were activated from the National Guard pool and subjected to a ninety-day training cycle to make them battle-ready for deployment to Saudi Arabia. They never made it, failing to meet training goals in a timely fashion.[30] While guard units have been mobilized for deployment to Bosnia, Kosovo, and later Iraq for peacekeeping duties, none in recent years has ever been committed to high-intensity battle. This is not a slam at the guard, but it is a different force compared to the regular army. The guard trains one weekend per month and two weeks every year. Training is more of a full-time occupation for the army. Given this difference, it would not be fair to expect guard and army units to perform at the same level. The guard complements the army—it is not a substitute.

Clancy has a fondness for smaller forces defeating larger enemies. So it's no surprise that in *Bear and the Dragon*, a fictional Sino-Russian War will see a repeat of what worked before.

The setup for war begins with Clancy's "good Russian" Bondarenko getting command of Russia's Far Eastern Military District, where he oversees six motorized rifle divisions, one armored division, and one artillery division—on paper. The units average about 70 percent effectiveness, but readiness varies wildly from division to division. The 265th MRD stands at about 85 percent effectiveness, lacking its organic tank regiment, though the BMP armored personnel carriers do mount antitank missiles. The remaining rifle divisions are at true regimental or cadre strength. The armored division is rated at regiment-plus. There is also several well-hidden supply and weapons depots that could furnish an extra division or two, but no one handy to man them. While the Chinese People's Liberation Army has been practicing for four years, the Russians haven't done much to maintain readiness or proficiency. Bondarenko starts his command with much work to do! Russian naval assets do not figure into Clancy's scenario at all, while the air force has a token presence of about fifty operational aircraft, with many more grounded.

Meanwhile, the U.S. is also operating with a diminished order of battle, thanks to military cuts made after the cold war. The four-division presence in Germany is now down to just one—the First Armored Division. It stands at 95 percent effectiveness. Training has been maintained, even if the defense budget has not.

About halfway through the narrative, the Politburo of the People's Republic of China decides it is time to move north. China has been on a shopping spree for foreign armaments so it is suffering from a shortage of foreign currency. Couple this with a trade breakdown owing to unfavorable news coverage of domestic repression. All this has put the PRC in a strategic bind. The leadership sees the seizure of newly found oil and goldfields in eastern Siberia, north of Chinese Manchuria, as the solution.

Clancy provides few landmarks that precisely mark the location of his make-believe theater of operations. The Amur River marks China's northern border with Russia, which is acknowledged in the novel. Clancy refers to a Russian assembly area located at Chita, which is several hundred miles to the northwest of Hailar, a major center in northwestern Manchuria. As the crow flies, Chita is over five hundred miles away from Blagovechensk, about one thousand miles away from Khabarovsk. Both are major cities on the Amur River and significant waypoints on the Trans-Siberian Railway, which hugs the Sino-Russian border.

Russo-Chinese history does not come into significant play in Clancy's scenario as a cause for war. China used to own a portion of eastern Siberia, which now makes up Russia's Maritime Province that abuts the Sea of Japan, ceding the territory to Russia in an unequal treaty signed around 1860.

Northern Manchuria has been the site of previous fighting in the twentieth century. When Japan briefly owned Manchuria in the 1930s, it fought a series of border skirmishes with Soviet Russia, culminating in a small division–sized battle over an area called Nomonhan/Khalkin Gol in 1939. Russia won that one. Indeed, the main channel of the Amur River may look like a good place to demarcate a border, but the river has a long history of running wild, oftentimes shifting channels after storms or spring floods. Borders should not move once set, but try telling that to a river that won't stay put.[31]

One traditional gold war flashpoint between the two Communist giants was the island of Hei-Tzia-Tsu, located at the confluence of the Amur and Ussuri Rivers, hard up by Khabarovsk. China still claimed the island even though Russia occupied it since 1858. Possession of the island would have placed Chinese forces uncomfortably close to Khabarovsk's airfields as well within artillery range of the crucial Trans-Siberian Railroad, whose final leg is between Khabarovsk and Vladivostok.[32]

The Soviet Union and China did fight a small war over the same frontier in the late 1960s–early 1970s. News reports about these incidents were pretty sketchy, but it did get to the point where Soviets were asking the U.S. for an understanding that would give them a free hand to go to war with China. This created the opening Kissinger and Nixon needed to engineer a rapprochement with China, creating a new balance of power that kept the ascendant Soviets in check while America was weakened by its debacle in Vietnam.[33]

Back to Clancy's War.

Like the fictional second Gulf War, the make-believe Sino-Russian War also takes place deep in unoccupied territory, well away from major cities. There are no civilians to kill accidentally in the cross fire. There is no collateral damage when the bombs are dropped. Only armies fight armies. Only soldiers die.

The Chinese attack comes late in the year—not quite winter, but late enough for some thin ice to form on the Amur. Infantry cross in rubber boats to take out the first two lines of Russian fixed positions, with the support of heavily concentrated Chinese artillery. Once the northern shore is secure, ribbon bridges are laid down for the crossing by the main elements of the Thirty-fourth Shock Army.

Clancy describes the Thirty-fourth as having four divisions—two mechanized infantry, one motorized infantry, and one armored. The Chinese war plan called for four type A armies like the Thirty-fourth

Shock to lead the invasion, followed by six type B armies that are sufficiently mechanized or motorized to keep up and occupy captured territory. Trailing all this are four type C group armies of mostly infantry to garrison the ill-gotten gains. All this totals forty-four divisions.

One strategic move the U.S. pulls off is to secure Russian membership in NATO. An attack on one member state is an attack on all, so it is no surprise that the U.S. will be pulled into the conflict. Yet other NATO member states make little to no contribution to the defense of Russia (though Clancy does briefly mentions the British readying one brigade). The First Armored entrains in Germany for the journey east. Russia also moves four more motorized rifle divisions toward Chita.

Bondarenko's plan is to trade space for time. It was something the Russians did in World War I against the Germans (Poland and the Baltic states were part of Russia in those days.) But this was not done in World War II, when Stalin attempted to defend the border with much of his army and did not easily allow any retreat in the face of the invading Germans. Bondarenko counts himself lucky to have Moscow's confidence and freedom to deal with the problem, rather than trying to hold, fail, and face a firing squad.

Bondarenko's staff figures the Chinese can advance about thirty kilometers a day—about twenty miles. The Chinese were planning on twenty kilometers on the first day, with gains of fifty kilometers a day after that. By either measure, the Thirty-fourth Shock Army will reach the goldfields in seven to eight days, with another two days needed to reach the oil fields. Given that week's grace period, Bondarenko figures he should have several good divisions handy to fight a real battle. Barely mentioned in the book is that the Chinese offensive immediately cuts the Trans-Siberian Railroad to all points east, including Vladivostok. The Chinese plan on turning east to mop up after two to three weeks, as the main objective of the offensive is to grab the gold- and oil fields.

Time is always a factor, even in Clancy's scenario. Can the Chinese bring more force to bear in Siberia faster than the Russians can bring in their reinforcements? Bondarenko can't match the forty-four Chinese divisions in terms of numbers. Aside from the U.S. First Armored plus four MRDs en route, a reserve division named Boyar is formed from older T-55 tanks manned by reservists. The entire mothballed unit consists of three hundred T-55s and 200 BTR-60s (an eight-wheeled armored personnel carrier). Bondarenko plans to use the First Armored to cut the PRC supply line north of the Amur River, while Boyar will be north of the Americans, advancing from west to east on a parallel line. This plan is a basic example of "maneuver warfare."

The Russian defense now takes shape, as the line to be held is about two hundred miles north of the Chinese breakthrough. Bondarenko has picked a ridge five miles north of the goldfield to make a stand with the 265th MRD. The recently arrived 201st MRD will take position to the west, ready to drive east into the Chinese left flank after the battle is joined.

The U.S. First Armored has formed up. The target is the Chinese type B army guarding the ribbon bridges across the Amur. This force consists of four infantry divisions with towed artillery and a single armored brigade. Technically, the U.S. is outnumbered by about 4:1, but the numbers do not tell all. Given the preponderance of recon assets enjoyed by the U.S., the First Armored has a clear picture of Chinese dispositions, while the Chinese are blind to the coming American onslaught.

First, the two infantry companies holding hilltop positions to guard the Chinese division flank each get hit with one battery's worth of artillery. The regimental HQ is hit with the First Armored's eight-inch guns. The First's multiple launch rocket system (MLRS) aims for the Chinese division's HQ. The First's aviation brigade goes hunting for the lone armored brigade attached to the Chinese type B army, taking out SAM sites and antiaircraft guns before turning on the laagered tanks. With HQs eliminated at every echelon, the Chinese can't even formulate a coordinated defense as the First Armored pushes through, seeking the Chinese rear areas.

The tempo of battle is now raised a few notches. F-16 CGs are tasked with taking out Chinese SAM radars while two squadrons of F-16s armed with JSOWs hit three of the four divisions in the Thirty-fourth Shock Army, reducing their total armored punch to little more than a brigade. This happens as the lead elements of Thirty-fourth Shock reach the ridge five miles north of the goldfields, where Bondarenko has chosen to make his stand with two motorized rifle divisions and three complete sets of divisional artillery. A third MRD is thirty kilometers (about twenty miles) south, ready to drive from west to east through the Chinese flank. South of that line is Boyar, ready to do the same with its obsolete horde of T-55s. The Thirty-fourth Shock army ceases to be an effective force.

A highlight of Clancy's has a company of Russian recon troops re-treating about one kilometer in front of the advancing Chinese forces throughout the book, maintaining constant contact without being seen and reporting straight to Bondarenko. At the ridge overlooking the goldfield, a grizzled old Russian Stalingrad veteran who lives nearby takes his best shot at the commanding Chinese general of the Thirty-fourth Shock Army, nailing him cold. At that point, the recon company bugs out before the Chinese can react.

Political developments in Beijing resolve the action, as China fails to launch a successful nuclear strike against the U.S. and a replay of Tiananmen Square sees the students overrunning the government compound this time, forcing a change of regime. China now seeks a diplomatic end to the misbegotten war.

Real Life After Make-believe

Ground war and air war have advanced a lot since Clancy penned his mid-1990s novels pitting the U.S. against his fictional "axis of evil." Given the advances in computer and communication technology, U.S. forces "punch above their weight."

During the Afghan war, the U.S. only put two hundred and fifty Special Forces troops on the ground. Their main weapon was the ground target laser designator coupled with the Global Positioning System. Using this combination, SF troopers could accurately call ground support from U.S. Navy and Air Force aircraft loitering in the skies above. At this point, airpower was restated from number of planes per target to number of targets per plane.

The second Gulf War took all of that a step farther, as all sources of information were integrated and provided to ground force commanders in near real time for decision and attack. Predator and Global Hawk provided visual information. AWACS controlled all air traffic into and out of the combat zone (the Iraqi Air Force was never a factor). JSTARs, which was in prototype in the first Gulf War, was a full-fledged version of AWACS for ground targets. Rivet-Joint provided all ELINT for the front. Take these systems and their sources of data, combine them, and the battlefield becomes transparent for any U.S. force in a conventional set-piece battle. Clancy only touched on this in his make-believe Sino-Russian War.

While all this stuff is pretty amazing, technologically speaking, it does not cover every dimension of war fighting. Technology is a great force multiplier in a conventional war. It does far less in counterinsurgency, peacekeeping, antiterrorism, and nation building—missions that the U.S. military confronts today. The United States won its second war in Iraq in two weeks flat, thanks to applied technology. But it has lost more men killed in action in the year following its "victory." Predator doesn't stop suicide bombers. JSTARs can't detect three die-hard Baathist guerrillas planting a roadside bomb. An M-1 tank, though impervious to AT missiles and RPGs, can't change the hearts and minds of occupation-weary Iraqis. Those truths return us back to the fundamental linkage between the use of force and politics: only soldiers can control or contest the political ownership of the ground.

Technology cannot substitute for this, even though in fiction the high-tech weapons are effective and thrilling.

Clancy has shown great willingness to rotate the various branches of the armed forces through starring and supporting roles throughout his books. Navy, army, air force, and marines all get their turns in the spotlight. Even the coast guard gets a major supporting role in *Clear and Present Danger.*

In any given deployment abroad to fight some small war, interservice cooperation has become the norm. Since the Goldwater-Nichols Act of 1986, more work has been done to increase the ability of the services to interoperate.[34] This need became apparent during the 1983 Grenada invasion, where army troops could not call in naval air strikes owing to incompatibility in their radios. Now compare that to Afghanistan in 2001–02, when army and air force Special Forces regularly called in air force and navy air strikes without any operational problems.

Clancy may have to mix and match weapons and service branches to add some variety to his novels. But in real life, that is going to happen anyway as each branch contributes some portion of their expertise to accomplishing a mission shaped by geography and political circumstances. Never again will each service try to fight and win its own war without regard to, or cooperation with, any other service in any given theater.

Terminate with Extreme Prejudice
The Role of Killing

The good guys do it. The bad guys do it. The difference is that Tom Clancy is willing to bend the rules to make it okay for the good guys to do it.

We are talking about killing, or "termination with extreme prejudice."

In war, killing has its place. The state holds the monopoly on violence. The soldier is its uniformed agent, authorized to kill enemy soldiers within the boundaries of widely accepted rules of combat. Soldiers cannot kill unarmed civilians—that would be a war crime, which is a nicer way of saying *murder*. Civilians do get killed when fighting takes place in suburbs and cities, but these deaths are a regrettable by-product of state-sanctioned violence so long as the civilians are not deliberately targeted.

Soldiers wear uniforms to identify themselves. Sometimes there are deviations from the rules, as civilians will pick up weapons to fight foreign soldiers occupying their country. Even when this is so, any civilians captured must be treated as a prisoner of war under the Geneva Convention, no different than a captured soldier.

In law enforcement, police officers are the agents of the city, county, or state who maintain law and order. They are issued sidearms that can only be used in specific instances when the use of deadly force is warranted. A police officer can kill a suspect if that person is armed and poses a clear and present danger to nearby people or other police officers. A cop can't shoot a fleeing suspect, or simply kill someone because he feels that person could be a threat. If a suspect is arrested, the officer has to notify him that he has the right to remain silent. If the suspect waives this right, anything he says will be used against him. He has a right to an attorney, even if he can't afford one. The suspect is innocent until proven guilty. He cannot be forced to incriminate himself. He has a right to a fair and speedy trial by a jury of his peers, with the right to confront witnesses and question evidence.

But in Clancy's world, most of these rules don't always apply. Killing wrongdoers is the quickest way to end a problem when the law does not apply or gives the bad guy too many breaks, thus making justice or national security difficult to obtain. In Clancy's world, killing always takes place within the context of paramilitary operations carried out by the CIA or suitably trained commandos in situations short of war. It may take place within the context of espionage if circumstances warrant it. It may be an extrajudicial killing in places where the force of U.S. law is weakened in the face of crime. Or it may take place within the context of counterterrorism.

The bottom line is that in Clancy's world, killing is pragmatic and effective.

Knowing Who to Kill—and When

The question of killing comes up quickly for Jack Ryan. *Hunt for Red October* is Clancy's first printed book, but *Patriot Games* is where the Ryan story begins. It is the early 1980s. Ryan is an ex-Marine who has left the Corps after suffering a backbreaking accident, and now works as a professor of military history at the U.S. Naval Academy. The book begins with Ryan taking a research break in London, accompanied by his family.

Irish terrorists belonging to the fictional Ulster Liberation Army attack the limousine carrying the prince and princess of Wales. Not knowing who they are or that the attack was a kidnapping attempt, Ryan intervenes. He tackles one of the gunmen, takes the guy's pistol, shoots him in the hip to disable him, and opens fire at the remaining gunman, killing him. In doing this, Ryan is shot in the shoulder. (No he does not go prancing around afterward with a big Band-Aid covering the wound. This is not a Hollywood movie.) Ryan's first kill happens within the context of a violent kidnapping attempt that has killed the prince of Wales's driver and bodyguard. The men Ryan shoots were armed and clearly demonstrated violent intent. The good deed does get Ryan a knighthood. It also lands one of the surviving terrorists, Sean Miller, in jail. By Clancy's description, Miller is a cold-blooded killer worse than most of his kind.

As *Patriot Games* unfolds, the bad guys in the ULA definitely want to get even. They spring Sean Miller as he is being transported to prison. They target Ryan and his family. Alert marine guards foil the ULA stakeout at Annapolis, but other ULA terrorists manage to machine-gun Cathy Ryan's Porsche shortly after she picks up her daughter at the Giant Steps day care center. Both mother and daughter survive, though daughter Sally's injuries are worsened owing to an unbuckled seat belt as the car slams into an abutment.

Now Ryan wants to protect himself and his family. He practices pistol shooting, courtesy of a senior marine noncom at the Academy. His freelance associations with the CIA allow him to there work part-time in the hope of developing more intelligence that could target the ULA for later action.

And, of course, the prince and princess of Wales will be stopping by for dinner later on in the book. As British police take down the ULA's ring in England, the ULA chief O'Connell commits his scanty Libyan-trained force to attacking the Ryan estate during the "royal" dinner party. The local police and U.S. secret service have the grounds well covered. But the terrorists penetrate from two sides. A smaller recon team gains entry by using an electric utility van to pay a service call on a nearby transformer. They use the two ladders on the truck's top to reach the bottom of a nearby cliff, allowing the larger seaborne strike team to reach the grounds.

The terrorists route the security detail at the gate. A smaller second team takes Ryan and his dinner guests captive—save Robby Jackson, who was elsewhere in the house, and is now looking for the household 12-gauge shotgun. The battle at the gate goes awry, and O'Connell calls for reinforcements. The six terrorists at the house are now three, and Jackson takes the opportunity to shoot two of them with the shotgun from a bedroom opening overlooking the living room. Ryan and his party guests take the dead terrorists' weapons and make their way to the boats the bad guys arrived with, the third terrorist in tow at gunpoint.

Called in by the beleaguered security detail, the heliborne FBI hostage rescue team (HRT) flies in through the passing storm, but fails to make it to the Ryan estate, landing hard about four hundred yards short after evading a Redeye fired by one of the terrorists. The HRT sniper infiltrates the Ryan estate, sizing up the number and disposition of bad guys. Meanwhile, Ryan and his guests have made their way down the cliff to the two waiting getaway boats. Ryan kills the two ULA boat guards, though his ULA captive also dies in the cross fire. Quickly, Ryan and his guests make their own getaway.

The ULA terrorists rally at the house, only to find their hostages gone. The FBI hostage rescue team is now in the woods, with their lead sniper doing recon on the house. As no hostage is present to be in danger, he holds his fire, unsure of who is in the house. By the rules of his agency, he cannot kill at this moment.

The terrorists are not bound by such rules. Sean Miller loses his temper and kills one of the renegade Americans helping out in the operation after being razzed for his failure. The terrorists then disappear over the cliff's edge, crowding into the remaining boat. The FBI and local police puzzle over the carnage at the scene—twenty-four dead bodies and no hostages. Elsewhere, the chase is on!

Ryan's boat makes it to the Naval Academy at nearby Annapolis. The marine guard is mustered to secure the harbor. They exchange gunfire with the terrorist boat, which then makes a fast getaway. Ryan and company pursue the terrorists in a larger navy patrol boat with a squad of marines onboard. They merely track the smaller terrorist motorboat with radar while notifying local police and the coast guard as the bad guys make their way to a Cypriot-registered freighter. The Maryland state police and FBI get there first, partially securing the freighter while cornering the terrorist motorboat between the freighter and the incoming navy boat full of marines.

At this point, Ryan gets his next chance to kill someone, as he sees Sean Miller on the freighter's deck. While Ryan puts his pistol to Miller's head, the accompanying marine sergeant reminds Ryan that killing the terrorist in cold blood is not worth it.

This is a point to dwell on as the rest of Clancy's work is examined. When is killing allowed? In *Patriot Games*, the terrorists kill the unarmed, but the good guys only take lives when the bad guys are armed or shooting.

The point is revisited briefly in *Hunt for Red October*.

Captain Ramius and his colleagues fake a nuclear reactor leak on the sub to force the evacuation of the crew, save one—a GRU plant who is working undercover as the sub's assistant cook. His mission is to scuttle the vessel in the event its crew tries to defect or surrender the vessel to the enemy. The agent kills one of Ramius's officers and seriously wounds Ryan's British counterpart. Ryan and Ramius hunt the agent in the sub's missile room. While the agent wounds Ramius, Ryan kills him. Again, the shooting takes place in the middle of a gunfight, a far cry from the agent coldly shooting the two men earlier in the plot.

In *Clear and Present Danger*, Ryan's time in combat is brief. An unauthorized rescue mission is arranged to extract a U.S. Army light infantry team that was infiltrated into Colombia to stage hit-and-run raids against cocaine processing facilities run by the Medellín and Cali drug cartels. The five teams were cut off and left to die to maintain deniability by the national security advisor, James Cutter. Ryan mans one of the door-mounted mini-guns on the big MH-53 helicopter. The mini-gun is a souped-up Gatling gun, able to pour out several thousand rounds per minute. Ryan hoses the tree line on his side of the aircraft while taking fire. His counterpart, Sgt. Buck Zimmer, is not so lucky, taking three rounds to the chest. It's not known if Ryan killed anyone, or even how many, as he was aiming his gun's fire at muzzle flashes in the tree line. But the "killing" takes place within the context of a battle, and the bad guys were shooting back.

Killing Without Warrant

Killing takes on a different meaning for John Kelly, alias John Clark, Clancy's other man of action. Clark gets several introductions throughout Clancy's timeline of sympathetic good guys. He plays a small role in *Cardinal of the Kremlin*, smuggling out KGB chief Gerasimov's wife and daughter. Clark, in *Clear and Present Danger*, plays a larger role as the covert advance man for the infiltration of the antidrug combat teams, and must also play a role in the unauthorized rescue mission to get them out.

In *Without Remorse*, John Clark appears in a starring role under his real name, John Kelly, U.S. Navy SEAL. Only now Clancy removes himself from the Reagan/post-Reagan years and plants his storyline in the early 1970s, just as the Vietnam War is winding down. Kelly fights a war of revenge against a Baltimore drug gang that tried to kill him but successfully whacked his girlfriend—an ex-gang member, ex-hooker and ex-addict.

So Kelly seeks revenge. He modifies his .45 automatic with a .22 caliber conversion kit and fits the pistol with a silencer. He uses his Special Forces training to stake out his area of operations, a blighted section of Baltimore where the drug gang that killed his girlfriend operates. Then he takes action, slaying the gang in ones and twos by various means. By the time it's all over, Kelly has killed over twelve people—more than Jack the Ripper—wiping out the drug gang along with several Mafia associates. Local detectives (among them Jack Ryan's father) figure out what happened and connects Kelly with the vengeance killings.

"It's only murder when innocent people die," Kelly replies.

In true bad-movie fashion, Kelly is given a one-hour grace period before arrest, which he uses to fake his own death.

Kelly then goes to work for the CIA as John Clark.

Killing criminals without due process is a form of crime fighting that is acceptable in dictatorships and Third World countries with lousy human rights records . . . but it's not practiced here. One contrasting example has been set by the New York City police department, which uses near up-to-date crime statistics compiled by computer to hold captains accountable for keeping crime rates down in their precincts. Aggressive police work within the boundaries of the law, not Dirty Harry vigilante tactics, cut the NYC crime rate by more than half.

Killing gets a more thorough examination in Clancy's most recent work, *The Teeth of the Tiger*. Here Jack Ryan Jr.—the young son of President Jack Ryan—goes to work for Hendley Associates, an investment firm. But the company is just a cover for "the Campus," an extralegal self-funded intelligence agency that recruits its agents from various armed services and government agencies. With access to raw intelligence acquired by the National Security Agency and the CIA, the Campus sends out its own agents to identify track, and kill anti-U.S. terrorists in Europe. The outfit was founded during the Ryan administration. A stack of undated presidential pardons signed by the elder Ryan sits in a Hendley vault, ready to bail any agent from any legal trouble they should encounter while fighting fire with fire. In effect, the pardons are presidential dispensations for necessary crimes yet to be committed.

At first the young Ryan is brought on as an analyst, following the same career path as a chip off the old block. Concurrent with the younger Ryan's employment is the recruitment of Dominic Caruso (FBI) and Brian Caruso (USMC). Dominic Caruso is introduced to the reader in a particularly violent context, as he tracks down a child molester shortly after a kidnapping. Finding the pederast's hideout, Caruso gets the drop on the guy as he watches TV. Making a deliberately noisy entrance, Caruso startles the suspect, and then guns him down. The knife used to kill his latest victim was within arm's reach on the coffee table, and the suspect did reach for the knife. But the thought that goes through Caruso's head before pulling the trigger was simple: *you are not going to jail today.*

Caruso is not subject to any penalty for gunning down a suspected child murderer, even though his training taught him that such suspects do not resist arrest. Meeting with his FBI superior in Washington, he is told that it is good to deliver justice, rather than enforce the law and give a criminal a chance to beat the rap in court. To Hendley is Caruso seconded, where he meets his brother Brian.

They are at first hesitant to join the Campus once they are told what the mission will be, but an ill-timed visit to a nearby shopping mall during a coincidental terrorist attack changes their minds. (Oddly, the Campus, CIA, NSA, FBI, or the Department of Homeland Security cannot identify or stop the terrorist attacks—parallel massacres at four separate shopping malls in the U.S.) The Caruso brothers are given a secret weapon—a pen that can be switched over to a stealth hypodermic that injects a fatal but undetectable paralyzing agent into its victim with a single jab.

Using intelligence gleaned from Hendley's stealthy association with CIA and NSA, the Caruso brothers go on a little killing spree in Europe. They jab and kill the terrorist ring's financial backer in London, kill another support guy in Munich, yet another support guy gets jabbed in Vienna and a key organizer is taken down in Rome. Jack Jr. filling in for one of the Caruso brothers, kills the last one. The younger Ryan taunts his victim as he lies dying. Unlike the elder Ryan, there is no clear context of combat that surrounds the killing. Ryan Jr. acts on the pragmatic needs of the moment and the mission, without any of the philosophical restraint shown by his father when a choice had to be made about whether to kill a bad guy in cold blood.

Time have changed, and so have the Ryans.

Dirty Deeds Done at a Price

Is the younger Ryan's action a murder or a killing in wartime? The cold war and the war on terror have their share of "dirty work" that fell outside the boundaries of traditional combat. Thus the matter is up for debate.

Killing noncombatant enemies was done in real life during the Vietnam War. Under the CIA-run Phoenix Program, Communist cadres doing political and support work in South Vietnam were targeted for elimination by trained U.S. servicemen. This was no different than the low-level political assassinations of mayors and schoolteachers that the Vietcong did to fellow South Vietnamese who did not support the Communist cause. Many killed by the CIA hit teams were Communist cadres, though some were domestic non-Communist opponents of the Thieu regime that got whacked because a local district leader or provincial chief wanted to eliminate a rival or two. The program was not perfect, but it did effectively gut the Communist insurgency in the south between the time of the Tet Offensive in 1968 and the U.S. pullout by 1973.[1]

Likewise, Israel traditionally exercised a foreign policy based on "an eye for an eye, a tooth for a tooth, a life for a life." Following the 1972 massacre of Israeli athletes at the Munich Olympics, Israel gathered intelligence on the gunmen who got away and targeted them for assassination. One by one, throughout Europe and the Middle East, the terrorists were hunted down and ruthlessly shot or bombed. The last such suspect was hiding out in Lillehammer, Norway, working as a waiter and married to a local woman. One night, several Mossad agents shot the suspect as he was on his way home from work. The suspect turned out to be a waiter, not a terrorist, in a case of mistaken identity.[2]

As for what the Caruso brothers did in fiction with their poison pen, be aware that even that stunt has an analog in real life. In the 1970s, the Bulgarian KGB used a similar device against dissident exiles living in London. Used for the killing was an umbrella with an injector hidden in its tip that shot a miniscule lead BB containing a small but fatal quantity of ricin—an extremely toxic substance derived from castor beans. One jabbing victim—Georgi Markov, a dissident broadcaster with the BBC—died.[3]

Assassination can be heavy-handed as well as subtle.

Another Israeli target was Yahya Al Ayash, a master bomb maker for Hamas, a Palestinian Islamic fundamentalist movement. The Mossad managed to find a way to get a special cell phone into his possession that had a miniature bomb planted inside. Upon answering an incoming call, the Israelis activated the signal that exploded the cell phone, blowing apart Al Ayash's head.

The Russians are not as subtle. During the first war with Chechnya in 1996, the Russians managed to zero in on the satellite phone of Chechen resistance leader Dzokhar Dudayev. The problem was that Dudayev was never on the phone long enough to get a fix on his location. Russian ground units managed to identify the gully containing Dudayev's HQ. A bomb was set off on the ground to destroy the installation, followed by a pair of airdropped guided bombs to complete the overkill.[4]

This was eerily similar to two instances in Clancy's work—the first in *Clear and Present Danger*, when a U.S. Navy F-18 drops a single laser-guided bomb on the house of a Colombian drug lord holding a conference. The second was in *Executive Orders*, when the UIR's Ayatollah Daryaei met a similar end in his executive mansion. John Clark, an acknowledged expert in such matters, handled the laser designator on the ground in both missions.

But the U.S. is cleverer than that in real life.

In 2002, as part of the war on terror, an important Al Qaeda lieutenant was found hiding out in Yemen. A Predator UAV fired a Hellfire missile to blow apart his car. It echoed a similar tactic used by Israel to eliminate unwanted Moslem extremist leaders, most notably Sheik Ahmed Yassin, head of Hamas, and his successor, Abdel Aziz Rantisi; both killed by antitank missiles fired by attack helicopters in March and April of 2004, respectively.

But looking at all these real-life instances of killing, one can see that fiction is pretty damn tame compared to truth. In Clancy's fiction, such killing can be pragmatist revenge masquerading as rough justice. John Clark and his sidekick Ding Chavez had the pleasure of capturing Somali warlord Mohamed Corp in a small side scene in *Debt of Honor*. Corp was a poor stand-in for Mohammed Farah Aideed, Somali warlord and ex-mayor of Mogadishu, whose arrest was sought by the United Nations in 1993. U.S. Rangers and Delta Force successfully captured several of Aideed's lieutenants, but never Aideed. (He eventually died of heart attack in August 1996.) Failure was met in the "battle of the Black Sea," which saw the loss of eighteen and the wounding of almost eighty, a defeat well-chronicled in Mark Bowden's *Black Hawk Down*. But Clark and Chavez use a high-powered flashgun to stun the warlord and his bodyguards, permitting a Special Force's heliborne "snatch and grab" without firing a shot.[5]

Capturing or killing a wanted leader of a pariah state is no easy matter. Clancy's commandos do this effortlessly, but our Delta Force and Rangers find it far more difficult. A writer can have super-elite shadow warriors storm any bastion at stiff odds with a few keystrokes and some well-chosen words. This is pretty damn hard in real life, judging by the results. Failure is more likely than success.

Perhaps the most obvious example is Cuban dictator Fidel Castro.

The Communist takeover of Cuba was a sore point during the cold war, given the island's proximity to Florida and the U.S. record for backing the wrong dictator during Cuba's revolution. The Bay of Pigs invasion, a plan crafted during the Eisenhower administration and carried out by Kennedy in 1961, was an attempt to seize an enclave that could be used to proclaim a provisional government that the populace could rally around and overthrow Castro. Instead, the puny invasion force of Cuban exiles was annihilated on the beaches.[6] This was followed by Operation Mongoose, a CIA-backed plan to undermine the Castro regime's legitimacy by building resistance networks in Cuba, as well as sabotaging sugar refineries and any other industrial targets. The plan included assassination as a subcomponent, and several attempts were made.[7] Perhaps the most comic aspect to become public was a plan uncovered by an investigating committee headed by Senator Frank Church (D-Idaho), which called for inserting a powder into one of Castro's cigars that would make his beard fall out. Without the beard, Castro would lose a measure of his charisma, and in turn be overthrown by the Cuban people.

As of the fall of 2004, Fidel Castro was still the Communist dictator of Cuba.

The U.S. has overthrown or killed undesirable leaders before, but always through a proxy in the target nation. That proxy could either be politically or financially backed by the U.S. Mohammed Mossadegh of Iran and Jacobo Arbenz Guzman of Guatemala were both democratically elected left-wing leaders of the 1950s who were both ousted by CIA-backed coups that had Eisenhower's political blessing. South Vietnamese dictator Diem was killed in November 1963, in a coup engineered by South Vietnamese generals that had the tacit approval of Kennedy. Socialist Chilean president Salvador Allende made his last stand in his presidential palace during a 1970s coup that brought General Augusto Pinochet to power, with Nixon's approval.

The U.S. once tried to kill Libyan dictator Muammar Qaddafi back in the 1980s. Libyan terrorists had set off a bomb in a Berlin disco, killing several American servicemen. As payback, Reagan ordered 16 F-111 medium bombers to deliver the tit for tat. While a Libyan air base was hit, several bombers also tried to flatten Qaddafi's personal tent mansion, killing two of his adopted children but missing the dreadful leader. This was technically a violation of President Ford's executive order prohibiting the assassination of foreign heads of state, but the rationale simply pointed out that Qaddafi was not deliberately targeted. (If he died in the attack, it would have been by an accident of war.)

More vexing is Osama bin Laden, the head of Al Qaeda, a nonstate sponsor of terrorism. The U.S. tried to get him extradited from Sudan to Saudi Arabia, only to see him fly the coop to Afghanistan. There he was welcomed by the fundamentalist Taliban regime of Mullah Mohammed Omar. But by 1998, bin Laden was outliving his welcome, and the Saudis were again seeking a way to deport him back to the home country, where he was a wanted criminal. That effort came close to being done, but was undone by a U.S. cruise missile attack. (President Bill Clinton kept two Los Angeles–class subs stationed in the Arabian Sea for such an eventuality, but the U.S. needed six hours' notice on bin Laden's precise whereabouts to nail him.) The missiles flattened an Al Qaeda training camp, but did not paste bin Laden. But the attack did renew bin Laden's relationship with Muhammed Omar.[8]

The CIA established a cell to track bin Laden's whereabouts, and if possible arrange for his assassination or extradition. The agency's efforts were sometimes fueled by each successive attack by Al Qaeda, then hobbled by the legal problem of how to handle bin Laden if captured and keep the CIA from becoming an accessory to any crime if he was killed. Bureaucratic and Clinton White House indecision did not help, either. Another problem was establishing bin Laden's whereabouts so he could be kidnapped, or killed, by covert Afghan allies or by agents of the anti-Taliban Northern Alliance.[9]

The U.S. would get its next chance to get bin Laden during the Afghan war of 2001–02. U.S. Rangers parachuted into bin Laden's Kandahar compound very early in the conflict, but their quarry had flown. Later in December 2001, troops from the Tenth Mountain Division, supported by troops provided by local Afghan warlords, assaulted the mountain bunker complex at Tora Bora, near the Pakistani border. It is believed that Al Qaeda and Taliban remnants successfully fought a rearguard action that allowed bin Laden to slip across the border to the tribal areas of Pakistan. (A similar battle fought at Shahikot in early 2002 also resulted in a lot of dead Taliban and Al Qaeda remnants, but did not yield the dead body of anyone important.)

Throughout late 2003 and early 2004 press reports indicated that the U.S. was seriously close to capturing bin Laden. A major Pakistani sweep in the northwest frontier early in 2004 nearly bagged bin Laden's chief lieutenant, Ayman al Zawahiri, but again the end result was the same—a lot of dead bad guys and no one of importance killed or captured. As of last summer, the British were getting good data on Al Qaeda agent whereabouts after turning Naeem Noor Khan, but the operation was blown when Khan's identity was leaked by some unnamed official in the Bush White House. The British arrested whom they could, based on Khan's e-mail traffic.

As of the time of this book's writing, Osama bin Laden is still at large.

Perhaps a more realistic example of killing and capture would be Saddam Hussein. The U.S. twice tried to bomb Hussein where they thought he might be. Upon the start of the second Gulf War in March 2003, a government building in Baghdad was flattened in the hopes of killing Hussein during a cabinet meeting. He survived the attack or was not present in the building. Several weeks later, Hussein's whereabouts were traced to a restaurant elsewhere in Baghdad. It was bombed and several innocent Iraqi bystanders died, but not Saddam. It was not until December 2003 that the dictator was captured in a sweep conducted by the Fourth Infantry Division, spearheaded by Delta Force troops. (Saddam's two sons, Uday and Qusay, were also hunted down, eventually meeting their end in a gangland-style shootout with troops from the 101st Airborne in July 2003, in the city of Mosul.)

In both instances, capture or killing took months to achieve, sometimes after several failed attempts and plenty of intelligence work.

The "bad guys" are not constrained by the rules in the assassination game. Assassination on a mass scale was the fiery ending of *Debt of Honor*, when a vengeful Japanese airline pilot plunged his Boeing 747 into the U.S. Capitol, killing the president, the entire Supreme Court, the service chiefs, most of the cabinet, and the Congress. Ludicrous? Perhaps no stranger than the suicidal jetliner attacks of September 11, 2001. One of the four doomed planes struck the Pentagon, while another aircraft whose control by the hijackers was fought over by some passengers crashed in Pennsylvania. Unknown is what target this plane would have chosen—the White House or the Capitol. (Some surmise that the Pentagon was hit as an alternate target given the difficulty of trying to dive into the smaller White House.)

Political assassination is revisited in *The Bear and the Dragon*, as FSB (ex-KGB) chief Golovko sees an armored Mercedes limousine much like his own destroyed by an RPG fired from a cement mixer. Was the killing meant for the occupant of the unlucky car—a noted Moscow pimp with ties to organized crime—or was it aimed at him? A big chunk of the book is given over to the Russian investigation of the killing, as agents try to sort out what happened. After much careful sleuthing, the Russians realize that conspirators in the killing had ties to an intelligence operative in the Chinese embassy. This finding comes at a time of heightened Sino-Russian tensions.

The Russians, with some help from the FBI station chief in Moscow, break the conspiracy just as it was gearing up to assassinate Russian president Grushavoy. While the assassination plot helps keep the potboiler plot going in the book, would the assassination be truly effective as an element of strategy? That depends on the system of government that the "target" heads. A foreign head of state eager to kill a U.S. president is wasting his strategic time. While the killing would certainly make a dramatic political statement, the vice president would simply replace the president and the United States government would continue operating, regardless of any crisis it was facing. This much was demonstrated when John F. Kennedy was gunned down in Dallas in November 1963. Within hours, Vice President Lyndon Johnson was sworn in and assumed the duties of the presidency, much as the fictional Jack Ryan did in *Debt of Honor.*

Perhaps the closest the U.S. government has ever come to elimination by assassination was in April 1865. While John Wilkes Booth successfully shot President Abraham Lincoln, coconspirators failed to kill Vice President Andrew Johnson and Secretary of State William Seward. Even if all three men were killed, constitutional succession would have tapped each cabinet secretary for the post in order of his department's seniority.

The fictional targeting of Grushavoy by the Chinese Politburo raises a different question—how much disruption will a state endure if succession is not plainly stated in its constitution? The Russia in *The Bear and the Dragon* is nominally democratic, as it is today under President Vladimir Putin, an elected strongman, so it is assumed that a constitutional succession would take place under the untested Russian constitution. But succession in the old Soviet Union was a little more complicated, depending on the outcome of office politics between the various factions in the Politburo. Stalin was certainly succeeded, but Malenkov lasted only several years before it became clear that Khrushchev consolidated power. Likewise, Khrushchev's ouster by a troika led by Leonid Brezhnev did not see power truly consolidated under one man for the better part of a decade, when Brezhnev truly became the clear winner.

Succession in a dictatorship is even more uncertain, as the sudden vacuum must be filled, usually by a player whose cunning and ambition is well-suited to screwing or stroking would-be competitors. When a dictatorship faces no external crisis, the succession drama can be played out despite the risk of civil war or subsequent coup d'état. To assassinate a dictator during a war is to disrupt the command and control of the state. The nation is plunged into chaos, as it must handle a succession crisis and an external threat at the same time. Nazi Germany certainly faced such an outcome during the bomb plot that nearly killed Hitler in July 1944. Had the plot succeeded, the conspirators would have to seize and consolidate power, all the time being pursued by the various factions of the Nazi Party (some of them armed, like the SS), and at the same time maintaining control of a multifront war against an array of foreign enemies.

Killing a world leader becomes more focused on the individual in *Red Rabbit*. There Clancy grafts the tale of a high-value defector from the KGB's communications office whose decision to betray the USSR is prompted by pangs of conscience when he finds out about a KGB plot to assassinate Pope John Paul II.

Historically, in the early 1980s, such a plot did come to pass, as Turkish gunman Mehmet Ali Agca succeeded in putting a few rounds of 9mm into His Holiness during his weekly procession around the crowd gathered in St. Peter's Square in the Vatican. Eventually, it was found out that Agca was allegedly working for the Bulgarian KGB—the same agency that killed Bulgarian dissident Georgi Markov. Bulgaria's KGB supposedly did all the "wet" operations (assassinations and killings) that the Soviet KGB did not want to undertake. The endgame of the cold war was afoot (though many did not realize it) as John Paul II's Polish origin was an inspiration to everyday Poles resentful of Communist control. The USSR leadership was very keen to eliminate the problem by killing the pope. Jack Ryan and his British compatriots fail to stop the shooting, but the Bulgarian KGB colonel is "caught" by British intelligence operatives and suffers an untimely death at their hands.

John Paul II forgave Agca for the attempt on his life. Though sentenced to life for the shooting, Agca was pardoned in 2000, with the pope's agreement. But that pardon came with extradition to Turkey, where Agca was rearrested for the 1979 killing of a journalist.[10]

As for state-sponsored assassination attempts against U.S. presidents, this concept has been grist for many movies and novels, but only once has such a plot been set into motion. Saddam Hussein did dispatch a team to take down ex-president George Bush shortly after the end of the first Gulf War. Shortly after the killer team was arrested in Kuwait, President Bill Clinton retaliated by launching a cruise missile strike against the Iraqi intelligence headquarters in Baghdad, unfortunately hitting the building at night when no one was working there.

Where dirty tricks truly goes awry is in *Cardinal of the Kremlin*, where KGB agents infiltrate the U.S. to kidnap one of the leading scientists working on the Strategic Defense Initiative (Star Wars). A blown traffic stop and the panic shooting of a state trooper by one of the agents eventually bring down the operation. The American "response" is a raid by Afghan mujahideen against a Soviet research facility just over the Afghan border in Soviet central Asia, which almost successfully overruns the base.

Killing Outside the Rules

Killing is pretty straightforward in battle. There is a cruel fairness in combat. The soldiers on both sides have guns and fight according to what few rules there are in battle. Terrorists do not play by these rules. To a terrorist, war means killing those who cannot shoot back. There is a ruthless and bloody logic that makes this sensible—the terrorist group has no hope of fighting any Western industrialized nation on equal terms. Any modern First World nation can field an army that could easily vanquish the terrorist group in a fair fight. The PLO found that out the hard way in 1982, when its thin battalions tried to blunt the Israeli invasion of Lebanon. The units broke down to squads, which the terrorists were more familiar with, and offered piecemeal and uncoordinated resistance. Terrorists can never hope to match the combat power of carrier battle groups, armored divisions or air wings, so they get by without them. The only thing they have are small arms, explosives, and a willingness to die for their cause, no matter how noble or dubious.

To date, terrorists are the "bad guys" in six of Clancy's thirteen books: *Patriot Games, Clear and Present Danger, Sum of All Fears*,

Executive Orders, *Rainbow Six*, and *Teeth of the Tiger*. In every book, terrorists undertake a direct attack on the United States, varying their means to suit the objective. But not all terrorists spring from the same source.

The terrorists in *Patriot Games* make up the breakaway Ulster Liberation Army, a fictional Maoist splinter group of the Provisional Irish Republican Army. The group specializes in kidnapping, assassination and bombing, relying on small arms and explosives backed by training in small unit warfare. The book was written in the 1980s, shortly after Europe passed through a hellish decade dealing with several terrorist groups of the same caliber as the ULA, like ETA (Basque separatists, Spain), the Baader-Meinhoff Gang (West Germany), the Red Brigades (Italy), and of course the IRA/PIRA (Ulster, Britain). Such groups were only capable, of small-scale massacre or spectacular assassinations and kidnappings.

The ULA's twice-attempted kidnapping of the prince and princess of Wales is not that far removed from the Red Brigades kidnapping and killing former Italian prime minister Aldo Moro or the kidnapping of U.S. brigadier general James Dozier. Then there was the spectacular assassination of a German industrialist by the Baader-Meinhof gang, or the IRA's bombing attack that killed Britain's Lord Louis Mountbatten.

Typically such groups are neutralized and soon eliminated by thorough police work, though keep in mind that systems of justice differs in Europe from the United States. In France and Italy, judges double as prosecutors and the trial is inquisitorial, not adversarial as it is in Britain and the U.S. Police also operate under different legal standards that would not pass constitutional muster here. In France, for example, police can hold a suspect for questioning for ninety-six hours without a charge. Here when an arrest is made, the suspect must be charged for a crime within twenty-four hours, and must be informed of his rights before questioning can begin. Nevertheless, Britain, Spain, Italy, and then West Germany managed to fight terrorism to some degree without a wholesale scrapping of the civil liberties of law-abiding citizens, even when imposing inconveniences like security checkpoints at airports and shopping districts.

The Colombian cocaine cartels are the terrorist-like bad guys in *Clear and Present Danger*. One may argue that they don't belong on the terrorist list given their lack of a political agenda (and political agendas can be a little flaky at times in the terrorist world). But they have wholeheartedly embraced the tactics of terrorism to undermine law and order in Colombia while easily financing their private armies from the cash-rich drug trade. Two drug cartels operated out of Colombia in the 1980s, one based in Medellín and the other in Cali. The larger Medellín cartel preferred to use violence to eliminate their legal opposition, so it's no surprise that hundreds of cops, judges, politicians, and citizens were gunned down. Chief among the cartel was Pablo Escobar, who died in a hail of police gunfire in 1993.

The Cali cartel preferred to coopt opposition with massive bribes. After the fall of the Medellín cartel, the Cali group took over 80 percent of Colombia's cocaine trade, reaping about $8 billion in annual profits. Yet by the end of 1996, all seven cartel leaders were dead or behind bars.

In Clancy's fiction, the drug cartel is targeted for action by light infantry teams infiltrated into Colombia by the U.S. military in a secret operation run from the White House. The teams would target for elimination the drug processing labs deep in the Colombian jungle. The squad-sized units could also operate with some advantage against the private armies of the drug cartels. Such gunmen might have rudimentary arms and tactical training, but nothing that could match an elite unit fighting in the field. The U.S. infiltration, while secret, is considered to be a legitimate military response to the unwanted importation of cocaine in the U.S., also assessed as an attack on the U.S. populace given the crime generated by the drug trade.

Since *Clear and Present Danger* was written, the cocaine trade has been a lucrative football whose possession easily finances any illegal activity. Control of Colombian drug production has passed to FARC, a former leftist insurgent group that has found the cash-rich drug business far preferable to fighting for a cause. Since the election of Alvaro Uribe as Colombia's president, the government (heavily financed by U.S. aid) has been destroying coca fields through aerial spraying and deploying specially trained army units to reclaim towns and provinces from FARC's control.[11]

In *Sum of All Fears,* there is an Iranian state-financed plot to attack the United States with a secondhand nuclear weapon. The agents of the attack are varied—Palestinian extremists troubled by the recent Arab-Israeli rapprochement (this is fiction, remember?), working with German Red terrorists and a disaffected Native American. This unlikely alliance successfully places a reengineered A-bomb in Denver, which does not explode as it should. The plot aimed at starting an accidental war between the U.S. and USSR comes to naught after reaching the brink.

The terrorists manage to kill tens of thousands of Americans at the Denver Super Bowl game, including the secretaries of state and defense. One would figure that prosecution in a Denver federal court would ensure the conviction of the two and a well-earned death sentence. Yet the two Palestinian defendants are "extradited" to Saudi Arabia, where they face the certainty of execution, whereas in the U.S. such an outcome is not a sure thing.

Fair trials can be like that, as was amply demonstrated in federal district court in New York City. One of two venues officially designated by the U.S. Justice Department for the trial of terrorist crimes, the New York court did not produce a single capital sentence in any terrorist case. Even the defendants in the 1993 bombing of the World Trade Center, which killed six and injured over one thousand, only got life sentences. When George W. Bush took office, New York lost its designation and the federal district court in Alexandria, Virginia, near Washington, D.C., became the official terrorist trial venue. The added bonus is that appeals go to the Fourth Circuit Appellate Court—the most conservative appellate court in the federal system. To this date, the only terrorists who were tried in court were U.S. citizens fighting for the Taliban in Afghanistan or working for Al Qaeda here. No foreign terrorists have gone to trial, as the Bush administration argues over the status of captured terrorists held in the legal limbo of captivity at Guantánamo, a leased U.S. naval base in Cuba. By the summer of 2004, the Supreme Court ruled that Guantánamo detainees had access to federal courts to contest their custody.

It should be noted here that only two death sentences have been handed down for a terrorist attack in the U.S. The first was given to Mir Aimal Kasi for the 1993 killing of a few CIA employees just outside the agency's headquarters in Langley, Virginia. Kasi ducked out in Pakistan's tribal areas after the killing, but was found, arrested, extradited, tried in 1998, and executed in 2004. The second was given to Timothy McVeigh, who played an active role in the April 1995 bombing of the Alfred Murrah Federal Building in Oklahoma City, which killed over 160 people. McVeigh was executed by lethal injection in June 2001. His coconspirator, Terry Nichols, drew life sentences in federal and state courts for his role in the killings.

The Iranian-backed terror threat gets its reprise in *Executive Orders*, where an effort by the United Islamic Republic (Iran merged with Iraq) to invade Saudi Arabia is complemented by a terrorist strike against the United States. An Iranian bio lab manages to culture a large quantity of Ebola virus. Iranian terrorist leader Badrayn has the virus packaged in cans of shaving cream that can be switched to an aerosol setting to vent the virus into a crowd. Ten teams of terrorists fan out to ten convention sites to release their deadly cargo, and then fly back as if nothing happened. Convention goers would then contract the virus and fly back to their home cities, where the epidemic would then break out and spread some more. This epidemic is stopped by a nationwide freeze of all interstate traffic ordered by President Ryan.

Likewise, bioterrorism is also the weapon of choice in *Rainbow Six*, where U.S.-based environmental extremists in control of a drug company genetically modify the Ebola virus, planning to spray it at the

2000 Summer Olympics in Sydney, Australia. Again, infected specta-tors would then fly home and spread the disease. The RAINBOW com-mando team stops this plot by arresting the traitorous U.S. army colonel who was about to insert the virus into the Olympic stadium's fogging system.

Clancy's two treatments of bioterrorism predate the two bio-attacks on the United States. Shortly after September 11, 2001, finely milled anthrax spores were mailed to the office of then Senate majority leader Tom Daschle (D-South Dakota). Still more envelopes were mailed to NBC anchorman Tom Brokaw, as well as the editorial offices American Media Inc., a publisher of supermarket tabloids. Stray spores randomly found their way into other people's mail that was being sorted in the same facilities as the tainted envelopes. Random cases of anthrax cropped up throughout the U.S. By the time the threat played out, half a dozen people sickened and died, while many more were put on antibi-otics. The Senate Office Building and several U.S. postal sorting centers had to be isolated and fumigated as well. A lesser reprise occurred in the spring of 2004, when an envelope filled with ricin also found its way to Senator Tom Daschle's office. No fatalities resulted and all those affected received antibiotics immediately.

In both cases, the U.S. has not tracked down the perpetrators and brought them to justice.

In Clancy's two books, the perpetrators are identified and punished by the last page.

Preceding the bio-attack in *Executive Orders* is the terrorist assault on the Giant Steps day care center. This place is a particular curse for the Ryan family (first being the place from where Catherine Ryan picks up her eldest daughter, only to see her Porsche machine-gunned from a passing minivan in *Patriot Games*). Now Ryan's youngest daughter (the first toddler) is the target for a squad-sized assault that pierces the thin secret service cordon but comes to naught. (An FBI agent visiting his little daughter disrupts the assault and hostage taking.) While the first attack in *Patriot Games* drives Ryan to seek revenge within the boundaries of national service, the second attack merely serves as a huge diversion in an already overburdened plotline. (That does not mean that Ryan shrugs off the attack. Don't expect any mercy from an angry president when you mess with his family!)

In *Teeth of the Tiger*, Arab terrorists make a comeback. Making arrangements with drug smugglers to gain entry to the U.S. via Mexico, four hit teams fan out across the U.S. to massacre shoppers at malls in Colorado Springs, Colorado; Des Moines, Iowa; Charlottesville, Virginia; and Provo, Utah. All four teams make "one-way trips," eventually being brought down by responding police, or in the case of the Charlottesville massacre, the gun-toting Caruso brothers.

Clancy's terrorists usually strike the United States.

In real life, that is not always true. The history of terrorism against the U.S. is largely foreign. Case in point: the suicide bombings of the U.S. embassy and Marine Corps barracks in Beirut in the early 1980s—both executed by the Iranian-backed Shiite group Hezbollah. This effort was complemented by the repeated kidnappings of U.S. citizens in Beirut, eventually numbering six to eight hostages held for several years during the Reagan administration. Killed after being kidnapped were a U.S. army colonel serving with UN peacekeeping forces and the CIA's top antiterrorism expert and station chief in Beirut. The follow-up to that incident was the expert hijacking of a TWA flight that originated in Athens, Greece, which resulted in still more hostages One thing all these incidents had in common was the lack of retaliation against the perpetrators.

For once, it looked like the U.S. would get even, when in 1985 hijackers of the cruise ship *Achille Lauro* managed to secure an airliner to take them to Tunisia from Egypt. The plane was intercepted by U.S. Navy F-14s and forced to land at Sigonella, a NATO air base in Sicily. The Italian government, however, was offended by the illegality of the "arrest" and allowed the hijackers to proceed, owing to insufficient evidence to prosecute. One American was killed onboard the cruise ship— Leon Klinghoffer, who was sickly and wheelchair bound. Abu Abbas, the mastermind of the attack, died in Baghdad of natural causes in March 2004.

The last big terrorist strike against the U.S. prior to the first Gulf War was the downing of Pan Am flight 103 on Christmas 1988. A bomb brought the Boeing 747 down over Lockerbie, Scotland, killing all on board and several on the ground. Some intelligence analysts argued that the bombing was an Iranian job done in retaliation for the USS *Vincennes* accidentally downing an IranAir Airbus that previous July 4, when the *Vincennes* was engaged in a fight with Iranian speedboats. But the finger eventually pointed at Qaddafi's Libya, with two Libyan intelligence agents identified as the culprits.

The Iraqi invasion of Kuwait stirred anti-American terrorism in a new direction. The ouster of Saddam Hussein's army required the U.S. to base its land and air units in Saudi Arabia. This was a religiously ticklish situation for the Saudis. As the keepers of the Moslem holy places of Mecca and Medina, the Saudis were very careful to make sure that foreign non-Moslem troops did nothing to undermine the faith-based legitimacy of the Saudi ruling family. No Western troops were stationed anywhere near the Moslem holy places. They could not bring in any alcohol, naughty pictures, or any symbols of their non-Moslem faith. After the war, a smaller number of American troops stayed to support air force units policing the southern no-fly zone over Iraq.

This arrangement was fine with the Saudi royal family; it did not go over well with Osama bin Laden. Bin Laden was a religiously motivated recruiter who supplied the Afghan mujahideen with Saudi volunteers during the anti-Soviet insurgency in the 1980s, but the presence of foreign infidels in holy Saudi Arabia deeply galled bin Laden. He turned to his Rolodex of contacts to form Al Qaeda—"the Base"—and recruited his Afghan veterans to make war on the U.S. Funding was not a problem, as Osama was one of many fortunate sons whose family owned the Bin Laden Group, the largest construction firm in Saudi Arabia.

Anti-American terrorism came home with a vengeance, as Al Qaeda–backed efforts saw the assassination of Jewish extremist Meir

Kahane in New York, as well as the 1993 bombing of the World Trade Center, which killed six and injured over one thousand. The conspirators, headed by blind Egyptian cleric Abdul Rahman, also conspired to destroy a number of New York City bridges and tunnels. Another World Trade Center operative was arrested in Manila, where he planned to bomb ten to twenty U.S. airliners. Eventually, all were brought to trial in New York City, but while many drew long prison sentences, none were given the death penalty by the various federal juries.

Al Qaeda's subsequent attacks became more deadly with the passage of time. A Riyadh office operated by the U.S. military was bombed in mid-1990s, killing several. U.S. personnel were moved out of Riyadh, to be kept in desert bases far away from the cities. At one such base, Al Qaeda operatives detonated a truck bomb that shredded the Khobar Tower apartment building, killing nineteen servicemen, in June 1996. Saudi police were quick to apprehend the culprits, trying and executing them before the FBI could question them.

Then came the August 1998 bombings of the U.S. embassies in Tanzania and Kenya. In retaliation, the U.S. launched cruise missiles against Al Qaeda targets in Sudan and Afghanistan. Two training camps in Afghanistan were destroyed but Osama bin Laden was not there. The Sudanese pharmaceutical plant suspected of making chemical weapons for Al Qaeda was destroyed as well, but the evidence of this activity was less certain.

Al Qaeda performed at least one more strike, blowing up a suicide boat against the hull of the destroyer USS *Cole* as it made a port call at Aden to refuel in October 2000. The U.S. did not retaliate. Following this strike, the World Trade Center and Pentagon were struck on September 11, 2001.

While Clancy's terrorists always strike the United States, state-sponsored terrorists backed by Libya, Iran, and Iraq were always smart enough not to. Killing Americans abroad was politically profitable enough, and any retaliation this prompted was always blunted by the political fallout between the U.S. and Western allies that were not in sympathy with American revenge. Striking back only reinforced the cowboy image of the United States that was a common perception among many Europeans, and underscored many reasons why the U.S. should not be trusted to undertake any unilateral military action to counter terrorism. While European governments may give the U.S. a free pass, vigorous left-wing parties and movements did not, and made their displeasure known in protests and articles. Even American efforts to track down and strike at Al Qaeda never received full cooperation from allies. That changed after September 11, somewhat. Western Europe understood the need to go after Al Qaeda and its Taliban sponsors in Afghanistan. Saudi Arabia refused to cooperate by allowing a state-of-the-art U.S. command post to coordinate the air war against the co-religionist Taliban.

Since September 11, 2001, fighting Al Qaeda has been a mixed success. Domestically, the Patriot Act has allegedly strengthened the hand of law enforcement in countering terrorism, but there are few arrests to show for it, and no convictions as of the summer of 2004. Throughout Europe and Asia, however, arrests have been more common. One advantage is that many European states practice domestic intelligence gathering, which can then allow information to be forwarded to law enforcement.

The U.S. has floated one electronic scheme to this end and is rumored to be part of another. "Carnivore" was the FBI code name for a massive data-mining scheme that has not been enacted to date. "Echelon" is a rumored worldwide electronic eavesdropping system run by the United States, United Kingdom, and Australia. So far, it is just a good story.

The U.S. once possessed a domestic intelligence capability exercised by the FBI under director J. Edgar Hoover, who preferred to compile embarrassing dossiers on political opponents throughout the 1940s to 1970s. Those abuses have made the U.S. reluctant to go down that path again, while the need for some action on domestic intelligence is debated.

Abroad, Al Qaeda's operations can be split into two categories: repeat performances and one-shots. Saudi Arabia has seen repeated bombing attacks, first aimed at foreigners by Al Qaeda in 2003 and then at fellow Arabs in 2003 and 2004. The Saudi royal family has been late waking up to the threat, but has been busy trying to counter it through aggressive police work while trying to manage a gradual modernization and shift to democracy. A major police strike wiped out a good portion of Al Qaeda's Saudi leadership in June 2004.

Pakistan is also plagued with repeat performances, ranging from several bombings of Shiite mosques and Christian churches to a pair of assassination attempts on Pakistani dictator Pervez Musharraf. Al Qaeda and Taliban remnants are also believed to be hiding out in Pakistan's autonomous tribal areas, where the national government holds little sway. Large-scale operations by the Pakistani Army have netted few kills or captures of suspected terrorists, but has driven them to the cities, where they are easier to spot and arrest.

One-shots are more common elsewhere. Al Qaeda–affiliated groups have set off bombs in Tunisia, Morocco, Indonesia, and Spain. Authorities are quick to bust up the terrorist rings, however, so campaigns cannot be maintained unless new networks are formed. Such large bombings tend to be spectacular, killing tens or hundreds of people. The Spanish railway bombings around Madrid in the spring of 2004 did alter an electoral outcome, ousting the conservative government and bringing the Socialists to power, who in turn withdrew Spanish troops from Iraqi peacekeeping/occupation duties.

Iraq has to be taken as a separate case here, because the forces opposed to the United States are varied and muddled. Al Qaeda does have a cell operating there under the Jordanian Abu Musab al-Zarqawi, which is credited with beheading several hostages. There is a captured document outlining Zarqawi's strategy for fomenting anti-American resistance concurrent with a terrorist campaign against the Shiites. But repeated assassinations of Shiite clerics and bombings of Shiite crowds during religious festivals could also have been done by Sunni-Baathist remnants who do not want to see themselves ruled by the Shiite majority they once kept downtrodden.

Special Forces: The Killer Elite

This "laundry list" of fictional terrorism is offset by numerous examples in Clancy's fiction of commando teams that lend credence to the maxim "Don't get angry—get even." The small elite unit whose derring-do changes the course of a battle, campaign, or war has long been the staple of war movies and books. Such films ran the gamut from *The Guns of Navarone, The Dirty Dozen, Where Eagles Dare*, and *The Eagle Has Landed*. Fiction here was not far removed from actual commando actions during World War II—whether it was the raid that destroyed the Nazi heavy water plant at Telemark, Norway, to the kayak raids on Bordeaux and Singapore, or the raid on St. Nazaire to destroy a large dry dock that could have accommodated the Nazi battleships *Bismarck* and *Tirpitz*. Whether it is history or fiction, the stories are exciting to read.

Commandos and Special Forces pepper Clancy's narratives. Head back to *Patriot Games*—the special force trying to arrive as the cavalry in the nick of time is the FBI's heliborne hostage rescue team (HRT). Trained to negotiate with terrorists and crooks who take hostages, the HRT is instead thrust into the awkward role of a light infantry squad, penetrating the shattered perimeter of the Ryan estate to assess the situation, but unable to take action because the situation does not fit within the context of its doctrine.

Clear and Present Danger sees U.S. light infantry retrained as a special force for covert operations in Colombia, fighting a guerrilla war against the drug cartels and destroying their jungle-based labs. All of the volunteers are of Hispanic background and speak Spanish as a first or second language. Complementing their efforts is John Clark, who is on the ground with a laser designator to illuminate ground targets for precision air strikes.

The tactics described in *Clear and Present Danger* got a real-life reprise in Afghanistan in the fall of 2001. The U.S. infiltrated about 250 Special Forces troops in the country, where they worked with the Tajik-Uzbek Northern Alliance and disaffected Pashtun in the south of the country. Trained ground controllers with laser designators linked to the global positioning system called in devastating but accurate air strikes from U.S. Navy and Air Force planes dropping GPS- and laser-guided bombs. Light infantry made a later appearance in the war, as elements of the 10 Mountain Division provided the ground troops for the hollow victory at Tora Bora. (Many Al Qaeda irregulars got killed but Osama bin Laden may have gotten away.)

Clark and Ding Chavez team up again in *Debt of Honor* as the spearhead of the Ryan doctrine, where, they help take out two of Japan's nine AWACS aircraft and rescue a future prime minister of Japan. Special Forces also come into play, setting up a temporary base deep in the mountains to support a flight of three RAH-66 Commanches, which do their bit shooting down Japanese AWACS and assassinating several members of the Japanese *zaibatsu*, the real power behind the government.

Kelly and Chavez once again carry out the Ryan doctrine in Iran, where the laser designator is used to illuminate Daryaei's home for convenient lethal placement of laser-guided bombs, carried live on a TV-satellite uplink.

But the commando concept really comes out to play in *Rainbow Six*, Clancy's other novel that gives John Clark a starring role. RAIN-BOW is a fictional NATO commando team whose sole mission is to carry out counterterrorism missions. By now Clark is pushing into his early sixties, and exercises a more executive role while Chavez leads one of two teams. ("Six" is the numeric radio designation for the leader following his call sign.)

Environmentalist renegades hire an ex-KGB agent to reactivate the remnants of Europe's quasi-Marxist terrorist groups of the 1970s and 1980s, and RAINBOW takes them down job by job—in a Swiss Bank, an Austrian mansion, and a Spanish amusement park. The counterattacks are varied and shaped by the tactics best suited for each situation: forced entry and close assault in the Swiss bank; a mix of long-range sniper shooting and forced entry in an Austrian palace; and a Spanish amusement park. By the time the Spanish job is done, foiling an attempt to gain the release of Carlos the Jackal—another 1970s-vintage terrorist—the renegade environmentalists at Horizon Corp. and their ex-KGB help have identified RAINBOW for what it is.

RAINBOW is struck close to home as some Provisional Irish Republican Army renegades paid for by Horizon attack the emergency room at a hospital in Hereford, England, not far from RAINBOW's HQ. Among the hostages are the wives of John Clark and Ding Chavez. The aim of the attack was to draw RAINBOW to the site and ambush the commandos. RAINBOW's team 1 is ripped apart by automatic gunfire. The terrorists' main aim accomplished, they try to flee the scene, but take casualties from survivors of team 1 and members of the just arriving team 2. The bad guys are either killed or captured. Several terrorists back in the hospital still holding hostages do not last long, as RAINBOW's hostage negotiator persuades the remainder to surrender.

This is the third time in Clancy's string of novels that terrorists target the family members of main characters, so pardon the author if this plot device is getting a bit familiar.

RAINBOW's final job is the destruction of Horizon's facility in Manaus, Brazil. As in *Clear and Present Danger*, the sovereignty of a foreign country does not count for much. RAINBOW flies in by cargo plane, inserts by helicopter, rapidly takes out Horizon's gun-toting "volunteers" in a brief jungle firefight, then using explosives, destroys the Horizon facility deep in the Amazon rain forest. The environmental fanatics are then told to strip and commune with nature, as the nearest settlement is seventy-five miles away. They are never heard from again after the RAINBOW team flies off.

RAINBOW makes its second appearance in *Bear and the Dragon*, as it is in Russia conducting training exercises with Russian SPETZNATZ commandos when China invades Russian Siberia. In a last-minute raid, the two groups of commandos strike a Chinese ICBM base not far from the Russian border in northwestern China. The joint strike takes out all the Chinese missiles, many in their silos, save for one, which is bound for Washington, D.C. Again, the scene is packed with action worthy of the big shoot-out at the end of a James Bond movie. Commandos once again make a long-odds attack against a high-value facility.

But do they do this in real life?

Small, fierce raids have long been a staple of Special Forces operations since World War II. Just looking at that conflict one finds many missions undertaken by both sides with mixed degrees of success. The U.S. Army retained its Rangers, while Britain did the same with its Special Air Service. In the early 1960s, the U.S. Army added the Green Berets (formally known as Special Forces) to its lineup to provide for effective counterinsurgency in the Third World.

The birth of modern terrorism in the 1970s created a need for yet more specialized forces to deal with the threat. Previous airline hijackings aside, terrorism did not seize the world's attention until the 1972 Munich Olympics, when the Palestinian terrorist group Black September captured and held hostage the Israeli Olympic team. West German police had to improvise on the spot how to handle the problem. The terrorists demanded a bus to take them to the airport, where helicopters awaited to take them away. At Ferstunfeldbruck Airport, the West German police tried to take out the terrorists, who quickly lobbed hand grenades into the parked helicopters, killing the Israeli athletes.

Lessons were learned the hard way, and by the end of the decade many Western nations had the capability to respond with force against the terrorist threat. Israel's response came in 1976, following the hijacking of an Air France Airbus A-300. The plane ended up at Entebbe, just outside of Kampala, Uganda, and about 250 hostages were herded into the airport terminal. The terrorists did release 150, keeping the remaining one hundred, who were Jewish. The Israelis sent four C-130s to free the hostages. Two taxied up to the terminal and deployed paratroops to assault the building directly, while teams of paratroops from the other two planes set up a light perimeter to forestall reinforcements and destroy any Ugandan MiGs found at the airport. The raiding party shot dead the five terrorists in the terminal, accidentally killing another three hostages, and suffered only one fatality[12] and ten wounded. Within fifty-five minutes, all paratroops and hostages were aboard the C-130s and off to Nairobi, Kenya, where the planes would refuel for the flight back to Israel while the wounded were transferred to a Boeing 707 refitted as an airborne hospital.[13]

The Entebbe raid was a pinch-hit affair, involving only several days of rehearsal on a mock-up of the airport using paratroops who were not specifically trained for counterterrorist strikes but still counted as elite, highly trained light infantry. They were armed with a high proportion of automatic weapons and used jeeps to cover the ground quickly at Entebbe to establish the perimeter. The Ugandans were not expecting the inbound flights, and a ruse further enhanced surprise when a Mercedes-Benz approached the terminal that was identical to the one used by Ugandan dictator Idi Amin.

The following year, in October 1977, four terrorists hijacked a Lufthansa Boeing 737, on a flight from Spain to Germany. After wending its way to Rome, Cyprus, Bahrain, Dubai, and South Yemen, the plane eventually ended up in Mogadishu, Somalia. Stalking its movements were two Boeing 707s, each carrying a thirty-man team belonging to GSG-9, a special unit belonging to West Germany's Border Protection Force. Shortly before the deadline expired for the release of some named terrorists in West German custody, GSG-9 assaulted the grounded airliner. The doors were blown off fore and aft. Two SAS members assisted, tossing in "stun grenades" that would dazzle the terrorists for four to six seconds. Commandos burst into the plane cabin, shouting for the hostages to get down, then shooting two of the terrorists. They then killed two more by the cockpit doorway. All told, only four passengers, one commando and one flight attendant were injured during the assault, which was over in eleven minutes.[14]

Both raids required a great deal of diplomacy to accomplish. Israel had to secure permission from Kenya to use Nairobi as a refueling stop for the return trip. West Germany could not execute its rescue mission without obtaining Somali permission to bring in its commandos. This permission was denied by Dubai because the government there insisted on the use of its troops in part of the rescue mission, which was a practical impossibility given their lack of antiterrorist training.

The U.S. was not blind to these developments, adding to its Special Forces lineup the army's Delta Force and the navy's SEAL Team Six, both trained in armed hostage rescue. Delta Force's debut was less than auspicious, as it made up part of the four-service Iranian hostage rescue effort that ended in fiery fiasco in Iran back in 1980. Eight Sikorsky CH-53s took off from a U.S. aircraft carrier in the Persian Gulf, slated to rendezvous with C-130s at an Iranian airstrip where they would be refueled. Only six of the helicopters made it, and one had a breakdown on the spot. In the rush to abort the mission, one of the CH-53s collided with a fuel-laden C-130 upon takeoff, killing eight U.S. servicemen.

The Iranian hostage rescue received a lot of criticism, and justly so. Had the plan gone forward, the helicopters would have flown the mix of Army Delta Force and U.S. Marines to a location outside of Tehran, where an advance man (U.S. Special Forces in real life, John Clark in Clancy's chronology) would furnish the team with trucks. In convoy, the rescuers would have assaulted the outer wall of the U.S. embassy, stormed the building, kill the Iranian students holding the hostages, pull them out, put them on the trucks, and drive them to a nearby stadium, where the helicopters would arrive and pull all out. Several AC-130 gunships would have been flying above to provide fire support. To sum up, had this plan gone forward, the commandos and their rescued hostages would have had to fight their way from the embassy to the stadium in a large city. To say this could be done without losses is a bit of a stretch.

The U.S. got a good taste of this problem in 1993, when a mixed force of Rangers and Delta Force met defeat in the streets of Mogadishu, during a heliborne raid to arrest Somali warlord Mohammed Farah Aideed. A truck-borne relief convoy tried to fight its way to relieve a force inserted by helicopter, as well as to two crash sites where the MH-60s were brought down by RPG fire. The battle lasted all day and night, resulting in the death of eighteen Americans and the wounding of over eighty in the company-sized force.

Special Forces were also given smaller missions of derring-do during the invasion of Grenada in 1983. Four Navy SEALs drowned when their assault boat capsized—their mission never publicized. Another four were lost in an effort to seize the yacht of Panamanian strongman Manuel Noriega during the 1989 invasion of Panama. Noriega was not on the boat, but its capture removed it as a means of escape.

During the first Gulf War, Special Forces did a lot of strategic reconnaissance behind enemy lines, but their success at hunting mobile SCUD missiles was nil. During the second Gulf War, U.S. Special Forces were given more substantive missions. Publicized was the rescue of POW Jessica Lynch, which turned out to be more for propaganda value. More substantive was the raid to seize the Haditha Dam prior to the Third Infantry Division's advance through the Karbala Gap. The Iraqis could have opened the dam's spillways to flood the local terrain, impeding the Third Mechanized Infantry Division's advance. Special Forces also surely played a role in the December 2003 capture of Saddam Hussein.

Perhaps the most beguiling comparison of fact and fiction took place in *Without Remorse*, where the navy tries to stage a raid to free American POWs in North Vietnam. The raid takes place in the 1971–1972 time frame, shortly after the raid on Son Tay prison camp. That raid saw the successful insertion of rescue teams, only to find the camp empty. In Clancy's fiction, the navy tried to do the same thing within its means, inserting John Kelly/Clark to keep a smaller POW camp under observation for several days to make sure the coast is clear for a small heliborne raid to free fifteen to twenty American pilots. Kelly/Clark calls off the raid when he sees an NVA company roll in to beef up the perimeter. On his way to his extraction point, Clark/Kelly runs into a passing car, and rakes it with gunfire from his silenced CAR-15. The bonus is a Russian colonel from military intelligence who had been interrogating the POWs, who eventually makes it known that the prisoners are soon to be shot. U.S. political pressure on the Russians in turn is placed on the North Vietnamese, who back off and release the POWs.

The little commando mission stands in stark contrast with Kelly's freelance commando raid against a Baltimore drug-dealing ring, and illustrates the legal boundaries of killing. In the heat of an assault, the aim for commandos is to kill the terrorists before they can kill the hostages, so it's no surprise that the Israelis and Germans took no prisoners at Entebbe and Mogadishu.

Likewise in 1995, the French faced a similar problem when Algerian fundamentalists belonging to the Armed Islamic Group hijacked a plane and planned to crash it into the Eiffel Tower after refueling. A special unit of French police rushed the plane and neutralized the threat, again taking no prisoners.[15]

Peru took a more heavy-handed approach. Terrorists belonging to the Tupac Amaru Revolutionary Movement infiltrated the Japanese embassy in Lima during a 1996 Christmas party and took the ambassador and many guests hostage. It took several months for the Peruvian Army to prepare and plan an assault on the compound, digging a tunnel underneath the grounds so that a company-sized assault could take place in April 1997. The troops blew a hole in the living room floor of the residence and poured out, timing the assault to coincide with an afternoon indoor soccer match when eight of the fourteen terrorists would be playing. The troops killed every terrorist—even the ones trying to surrender—and freed seventy-two hostages while losing two soldiers and one hostage.[16]

Russia has been more heavy-handed in dealing with its Chechen terrorist threat. Chechen rebels in 1995 twice assaulted and captured hospitals just over the provincial border in Russia proper, at Budyonnovsk and Kizlyar respectively. The army undertook the job of assaulting the buildings, but was repeatedly beaten back in both instances. The Budyonnovsk incident was far worse—with about one thousand hostages—and the loss of about one hundred civilians, police officers, and soldiers in the assault.

The second Chechen war also started with a bang in September 1999, as powerful bombs set off in the dead of night flattened several apartment buildings in Moscow and Dagestan, killing about three hundred. This occurred as a rebel movement began in Chechnya that embraced Wahhabi Sunni Islam instead of the more tolerant Sufi branch common there. Russia struck back hard, as usual, suffering many casualties as its inept army could only accomplish with great difficulty what the U.S. Army did easily—take a city with few casualties. Grozny was wrecked in February 2000, at heavy cost to Russia, while the Third Infantry Division's "Thunder Run" took Baghdad with few casualties.

Chechens struck back at Moscow, taking over a theater during a performance of the Russian musical *Nord Ost* in October 2002. With the failures at Budyonnovsk and Kizlyar fresh memories, Russian SPETZNATZ troops changed tactics. Rather than assault the theater and risk the lives of the seven hundred hostages, a "knockout gas" was used that immobilized the hostages and the forty to fifty terrorists. The Russians took no prisoners, but also lost 115 of the hostages while hospitalizing most of the survivors. The army would not tell nearby hospitals what kind of gas was used, so emergency room doctors could not deliver sure treatment of the victims, but it is suspected that Fantanyl, a fast-acting opiate, was used.[17] Chechen terrorists were wise to this when they took over a school in Beslan in September 2004. They punched out the windows, meanwhile holding over 1,000 hostages for two days. A rushed assault by SPETZNATZ resulted in over 350 hostages killed, over 700 wounded. Half the victims were children. All but one of the 26 terrorists were killed.

Even the Russians have taken a page from the Israeli counterterrorism book, dispatching their own hit team to take out former Chechen president Zelimkhan Yanderbiyev in Doha, Qatar, in February 2004. The two Russian agents were captured and given life sentences.[18]

Terrorists choose the time and place of attack, which gives them the initiative and the advantage. Countering the threat will take more than Special Forces and preemptive wars. There is a lot of intelligence and police drudgework, monitoring suspects abroad and at home to develop the information needed to stop them before they can act. There are no smoking guns, no important clues that unravel the whole secret scheme. It's a low-key incremental war that will be punctuated by a few gunfights here, a few bombs there. You will only see it in the headlines at those times.

Send in the Spooks

Spying will be placed here in summation as the poor cousin to killing. Clancy can be a bit conflicted when he writes his typical action-packed techno-thriller, as he wants to put a spy novel somewhere in there. It is harder to assess how decisive espionage is as an element in statecraft, as the success stories stay secret and the failures are more likely to be known. It is hard to know in real life whether espionage was a decisive factor in delivering victory to the U.S. during the cold war.

In real life, Americans get their spy story in uneven episodes. Many times, it is failure, as some Americans prove all too willing to sell secrets to a foreign power. The Walker spy ring, CIA's Ames, FBI's Hanson, Harry Wu Tai Chin, and Jonathan Pollard all got their thorough write-ups after years of undetected work. Then there are the few success stories—Oleg Penkovsky, "Top Hat" and "Fedora," and the defection (and loss) of Vitaly Yurchenko, number five in the KGB hierarchy. Then there are the failures—how CIA missed the breakup of the Soviet Union; how various branches of U.S. intelligence could not piece together Al Qaeda's September 11 conspiracy; and the total misestimate of Iraq's arsenal of weapons of mass destruction.

The intriguing stories overlook some sad facts in U.S. intelligence gathering. First, the largest agency involved in the gray business is the

National Security Agency, not the CIA. NSA's forte is electronic intelligence and signals intelligence. The National Reconnaissance Office runs the U.S. constellation of spy satellites and interprets their images. The State Department has its own intelligence unit. So does the Pentagon, through the four uniformed services. The Treasury Department also gathers information in accord with its own interests.

And then there is the CIA, still placing its agents under diplomatic cover in various embassies. If they get caught, they get bounced out of country, persona non grata. CIA is trying to recruit its own corps of agents to work without diplomatic cover, which means they operate without a "get out of jail free" card to bail them out if they get caught.

This is not the CIA of the 1950s, which used covert means to engineer coups against left-wing governments in Iran and Guatemala. It's not the CIA that screwed up at the Bay of Pigs. Nor is it the CIA that covertly financed anti-Communist insurgencies in Nicaragua, Angola, and Afghanistan.

Rebuilding a CIA "human intelligence" network is going to take much time. It will add another source of information to the huge flood stream of data that analysts (and their computers) must wade through. It must be worth doing, otherwise why spend the billions of dollars? Yet in the end, it is hard to know just what value spying has, compared to other sources of intelligence.

Spy novel author John le Carré, also a former intelligence agent, once addressed the topic in the early 1990s while speaking before the Boston Bar Association. He noted the billions of dollars spent on espionage, the untold human effort to find out what the bad guys were thinking and to use that information against them. While that great effort was expended in the cold war, it was not the spy who provided the key bit of information that brought Communist Russia crashing down, le Carré noted. It was the strength of an open society and democratic government in the United States.

In the end, the spies had nothing to do with ending the cold war.[19]

FIVE

Secondhand Clancy
Jack Ryan on the Silver Screen

One common complaint heard is that a movie is never as good as a book.

The rule holds true for most movies based on Tom Clancy's novels.

Only four of Clancy's novels made it to film: *Hunt for Red October*, *Patriot Games*, *Clear and Present Danger*, and *Sum of All Fears*. Once a Clancy novel passes through the Hollywood left-wing filter, it comes out with contradictions that range from slight or grotesque compared to Clancy's more conservative worldview.[1]

So let's start at the beginning of Clancy tales retold by the left coast.

Cue Russian Choral Music. Take One.

Hunt for Red October had the misfortune of being released in 1989, shortly before the cold war ended. The chronology shifts *Red October* to 1984, "shortly before Gorbachev comes to power." (The movie does not specify who is the current U.S. president in the story.)

In Clancy's book, Ramius's motivation to defect and deliver the *Red October* to the U.S. is clearly anti-Soviet. He never liked the system. He grew to hate it even more when his wife died at the hands of a shoddy medical system. But in the movie, Ramius (played by Sean Connery wearing a spiky hairpiece) seems vaguely antinuclear and troubled by size of the USSR's nuclear arsenal. The *Red October*'s caterpillar drive makes the sub near silent, allowing it to creep up to the U.S. coast and be able to launch with little warning and short flight times. In real life, the SS-N-20 solid-fuel missiles handled by the Typhoon-class submarine has a range of about 5,100 miles, so the need to get close to the U.S. to launch is not as pressing. The basic rule of thumb is the longer the range of the missile, the more ocean there is to hide in.

The *Red October*'s *zampolit*, or political officer, notes Ramius's recent diary entries about "the end of the world," including passages from the book of Revelations[2] and J. Robert Oppenheimer's quote at Alamagordo: I am death. Needless to say, he begins to suspect Ramius is becoming politically unreliable. As Ramius and *zampolit* Putin (no relation to current Russian president Vladimir Putin) open the safe, Ramius gets the jump on him and breaks his neck, making it look like an accident. Bogus orders are substituted. Instead of going north to undergo exercises with an Alfa-class attack sub as "hunter," Ramius tells the crew they are going south to evade the Russians, evade the Americans, park the sub off the East Coast to show who is boss, then go to Cuba for some shore leave. (Just picture the video—"Russian Sailors Go Wild.")

So far, so good—the movie is moving parallel with the book. Yet note this: the action is compressing about fifty pages of narrative into a space of about five minutes. That in a nutshell illustrates the basic problem of turning a book into a movie. The format is brutally limited by a short running time, so the screenwriter must cut to the chase and focus the plot only on the basic elements of conflict in the story, while also discarding character development. But that brings up the next problem—how faithful must the movie be to the book? *Hunt for Red October* is a pretty tall sea story set in a cold war context. It doesn't need a lot of embellishment, as the story is exciting enough as it is. Yet embellishment is what the director and screenwriters must deliver, as they must fashion new plot conflicts to drive the story forward for lack of time, budget or imagination.

Hollywood clichés serve a sad but useful purpose here. The movie audience unconsciously knows the tried, tired but true conventions of any genre, so they act as visual shorthand to drive the movie forward without expending too many minutes in exposition. As Ramius tells his crew where they are going, the USS *Dallas*, on patrol in the Barents Sea, picks up the *Red October*. The Russian sub engages its caterpillar drive and goes silent as the pumped-up crew belts out a very lame rendition of the Soviet national anthem. Jones, the chief sonar man on *Dallas*, reports to Captain Mancuso that the sonar contact went silent, and then he heard singing.

Where did we see this cliché before?

World War II movies.

The "bad guys"—err, Nazi Germans—were really into loud male chorale singing. We see this in *The Enemy Below*, a really good destroyer escort versus U-boat movie starring Robert Mitchum and Curt Jurgens. We see the same thing with the U-boat crews singing their service song in *The McKenzie Break* or the underage SS Panzer troops belting out the "Panzer Lied" in *The Battle of the Bulge*. Americans do this, too, but they limit themselves to singing "The Star-Spangled Banner" before ball games. You don't see American servicemen singing "God Bless America" before staging a bloody frontal assault on a Nazi machine gun nest or dropping the bomb on Hiroshima.

Two more movie conventions come into play early in the film.

The first is a staple of all war movies—dramatic disagreement among the servicemen in uniform. In the military, subordinates do not challenge authority, as that would be a breakdown in discipline. Without discipline, no unit or crew could function. Having a subordinate question Ramius's killing of the *zampolit* in a sharp tone in front of the officers makes for good drama, but it looks pretty stupid. Again, this convention has been used in tons of war movies. *Master and Commander*, *Crimson Tide*, *Platoon*, *The Guns of Navarone*, *The Caine Mutiny*, *Run Silent Run Deep*—the list here is randomly assorted, but endless.

The second convention is heavy-handed foreshadowing. When the director wants to signal the audience to pay attention to something that will become important later, he lets the camera linger on a particular character or object. On the *Red October*, this technique is used on the assistant cook, after Ramius makes some remark to his *zampolit* earlier in the film about how many KGB or GRU operatives are hidden on his vessel. This robs any future plot twist of its surprise. (For a good reference point illustrating the opposite, recall *Alien*, when the larval beastie eats his way out of a crew member in front of his shocked shipmates. No one in the audience expected it, and the screams that followed were real.)

Now Jack Ryan has to be brought into play, played by Alec Baldwin. He is dropped off at the airport by his wife, briefly played by Gates McFadden (she of *Star Trek: The Next Generation*), now sporting a British accent. (I thought Cathy Ryan was an American eye surgeon?) Ryan fears flying. That's okay . . . heroes should have fears. (Even Indiana Jones was scared of snakes.) Ryan arrives at CIA headquarters, not looking tired even though he says he is, to drop off the latest photos of the *Red October*, puzzled by the twin openings in the hull fore and aft. CIA's Admiral Greer (played by James Earl Jones) gives Ryan the okay to go see Skip Taylor.

As in the book, Taylor plays a key secondary role interpreting what purpose those inlets and outlets served on the *Red October*. Heavy-handed foreshadowing comes back into play, as Taylor shows Ryan the experimental docking collar he is working on for the navy's deep-sea research vehicle (DSRV), basically a mini-sub. This docking collar will fit all makes of submarine.

Meanwhile, back on the sub . . .

True to the book, Ramius's letter reaches his father-in-law, who is the Soviet Navy's chief political officer, announcing his intention to steal the sub and defect to the United States. This musters the entire Red fleet into action, pursuing the *Red October* into the North Atlantic.

Now the limitations of the movie kick in with a vengeance.

Were *Hunt for Red October* made today, computer-generated imaging would have given us great footage of Soviet Kiev-class carriers and Kirov-class cruisers forming into battle groups with destroyers and frigates, speeding at thirty knots into the North Atlantic behind a swarm of Alfa- and Victor-class attack subs. Ships are very expensive props, however. It is nice that the U.S. Navy lent its cooperation to make the movie, as this allowed some limited use of a ship here and a sub there to add some verisimilitude. It's pretty obvious the Soviet Navy didn't. The filmmakers had to content themselves with a floating Typhoon-class sub mock-up for a couple of external shots, a cool-looking model of a Tu-16 Bear on ASW patrol, really big sub models in a dunk tank for the underwater scenes, and a really roomy control room set for Sean Connery and his officers to prance around in.

Even then, the navy's generosity is limited to one or two assets at a time. Footage shot aboard a real aircraft carrier is mixed with stock footage of flight operations. A scene of an ASW helicopter passing overhead is contrasted with a canned film clip of an airdropped torpedo hitting the water. Approach video of an F-14 is mixed with Korean War–vintage crash footage of an F-9 smashing into a flight deck. A helicopter tries to lower a stuntman onto the conning tower of a submarine. A lone Perry-class frigate steams toward the camera. A nuclear attack sub broaches the surface. Never does the moviegoer see more than a real vessel or two in any scene. Dialogue, film editing, and clever use of models must suffice to give the viewer the illusion of larger actions taking place.

Back to the movie.

Ryan has to maneuver through the rapids of compressed action to go from his office to the *Red October*. Ryan gives an impromptu last-minute briefing to National Security Advisor Jeffrey Pelt (played by Richard Jordan) and the service chiefs. Ryan makes a leap of intuitive analysis, believing that Ramius is trying to defect while the service chiefs interpret the Soviet fleet moves as provocative. In a post-meeting aside with Pelt, Ryan is given three days to bring in *Red October*, or it will be sunk.

The movie plot receives a further push when the Soviet ambassador meets with Pelt. First, he calls the huge Soviet naval deployment into the Atlantic a rescue mission to find and recover the *Red October* and its crew. But the second meeting finds the ambassador changing his story, calling Ramius a madman who will launch his missiles at the U.S. if allowed to get to a firing position. This gets the U.S. Navy involved in hunting the *Red October*—to kill it, not steal it. Only Ryan believes Ramius is trying to defect, based on what he knows about him.

Back to the book.

A character missing from the movie is in play, a CIA spy in Moscow with access to the Politburo code-named CARDINAL. His information goes straight to Ryan's superiors, who know for certain that Ramius is trying to defect. The navy improvises a comprehensive response to take advantage of this situation, deploying the Atlantic fleet to screen the Russian fleet from proceeding farther west in a massive game of "chicken." The old missile sub *Ethan Allen* is readied for its last voyage, to be scuttled in the western Atlantic to fake the wreckage of the *Red October*, so that the Russians could not suspect the U.S. gaining possession of the sub. None of this comes up in the movie.

Also missing from the movie is the British carrier HMS *Invincible*, which plays a role in getting Ryan to his momentous rendezvous. The British are nowhere in the movie, even though they play a significant but supporting role in Clancy's narrative. Extra characters and smaller plotlines fall by the wayside in the movie. The staff member belonging to a liberal senator is captured as a Russian spy and turned. U.S. Navy Russian experts die in a helicopter crash, forcing Ryan to play a more active role in the plot. A Soviet sub suffers a reactor meltdown after a check valve breaks off in the cooling system. Navy and air force fighters play chicken with Russian ships and aircraft.

All that stuff is in the book.

All of it never appears in the movie.

The necessity of focus forces these parts to be cut from the film, lest the running time double. Yet all these smaller parts lent much texture to the book, as well as some global perspective and verisimilitude.

Back to the movie. Ramius has problems of his own. While making the speed run through the rocky troughs of the Rejkjanes Ridge, the caterpillar drive fails owing to sabotage. *Red October* switches to its propellers, only to be detected by a sonobuoy dropped by a patrolling TU-16 Bear. The bomber follows up with an airdropped torpedo, which the *Red October* must foil. Countermeasures fail as the faster torpedo closes on the sub. Ramius delays taking the turn in front of the Neptune Massif, calling for the turn at the last second. The torpedo is too fast and too late to match the turn, so it slams into the rocks. This scene was concocted for the movie, not the book.

Many of the scenes showing *Red October* shooting through "Red Route 1" are reminiscent of *Star Wars*. The speed run through the rocky trench is not much different from the rebel fighters doing a low-level strike against a weak point on the Death Star. Indeed, the *Star Wars* reference is not limited to this part. USS *Dallas* is introduced to the viewer much like an imperial cruiser—with a long shot of the vessel passing over the top of the frame.

Ryan is taken by plane to a carrier. He hates flying, especially in stormy weather, being bucked by turbulence while a crewman recounts a more nauseous flight in the recent past. No one gets airsick. Ryan persuades the admiral of the carrier battle group (Senator Fred Thompson, R-Tennessee, a part-time actor) that the *Red October* is trying to defect. He secures a helicopter flight to take him to the *Dallas*'s position.

In the book, Ryan flies out to the carrier *John F. Kennedy*, and from there to HMS *Invincible*. The Americans are too busy screening the three Russian battle groups, so the British do the work of contacting *Red October* and getting Ryan onboard. In the movie, that job shifts to *Dallas*. Ryan's helicopter flight hits the threshold of its range and Ryan yells at the pilot to use his reserve fuel to make the rendezvous with *Dallas*, which has just been sighted. Again, to heighten suspense, the helicopter tries lowering Ryan with its rescue sling to the top of the *Dallas*'s conning tower. (Why not hover above the deck? Is that too easy?) The helicopter is about to break off for lack of fuel when Ryan hits the release and drops into the water beside the *Dallas*. Ryan is pulled aboard by a *Dallas* diver who was standing by, and comes aboard quite wet, but not shivering, even though the water is cold enough to kill a man in less than four minutes.

Mancuso is not pleased having to break off the pursuit of the *Red October* just to pick up Ryan. Mancuso just got the order to sink the Russian sub and Ryan only has two minutes to convince Mancuso that Ramius is trying to defect. Using a corny plot device, Ryan tells Mancuso that he knows Ramius well enough to call his next move—a turn to starboard to check his baffles to make sure he is not being tailed. Mancuso is convinced, orders *Dallas* to go briefly to full speed to announce his presence, and maintains a firing solution as *Red October* goes to periscope depth. *Dallas* follows.

The book differs here by wide degrees. Mancuso's persistent pursuit of *Red October*, aided by his top sonar man Jones, enables *Dallas* to maintain contact and pick up Ryan and a British colleague from *Invincible*. It's *Invincible* that makes contact with *Red October* and arrangements go forward for the defection.

Another dropout from the film is the navy rescue ship USS *Pigeon*, with its DSRV on board. *Pigeon* plays a key role in getting the *Red Oc-*

tober's crew off, after Ramius gets one of his officers to fake indication of a nuclear reactor leak by using the X-ray machine in sick bay to irradiate the crew's warning badges. (The badge is a strip of unexposed film that is fogged by radiation.) This convinces the crew to leave quickly! In the movie, the chief engineer fakes the leak by triggering the radiation alarm. *Red October* surfaces, and the crew take to the deck to inflate the life rafts in rainy, windy weather. Funny how the life rafts don't blow away as the crew manhandles them. A Perry-class frigate approaches the *Red October*, ready to rescue the crew.

The movie sharpens its departure from the book by magnifying suspense without the surprise, and by marring continuity. As the *Red October*'s crew paddles toward the frigate *Reuben James*, the frigate's ASW helicopter drops a torpedo aimed at the *Red October*. As a crewman on the *James* calls off the torpedo's closing distance, a hand reaches down to press the self-destruct button. It's the CIA's Admiral Greer. He tells the crewman he did not see him on the ship, nor should he remember what happened.

Meanwhile, back on the *Red October*, the DSRV docks and drops off Ryan, Mancuso, and Jones. (Funny, the *Dallas* didn't have that DSRV handy until now, and the movie never shows how it got there.) They have sidearms. Mancuso is not sure what will happen next. The hatch opens and the Russian officer beckons the trio onboard. They go to the conn, where they encounter the perfect movie tableau—the *Red October*'s officers arrayed around the room. So what do the characters do? They make clichéd small talk typical of war movies. Ryan makes a hand gesture to ask for a cigarette, but then begins to chat in Russian with Ramius. ("It is good to study your enemy, blah, blah, blah . . .") Ramius presents his boat to Ryan and associates, requesting asylum in the United States.

But wait, another source of danger must be added, or there would be no suspense (yawn). Tupolev shows up in his Alfa-class attack sub. He launches a torpedo at the *Red October*. Jones picks it up on sonar. Ramius orders the sub turned into the path of the oncoming torpedo, increasing the closing speed so that the sub can hit the torpedo before it has traveled far enough to arm itself. The reassuring thunk against the hull is proof of concept. Quickly, Tuploev's Alfa launches another fish, but with the peacetime minimum safety setting on, so it fails to explode as it zips by *Red October*. Ramius, who trained Tupolev, doubts his ex-pupil will make the same mistake again.

As if there wasn't enough tension in the plot, the assistant cook bursts forward and riddles the conn with pistol fire, totaling the torpedo fire control and killing the Russian first officer (played by Sam Neill, who affects a stilted Russian accent). This was coming since the camera lingered on the assistant cook over an hour ago.

Ryan and Ramius now go hunting for the assistant cook/GRU agent in the *Red October*'s missile room, as Mancuso takes command. The duo is ambushed at the threshold, and Ramius takes a bullet to the shoulder—the standard serious flesh wound seen in many Hollywood action flicks. Ryan must proceed alone, as Ramius points out to him that there is much in this part of the sub that does not mix well with bullets. Ryan reacts sarcastically. "Be careful what I shoot at? What about him?!" Ryan stalks his prey, clambering up the ladder to the catwalk and then forward to missile silo 20, where the assistant cook wants to ignite a missile to scuttle *Red October*. (At this point, Alec Baldwin does an impersonation of Sean Connery's Scottish accent—"Be careful, Ryan, things here don't react well with bulletsh [*sic*]"). He then confronts the Russian, who is holding the two wires that need to be crossed to do his dirty deed. The camera focuses on the standoff for a good ten to twenty seconds, until Ryan gathers enough composure to shoot the Russian full of bloody holes.

As if this wasn't bad enough, Tupolev fires another torpedo, this time with zero safety distance. Mancuso orders a hard turn, with the Alfa hot on his tail. The *Red October*, weighing in at 29,000 tons submerged, is slower and has a wider turn radius. It is clear it will not be able to shake the torpedo, and with a damaged fire control, cannot shoot back. At this point, *Dallas* (under command of its executive officer) cuts into the torpedo's path, drops countermeasures, and then blows ballast for an emergency surfacing to shake the fish. *Dallas* broaches the surface like a whale, then crash dives. These scenes are interspersed with Ryan's hunt for the Russian amidst the missile silos.

The torpedo is still active. It locks onto *Red October* as Mancuso orders a course aimed straight at the oncoming Alfa. At the last minute, Mancuso calls for hard right rudder, 30 degrees down dive. *Red October* shakes the torpedo, which then slams into the Alfa, sinking it. (Serves Tupolev right, as he is the onscreen villain the audience roots against.)

Now the *Red October* is seen going up the Penobscot River in Maine, where it can hide from the prying eyes of Soviet spy satellites, which will be scoping out all the U.S. naval bases on the East Coast. Ramius makes a little speech about how the *Red October* was built to attack the United States, and how a little revolution every now and then is a good thing. The movie ends with a scene showing Ryan flying back to England, his daughter's new teddy bear in the seat next to him. Ryan, who fears flying, is sound asleep.

Cue rousing Russian chorale music.

Fade scene.

Run credits.

Well, the ending was mostly faithful to the book. There was a life-or-death duel with Tupolev's Alfa. *Dallas* did play a role shepherding *Red October* to safety. And that assistant cook was a GRU agent assigned to scuttle the sub. That's about it. Missing was the scuttling of the *Ethan Allen* to fake Russian sub wreckage in deep waters. Missing was the ejection of the dud missile after Ryan kills the assistant cook, adding some verisimilitude to the false Soviet sub wreckage. Ramius helps Ryan stalk the assistant cook/GRU agent, taking a bullet in the upper leg, not shoulder. The USS *Pogy* helps *Dallas* escort *Red October* to the U.S., bound for a covered graving yard in Norfolk, not a river in Maine. And in the mix, a left-wing American working as a Soviet spy is uncovered on the staff of a liberal senator assigned to the intelligence committee, and is turned. None of this is in the movie, regardless of whether the cuts were made in the interest of focusing on the plot essentials or possibly leavening Clancy's right-wing worldview.

In the movie, that left-right contradiction comes through in a subtle way in the final meeting between National Security Advisor Jeffrey Pelt and the Russian ambassador. The ambassador regrets to inform his American counterpart that the Soviet Navy has lost another submarine. Pelt delivers a puckish reply, something like, "Oh, no, you mean you lost another one?" Look at the office wall in the background, and note the photographs of presidents Franklin Delano Roosevelt and Jimmy Carter, both Democrats. Wasn't there a Republican president in office back in 1984, which was the movie's time frame?

Was this intentional?

Ah, it's a small detail, best overlooked. It is doubtful any viewer ever noticed this, anyway.

Cue Mournful Irish Music Sung by a High-pitched Female Voice. Take Two.

Patriot Games (1992) marks the second foray into turning the Clancy canon into action films, and also marks a changing of the guard, as Harrison Ford takes over the part of Jack Ryan from Alec Baldwin. Basically, a moderate left-wing Democrat replaces an extreme left-wing Democrat.

In movies, the bad guy least likely to offend any ethnic group is a European terrorist. (Never cast Arabs as terrorists, that would be racist, even if the daily news contradicts that rule!) The Clancy name hails from Ireland, but he is an Anglophile first, and it shows clearly in *Patriot Games*—the book and the movie.

Not much longer than *Hunt for Red October*, *Patriot Games* will suffer from the same time challenge that all books must surpass once transposed into movies—the screenwriter can't fit all of the book's actions and characters into the 90–120 minutes of allotted screen time. Something has got to go.

Hollywood took greater liberties turning *Patriot Games* into a movie, much to Clancy's consternation. Clancy vehemently vented his frustrations at the changes, many of which were just plain stupid.[3]

One draft of the script called for the boat chase to end in a crash on a coral reef. There is only one problem: there are no coral reefs in Chesapeake Bay. This drove Clancy nuts, and it led to shouting matches with film producer Marc Neufeld, as well as alleged fourteen-page single-spaced memos penned by Clancy picking out the technical flaws in the script.

Fellow author Joseph Wambaugh, who penned many a cop novel massacred by Hollywood, was philosophical. "Clancy shouldn't get upset because these people who make the movies know something by now: the ticket buyer is incredibly stupid. It doesn't matter where they put the coral reef."

Clancy was eventually assuaged. No longer threatening to remove his name from the film, Clancy did get a promise from Paramount executive Brandon Tartikoff for closer collaboration in the future, but no veto power over a script. Paramount had not yet purchased the rights to *Clear and Present Danger* and *Sum of All Fears*, so pleasing Clancy did result in two more books making it to film.

And the coral reef in Chesapeake Bay was replaced in the script by jagged rocks. At least this changed allowed the author and the studio to save face.

Now back to the film.

Book and movie start alike: Jack Ryan is a professor of history at the Naval Academy at Annapolis, in London with his wife and daughter. In the book, he is researching some British naval history ancillary to his main research for a book on Admiral William Halsey. In the movie, he is delivering a lecture to officers of the British Navy about the state of the Russian Navy after the fall of the Soviet Union.

Yes, Jack Ryan does get to thwart Irish terrorists hell-bent on shooting up a royal limousine with some very important people inside. In the book, it is the prince of Wales, his lovely young wife, and their infant son. (Nowhere in the book are they ever identified as Prince Charles and Princess Diana.) In the movie, the VIP is Lord Holmes, cousin of the queen mother and minister of state for Northern Ireland. The bad guys are still the same—terrorists from Northern Ireland, presumably belonging to the provisional wing of the Irish Republican Army.

The action is fast and furious—a London Taxi makes a U-turn to block the path of the limousine, which screeches to a halt. A trailing car with the gunmen stops, and they riddle the front of the black car, killing the driver and lone bodyguard. An explosive charge demolishes the front end. Detonation cord is being placed on the rear passenger door as Harrison Ford charges in, tackling the first gunman (Sean Miller), shooting at a second (whose shot hits Ryan in the shoulder), and nailing a third gunman holding an AK-47. The London taxi gets away with the remaining members of the hit team.

If this were any other movie, Ryan's shoulder wound would not be serious. Remember, that's the standard Hollywood flesh wound, a little worse than a cut finger. But not this time. Harrison Ford's Ryan loses a lot of blood and starts going into shock as his doctor wife gives first aid. Sean Miller is captured—and bitter. Ryan killed his younger brother Patrick in the attack.

Cut away to Ireland. The attack on Holmes does not go over well with other IRA brigade commanders. Kevin O'Donnell is having a talk with "Jimmy" and is told that "Charlie" will be by later that night to straighten things out. In the meantime, Jimmy is eyeing this really attractive redhead at the pub. After the meeting, they go upstairs.

O'Donnell is no idiot. As three visitors arrive (one at the door, two at the back), he gets the drop on them in two separate ambushes, gunning them down with a 12-gauge "street sweeper" assault shotgun. The "redhead" is O'Donnell's girlfriend, who puts two bullets into Jimmy's head with a silenced automatic pistol while Jimmy was expecting a wild night. The two make their getaway. It's pretty clear here that O'Donnell is making a break from his organization, but nowhere in the film is it made clear that this IRA splinter becomes the Ulster Liberation Army,

Clancy's fictional Maoist-based Irish terrorist group. O'Donnell delivered a little policy statement to Jimmy shortly before breaking off the pub meeting, where he states that the focus must be on taking down the British royal family and ruling class. This is about as much watered-down Marxist dogma a screenwriter can fit into one sound bite. The girlfriend character was made up for the movie, and is typical of Hollywood's femme fatales, as seen in other films like *The Crying Game*, *Black Sunday*, and *The Eagle Has Landed*. (The girlfriend makes no appearance in the book, where deadly eye candy is not needed.)

Miller goes to trial. Ryan, his arm in a sling, identifies him as one of the IRA gunmen and testifies against him in court. As in the book, Ryan endures a rough cross-examination at the hands of Miller's defense attorney. Miller threatens Ryan as he leaves the courtroom. None of this changes the outcome—Miller is found guilty and faces a long stretch in prison. His British hosts also give Ryan an honorary knighthood, but the movie makes light of this and glosses over the point.

Now the film must employ a ton of heavy-handed foreshadowing. Cathy Ryan says she is pregnant. Sean Miller is in his cell, obsessing over Ryan by staring at a press clipping. Paddy O'Neill (played by Richard Harris) is making some lame IRA statement on TV. All of these elements will come into play later in the movie.

Cut to the attractive redhead with the bouncing ponytail. She is visiting a rare bookstore with an old book in hand, looking to have it rebound. She chats with the store's proprietor, Dennis Cooley, asking if the book can be repaired quickly. Inside the book is a note asking for information about Sean Miller's scheduled move to Albany Prison at the Isle of Wight. How many guards? What armament? Which route? When? Cooley, who acts as a go-between for a spy in the British government, promises no miracles, but will do what he can.

In the next scene, three police vans, each with two-car escorts, leave by three different routes. They are playing a shell game. In one of those trucks is Sean Miller. Just as the police vans part ways, so do the book and movie. In the book, the police van is taking a ferry in stormy seas when it is attacked by Miller's pals, who disable the ship's bridge, destroy the radar and radio, and make off in an inflatable Zodiac motorboat. The escorting police inspector is wounded. In the movie, the ambush takes place at an open drawbridge that brings the convoy to a halt. O'Donnell and his gang approach by motorboat. They take out the two escorting police cars with RPGs and demand that the door to the police van be opened as they hold a hostage at gunpoint. Miller is freed. O'Donnell gives Miller a pistol and he finishes off the surviving cops, including the police inspector.

Back to the United States. Ryan receives some unwanted visitors—Admiral Greer (played by James Earl Jones, again) and Marty Cantor (played by J. E. Freeman). Greer tells Ryan that Miller is free and has left Great Britain. Greer believes it highly unlikely that Miller will make his way to the U.S. to get even. He offers Ryan a chance to rejoin the CIA, which Ryan turns down. His wife seconds that decision.

Meanwhile, back in London, Lord Holmes suspects that an IRA spy has penetrated his agency. Thirty-one people had advanced knowledge of the Miller move, and five of them are now dead. One detective leading anti-IRA investigations wants to get his hands on the traitor. Geoffrey Watkins, who assists Holmes, wishes that, too. (Heavy-handed foreshadowing—Watkins is the IRA spy.)

Meanwhile, O'Donnell and his small crew of happy henchmen are on a small rusty freighter, outbound from Britain to receive more advanced training somewhere else. Miller wants to take another swipe at Ryan, while O'Donnell reminds him that the British royal family is the real target.

The film now downshifts to provide a little character exposition. Ryan is teaching at Annapolis, where he is presented a medal—the Order of the Purple Target, with the words *Shoot Me!* emblazoned on a brass bull's-eye. Commander Robby Jackson is more than pleased to present Ryan this medal in front of his history class. They later chat in Jackson's office, where Jackson asks Ryan why he forcefully intervened in a terrorist hit. Ryan attributed his unthinking assault to "rage," as he could not let the terrorists murder harmless, innocent people. (Ignore the political significance of the harmless, innocent people, of course.)

The trough in action is misleading. As Ryan leaves the Annapolis campus, he spots a young man standing on the street corner. Not far away, Sean Miller and several colleagues are sitting in a Ford van, outside of the school where little Sally Ryan is waiting for her mother to pick her up. (Forget about the book's Giant Steps day care center.)

Another parallel divergence from the book occurs here. In the book, the marine guards spot the loitering young man and disarm him as he waited for Ryan to walk past. In the movie, Ryan spots the would-be assassin, and gets the drop on him. An uneven fistfight follows. Ryan is at a disadvantage here, but the marine guards gun down the thug. A getaway car is seen driving away. (It seems Harrison Ford has to get pounded in just about every film he stars in, and this one is no exception.)

Also in the book, Alex Dobbens, a radical black terrorist, aids Sean Miller in machine-gunning Cathy Ryan's Porsche. In the movie, Dobbens is absent. (Is it politically incorrect to have a black villain?) A Maryland state trooper is also gunned down on the highway, but that detail is left out of the movie to focus the plot on killing Cathy and Sally Ryan. The Porsche crashes into an abutment—plot divergence is now over. Now Ryan must pace the corridor at the hospital, awaiting news from the surgeon over whether his wife and daughter will survive.

Paddy O'Neill is seen on the TV again. The U.S. fund-raiser for the IRA was denying any connection between his organization and the shooting, and makes a condolence statement to the Ryan family. In the book, O'Neill is a minor figure who also does the same job—raising cash for the cause and maintaining some plausible deniability for some of the bloody work done back home. Ryan confronts O'Neill in three scenes. First is at the hospital, where he glares angrily at O'Neill and says nothing as O'Neill tries to personally deliver his condolences. The second is in an Irish pub, where Ryan demands from O'Neill information on Sean Miller, or else. O'Neill makes it clear he would never betray another Irishman. In the third scene, O'Neill gives Ryan a package at the hospital cafeteria.

In the package is information about a female suspect that Ryan had spotted briefly at the London hit and again in Annapolis. O'Neill is true to his word—he would never betray another Irishman. The suspect is British.

The movie plot must now take some liberties to move the story forward. Ryan does rejoin the CIA, but he does not practice his pistol shooting under the guidance of marine gunnery Sgt. Breckinridge, as he did in the book. The Irish terrorists are seen at a terrorist training camp, "somewhere in North Africa." The book is less discreet—the damn camp is in Libya, with a whole bunch of other camps. (It seems that Colonel Qaddafi takes a strong interest in state-sponsored terrorism.) Miller and O'Donnell have their usual spat about getting even with Ryan versus killing British royalty, which worsens now that Miller is told the Ryans survived.

Ryan is now working long hours at the CIA, poring over spy satellite photos, intelligence files, and tons of raw data. He pieces together the gang's freighter getaway from London and subsequent trip to "North Africa." (In the book, the training camp is in Libya.) Re-tasked spy satellites uncover which camp the terrorists are staying at. Dennis Cooley, the rare bookstore owner, flies the coop and shows up in the spy satellite photos, reconfirming Ryan's hunch after O'Donnell's girlfriend is also spotted.[4]

It is time for the book and movie to diverge, again.

Ryan's information is used to stage a counterstrike at the terrorist training camp, using Special Air Service commandos provided by Britain. Two UH-1 Hueys swoop low over the desert to drop off their lethal passengers, then circle to provide fire support as the eight commandos wipe out the camp and every living person in it. This was shown in the movie as a live TV feed from a spy satellite, shown in infrared.

But this did not happen in the book, at least not quite the same way.

The commandos were French (yes, French) paratroops, who were delivered by helicopter from the flight deck of the USS *Saratoga*. The French stage two raids—one against Action-Directe, their own domestic terrorist pain. The narrative of this raid provided the plotline for the SAS raid in the movie. The second raid a few days later was to have hit O'Donnell's camp, but the IR spy satellite showed it to be vacant and the commandos encountered a Libyan army unit on unexpected maneuvers, and had to turn back. (A Frenchwoman is mentioned briefly as an accomplished assassin for Action-Directe, providing the model for O'Donnell's girlfriend in the movie.)

By discarding this, and sticking to the raid footage, the film introduces a "false ending" that reassures the characters that everything has been taken care of. But this does not fool the average jaded moviegoer, who knows the film has another fifteen to twenty minutes to go. Some action is needed!

Holmes stops by the Ryan home to present the queen's medal. He has a security detail of four to six guards armed with Uzis. A Maryland state police trooper guards the gateway to the grounds of the Ryan home, a spacious house overlooking the shore—with a view of the horizon? Chesapeake Bay is only ten miles wide north and south of Annapolis, where the Ryan home is located in the book. Geoffrey Watkins, the traitor in Holmes's entourage, cuts the power in the Ryan home and kills one of the security detail. O'Donnell's terrorists, now trained as commandos, take out the perimeter guards in the darkness, having an advantage with their night vision goggles. They only number five or six.

This is a far cry from the intricate two-squad attack on the Ryan estate shown in the book. Yes, the bad guys approached by boat, but that's about it. In the book, Alex Dobbens lowers two utility ladders from an electrical service van to allow the terrorists to ascend the seaside cliff to begin their attack. Funny, nothing is shown in the movie that tells the viewer how the terrorists got their ropes anchored at cliff top to do the same. The filmmakers wouldn't want to slow down the action.

The movie resolves in five or ten minutes what takes Clancy several chapters to describe. Robby Jackson knocks awry the terrorists' plan in the house by finding the household 12-gauge and letting lose at the terrorists. Not so in the movie, where Cathy Ryan find the 12-gauge, but can't find the shells. She hits O'Donnell's girlfriend with it as the villainess opens the door of the upstairs walk-in closet.

Ryan and his guests make it to the basement, where they see things are going wrong. Watkins is captured. Ryan takes Watkins's silenced pistol and puts a round through his kneecap (traditional IRA punishment, by the way) and demands to know how many bad guys are stalking around the house and how they got there. (The six arrived by boat.)

After much stalking around in the dark (Ryan knows the house layout but does not have night-vision goggles), Ryan gets his wife and daughter out of the second story and into the basement, ambushes two of the terrorists entering the basement, then exits the house from the basement outdoor entrance as O'Donnell, the girlfriend, and Miller enter from the top.

Suspend some disbelief, as Ryan, his pregnant wife, Sally, and the dinner guests are next seen at the base of the cliff. How did they all rappel down there? The terrorist trio follows. Ryan gets away in one of their boats. They pursue. The storm is upon them. It's windy. It's rainy. O'Donnell sees Ryan alone at the wheel and insists that Miller turn the boat around so they can get Holmes—the real target in the mission. Miller guns down O'Donnell and the girlfriend, so eager he is to get Ryan.

Well, this cliché has been seen before. How many more can be added? Ryan's boat is on fire. Sean Miller jumps from his boat to Ryan's. They have a fight. No guns, even though shooting would be quicker and more sensible. (Ryan could have easily taken a loose Uzi from one of the dead terrorists in the house—that would have helped.) Ryan has the boat pole. Sean Miller swings the anchor. Blows are blocked. Blows miss. The anchor goes *ka-chunk* into the boat's fiberglass deck. Now the two struggle with the boat pole. Ryan pushes

Miller, who falls over backward and is impaled on the upturned horns of the boat anchor, dying the traditional, painful, bad guy movie death. And, of course, the boat was headed for the rocks while all this was going on, so Ryan has to jump into the stormy waters just as the FBI hostage rescue team helicopter shows up. Too bad the chopper doesn't have a rescue winch, but Ryan has been pulled safely out of the water and is next seen wet and blanket-clad, surrounded by his family.

The scope of action in *Patriot Games* is much smaller than in many Clancy books. There are no fighter wings, armored divisions, or carrier battle groups in action. In the book, the biggest fight is the two-squad terrorist attack on Ryan's home, cut down to just six bad guys. You never see more than one or two helicopters in action. The SAS commando raid is an animated special effect. The freeing of Sean Miller is done without ever seeing the RPGs and automatic gunfire raking the police convoy. The assault on Lord Holmes's car is actual size, but hey, that was a smallish affair. There is nothing big budget about the entire film.

By comparing the book and movie versions of *Patriot Games*, one gets a better example of how to cut down a book plot to fit a movie screen. The plot was ruthlessly condensed to focus only on the basic conflict. The character list is pared down to the minimal number needed to drive the plot, minor continuity problems be damned. All action fits the screen, so it's always small fight scenes with minimal gunfire. And there is the same ham-fisted clumsiness in storytelling that shows a poor grasp of suspense. Plot twists are expected and unsurprising.

Clancy's worldview, of course, is absent.

But the ending does leave the audience hanging in one small way. Cathy Ryan gets a phone call from her obstetrician, inquiring if she wants to know if the baby she is carrying is a boy or a girl. The film ends before the answer is given.

Cue mournful Irish music sung by a high-pitched mournful female voice. Run credits.

Cue Patriotic Martial Music. Show American Flag. Take Three.

In *Clear and Present Danger*, patriotism matters.

Even the poster art shows it—Harrison Ford (as Jack Ryan) is seen wrapped in the American flag. It's really subtle. Decatur's toast—my country, right or wrong—is the more traditional definition of patriotism, but it is faintly heard here. Samuel Johnson's definition—that patriotism is the last refuge of the scoundrel—is echoed. The loudest definition of patriotism in this movie is the shrill toot of the whistleblower, and certainly does not square with Clancy's view of the presidency and its relationship with Congress.

Again, compression and deletion come into play. A major subplot in the book is the voyage of the Coast Guard cutter USS *Panache*, and its crew of lesser characters, Capt. Red Wegener, Chief "Portagee" Oreza, and others. They are not to be seen. Also gone are search-and-rescue ace Col. Paul Johns of the U.S. Air Force, Sgt. "Buck" Zimmer, and the MH-53 "Pave Low" helicopter. Also gone are most of the covert light infantry teams that will be taking the fight to the Colombian drug cartels. The movie will make do with a single squad.

Other than that, it is still a war on drugs. The movie plot will shadow the book plot over the course of basic dramatic conflict, until the storyline goes flying off the rails to the left.

Book and movie start with the Coast Guard overtaking and boarding a yacht in the Caribbean (in the movie, *Enchanter*, in the book, *Empire Builder*). The sailors find a bloodied cabin and two crew members that don't look like the owners. It turns out that yacht—and family—belonged to a good friend of President Bennet (unnamed in the book, but known by his secret service code name WRANGLER). Bennet is informed that the multiple murders were done on orders from a Colombian drug cartel. Instead of acting, he reacts. Massive drug smuggling by the Colombian drug cartels constitutes a clear and present danger to the United States, and what he wants to do about it is what he is not allowed to do about it.

Donald Moffat plays Bennet with a measure of Reaganesque absent-mindedness. He makes his views known to his national security advisor, James Cutter. In the book, Cutter is a vice admiral who shows above-average cunning when it comes to office politics and bureaucratic infighting. In the movie, Harris Yulin plays Cutter as an amoral, cunning weasel who tries to enact covert policy without overt responsibility. The policy will be to use military force to take the war to the Colombian drug cartels, without informing the Colombian government. Implementing that policy will be the deputy director of operations at the CIA, Robert Ritter. The DDO has a bureaucratic incentive to do this in the book, as the deputy director of intelligence (DDI—James Greer) has pulled off two intelligence coups that should have come from his department: the defections of the Soviet SSBN *Red October* and KGB chairman Gerasimov (both thanks to Jack Ryan). This does not come out in the movie, as Rob Ritter (played as a slimy, amoral yuppie by Henry Czerny) undertakes the operation without Ryan's knowledge, but insists on written authorization from Cutter, who issues it in the president's name. (This is the "get out of jail free" card that the Iran-Contra conspirators wished they had.)

One key point in the movie, not the book, is Ryan's sworn testimony before a Senate subcommittee where he explains the government's $75 million antidrug funding for Colombia, limited to support and intelligence. A senator takes Ryan to task, asking him under oath to reassure the committee that it is receiving all the facts and that no troops would be committed to Colombia. Ryan promises. But the whole artificial exchange echoes of Vietnam and Iran/Contra—incidents where Congress surrendered power to the White House, or was bypassed.

Next, Ritter flies down to Panama to confer with John Clark (Willem Dafoe). Clark is clearly a CIA operative throughout most of Clancy's novels (exception: *Without Remorse*), but here he is an implied freelancer who will do the job once the money appears in his bank account. Clark has no wife or kids, unlike his fictional counterpart in print. All Clark needs is about twelve men to do the work, a fraction of the forty or so needed in the book.

The team is inserted by a pair of MH-60s—the Special Forces version of the UH-60 Blackhawk. (Sorry, no MH-53 here.) In the book, the teams were to stake out airfields belonging to the drug cartels and radio any observed takeoffs. A U.S. Navy E-2C Hawkeye (the carrier-borne version of AWACS) would then acquire the illegal flight and vector an F-15C to intercept, and then escort the illegal flight to a U.S. airfield for arrest—or shoot down the drug plane if the pilot did not comply. Such subtleties take too long to show in a movie, so cut to the chase and have the covert team blow up the drug planes and drug labs wherever they are found.

Escalation is an inevitable result. But the order of events is skewed. FBI director Jacobs is assassinated in Colombia. In the book, the downed drug flights triggers the retaliation by the Colombian drug lords, which takes aim at Jacobs. His end is quick—three out of four RPGs slamming into his lone car on its way from the airport to the U.S. embassy in Bogotá. In the film, ex-Cuban intelligence operative Felix Cortez (working for drug lord Escobedo) spots the spent shell casings from the firefight around one of the blown planes and knows they came from M-16s used by the U.S. Army (drug gangs prefer the Russian-made AK-47). That evidence triggers the retaliatory hit in the movie, arranged by Cortez on his own initiative, without telling Escobedo.

Clancy disposes of Jacobs in about two pages. There is nothing elaborate about four RPGs shredding a car. In the movie, it's an elaborate ambush against a convoy of four Chevy Suburbans en route to the embassy. The drug gang uses two buses to cut off the convoy from escaping at either end of a narrow street. The gang members then rake the convoy with RPGs and AK-47 gunfire. Jack Ryan survives, but most are killed, including FBI director Jacobs.

The U.S. retaliates, of course. John Clark goes in country to keep an eye on a gathering of major drug lords, which the U.S. knows about in advance. Clark sets up a laser designator to illuminate a parked pickup truck. (In the movie, Chavez does this alongside Clark.) An air strike is called in and a passing navy jet drops a laser-guided bomb. The bomb is made with a cellulose casing, allowing more high-powered explosive to be packed into its limited volume. The hit is accurate and the blast destroys the house, and everyone in it, including some innocent women and children.

At this point, it is pretty safe to say that the film flies off the rails from the course set by the novel. In the movie, Ryan suspects things are not what they seem when he finds out from his wife that Jacobs's secretary, Moira Wolfe, was murdered the same day. (In the book, Cortez seduces Wolfe to gain information through her inadvertent chat about work—but he does not kill her. Worse, he jilts her.)

Throughout the movie and the book Ryan has been skirting along the edge of the illegal, covert Colombian operation. He has to get more information. In the book, that means working late, getting into Ritter's document safe, copying lots of documents, and reading about the details of the operation. In the movie, it's a little more exciting, as Ryan is aided by a CIA hacker to gain access to Ritter's PC. It turns into a chase scene with computers, as Ryan begins accessing and printing Ritter's files as Ritter deletes them. And it's all done in MS-DOS, which really makes the movie show its age.

True to book and movie, Cortez contacts Cutter. They meet in Panama City. Cortez knows enough about Cutter's operation to expose it. The price for Cortez's silence is Cutter cutting off support for the operation. In return, Cortez promises advanced word on large drug shipments to allow for some spectacular arrests, so long as a significant remainder of cocaine makes it through to the U.S. In the movie, Cutter gives the location of the U.S. covert team to Cortez, who orders them hunted down by the cartel's gun-toting militiamen.

Current DDI James Greer embodies another counterpoint between book and movie. Clancy finishes him off with pancreatic cancer. In the movie, James Earl Jones dies a good death, stoically facing down his illness without losing any weight. Cancer doesn't do that in real life, and the disease slowly wastes Greer's body as Ryan dutifully visits his boss three times a week. Greer's death is needed as a setup in the movie, as he repeatedly tells Ryan to watch his back and do the right thing for the good of the United States. He reminds Ryan that he took an oath to uphold and defend the Constitution, and not the president or anybody else in government. In short, Greer is the conscience of the American spirit. The movie does a great job of interspersing scenes of Greer's funeral, with the president's oration about honor, duty, and patriotism, with the fruit of Cutter and Ritter's betrayal—the U.S. soldiers getting gunned down one by one as the cartel's private army closes in. Several are captured alive.

The milquetoast Cutter eliminates encrypted communication between the squad in the field and Clark in Panama. (In the book, Cutter flies down to Panama and shuts down the communications station, removing the computer floppy disks needed to guarantee encrypted communications.) Moreover, the movie Ritter tells Clark that Ryan was threatening to squeal. Kill Ryan and the operation goes back on line. Of course, Ryan is flying down to Colombia without knowing this. Clark meets him at the airport, gun discreetly in hand, and kidnaps Ryan at the terminal. Clark calls Ritter and tells him Ryan is dead. (Ryan is alive—bound and gagged). Ritter says nothing over the phone. Clark is now convinced that Ritter is the culprit.

Keep in mind that the intricate plot of *Clear and Present Danger* has just been rearranged to fit the demands of the action movie genre. Needed here are shoot-outs, fight scenes, and clear-cut good guys and bad guys. There is no time to explain anything. The movie Clark and Ryan buy a helicopter and fly in country, finding the body of a dead soldier in a creek. They also confront an angry Ding Chavez, who successfully evaded Cortez's hunting parties. Ryan accepts blame, either as an act of courage or as an attempt to end the argument.

The movie now follows its own path, in non-Clancyesque fashion. Ryan goes to Escobedo's mansion and asks for a meeting, flashing his CIA business card. He explains to Escobedo that Cortez is looking to take over his drug empire, and states his case for recovering any captured Americans. Escobedo is swayed, and arranges for a meeting with Cortez at the Lindo coffee roasting plant.

Well, things go from bad to worse. Fight and chase scenes are needed—Escobedo is killed. Ryan fights Cortez. Chavez is shooting silenced rounds through the window. Cortez gets away and rousts the guards. Ryan runs into Clark. Together they find the captured Americans. Clark gets them to the waiting helicopter. Cortez chases Ryan through the coffee roasting plant. Ryan gets the drop on him in an ambush. A big pile of wood collapses on Cortez. Ryan makes it to the roof and outruns automatic gunfire to make it to the hovering chopper. He hangs onto the skid. Clark pulls him up. Chavez spots Cortez and kills him at long range.

They get away.

It's Miller Time.

Well, a lot of that just didn't happen in the book, and it does not improve the plot. The four light infantry teams have to be extracted by Paul Johns and his MH-53, with cooperation from a MH-130 and the twin Beech piloted by Clark and his partner Larson. One team is mauled when a confrontation with one of Cortez's hunting parties goes awry. "The battle of Ninja Hill" is overlooked, as Capt. Ramirez (Chavez's squad leader) organizes several ambushes of drug militiamen operating in platoon and company strength. Too bad this didn't make the movie, as the battle scenes are taut and well-drawn. The last extraction is the remnants of Chavez's squad, as well as another squad. Prior to the extraction, Cortez and Escobedo are captured. (Escobedo is flown to Bogotá by Clark and Larson and delivered to his fellow drug lords—who don't trust him and will put their bullets where their suspicions lay.)

Johns and the MH-53 have a problematic recovery, as one of the engines on the chopper begins to malfunction just as the leading edge of a hurricane blows in from the Atlantic. He barely makes it to the Coast Guard cutter USS *Panache*, making a highly difficult landing despite gale-force winds and forty-foot seas. In fact, the ending to the book is probably too wild and unbelievable to fit comfortably within the confines of an average Hollywood action-adventure movie.

Another book part conspicuously left out is Cutter's fate. In the book, he is paid a visit by one of Clancy's constellation of reliable Irish Catholic FBI agents. Cutter is told what awaits him if he is prosecuted for his role in the illegal war in Colombia. Cutter, while jogging along a parkway, darts out in front of a speeding bus to end his life.

Such a quick, merciful death would have been a blessing for Cutter in the movie. Ryan has to have his final confrontation with the president. A political animal to the core, the president tells Ryan how it will be—Ritter and Cutter will take some blame, do a little jail time, and rake in big bucks on the lecture circuit. The bulk of the blame will be placed on the late James Greer (dead men can't rebut charges), and Ryan will bring Greer down. Ryan balks and tells off the president. He is seen stalking out of the White House, past a powerless Cutter and Ritter. Ryan heads straight for Capitol Hill, and with the film's ending credits running, he raises his right hand and swears to tell the truth to a full Senate committee, much like the Iran-Contra or Watergate investigations.

The message is clear. The president is bad. The Congress is good.

Liberalism gets to rear its head in Clancy's conservative world whenever the book becomes the movie. To Clancy, Congress is the weaker branch of government that should not be allowed in the driver's seat. In the book, congressional difficulties are resolved in an informal meeting between the chairmen and ranking members of the Joint Intelligence Committee. Throughout Clancy's novels, it is the president who has the power and ability to shape the national agenda and take action. Congress can only betray the policy or hobble it—or better yet, be informed and stand aside as the president acts. Not so in the movie, which romps through material familiar to many Americas: scandals involving abuse of power, unwanted and secret wars, and cover-ups of illegal activity. Watergate, Iran-Contra, Abscam, Koreagate, the Keating Five, the 9/11 Commission, and even recent hearings by the Senate Armed Services Committee over the Abu Ghraib prison abuses lay down a context that makes the *Clear and Present Danger* scandal so easily recognizable with a minimum of explanation and exposition.

Cue Ponderous Serious Music. Take Four.

"I'm Tom Clancy. I wrote the book they ignored."

So begins Clancy's commentary on the DVD version of *Sum of All Fears*. The quip can be applied accurately to any of the four movies that have been made based on Clancy novels.

In *Sum of All Fears*, terrorists get their hands on an Israeli nuclear bomb lost during the October war in 1973. They sneak it into the United States, set it off, and successfully trigger a confrontation between Russia and the U.S. Jack Ryan finds out what really happened, gets the information into Russian hands, and the Russians take the first step in standing down from the nuclear confrontation.

That is where the book and movie are similar. But they are far, far apart.

With a running time shorter than two hours, the moviemakers have no time to give to any subplot in the Clancy book. Bad guys have to be the bad guys a movie audience can understand. Arab terrorists are not marketable or politically correct, even though they've been pretty commonplace as terrorists in deed these past three decades. The movie bad guys have to be people that everybody hates—neo-Nazis bent on taking over the world (again), and not some oppressed Third World minority struggling to find its own political voice, with guns and bombs if need be.

Jack Ryan is not the married man with a brilliant wife and two smart kids we've come to know. He's single (played by Ben Affleck), having just met Dr. Cathy Muller. Ryan the movie character is definitely going to be the man of action in this film, even if other characters are better at it. Now the film has tapped Generation X, is acceptable as a date film, and possibly reaches a larger audience?

Admiral Greer is dead and buried, but has his doppelgänger on duty in the form of CIA director William Cabot, played by Morgan Freeman. In the book, Ryan is already deputy director of intelligence at CIA. In the movie, he is a lowly analyst brought up under Cabot's mentoring wing.

As for the lesser cast of characters? Let's play hide-and-seek.

There is no SSBN USS *Maine* and its hard-driving captain, Harry Ricks. There is no Elizabeth Elliot to be the national security advisor, and she is not sleeping with President Fowler. The vice president, Roger Durling, is nowhere to be seen. There is no Arab-Israeli rapprochement. There is no violent Palestinian splinter faction to oppose the peace. There is no 1970s-vintage Marxist German terrorists to team up with. There is no Native American renegade to help get the bomb into the U.S. Many of the secondary cast of Clancy characters are not there, like FBI's Dan Murray or navy's Bart Mancuso. John Clark is there, acting much as he does (played by Liev Schreiber). Mary Pat Foley is on the intelligence, not operations side of CIA, and she is very pregnant.

Yes, the movie begins with the fateful flight of the Israeli A-4 Skyhawk with one nuke onboard. The book shows a rushed takeoff as the Syrians are breaking through the Golan front, but the movie is more sedate, merely showing the plane on patrol. A photo of his wife and kid momentarily distracts the pilot when he spots a surface-to-air missile (SAM) coming straight at him. Of course, the plane is blown apart and the bomb slams into the desert floor, unexploded, and is buried by the shifting sands over time.

Meanwhile, halfway around the world, Russia undergoes succession. A heart attack takes down the ailing president, who is replaced by a younger, healthier Nemerov. The fellow was the subject of a paper Ryan had done fourteen months previously, and that makes him the CIA's in-house expert on the new Russian president.

One nice contrast in the movie is the president participating in a simulated crisis involving the Russians. The next crisis is the real thing, as Russia launches a massive nerve gas attack to retake Grozny, the capital of Chechnya, then as now a breakaway province. The U.S. provisionally recognizes Chechnya and will be calling for UN peacekeepers to stabilize the situation. The incident also discredits Ryan, who claims that Nemerov is not the type who would do this, having come to power without the help of the military. In private, Nemerov finds out the strike was ordered by a pair of renegade generals. He turns to his KGB chief, Grushkov, telling him to make the generals "disappear."

It is odd to see the U.S. going to bat for Chechnya in the film. Russia certainly heard some U.S. displeasure over human rights abuses there in the 1990s, when the ailing Yeltsin ran Russia and Clinton was the president. The former Red Army took Grozny, but was run out of town by a surprise Chechen attack. Yeltsin negotiated an armistice of sorts and Chechnya enjoyed an undefined autonomy that was not recognized as independence by other nations, particularly the U.S.

The second Chechen war, began in September 1999, saw the introduction of fundamentalist Wahhabi Sunni Islam from Saudi Arabia in normally Sufi Chechnya. As the new rebel Chechens waged war along the border with Russia, several Moscow apartment buildings exploded and collapsed, killing scores. Russia quickly blamed Chechnya.

Russia, now under the leadership of a younger, healthier Vladimir Putin, did not hesitate to destroy Grozny in order to retake it. No nerve gas was used. Now comes the summer of 2002 and the U.S. fictionally supports Chechnya in the movie. Later that year, Chechen terrorists seized a Moscow theater and took over seven hundred hostages, and the Russians retook the building, unfortunately killing over one hundred hostages after using a "knockout gas" to incapacitate all inside. Had this event come to pass before *Sum of All Fears* was made, it is highly doubtful the film's producers and director would have the U.S. granting recognition for a regime resorting to terrorism, especially after what the U.S. suffered on September 11, 2001.

Let's return to the movie.

An Arab grave digger discovers the bomb and sells it to a Syrian-based British arms dealer. The arms dealer sells it to the neo-Nazis for $50 million and ships it from Haifa to the Ukraine, where Russian nuclear scientists (looking for a quick buck) rebuild the bomb and place it in a cigarette vending machine. Then they ship it to the U.S.

In real life, the border between Israel and Syria, as well as Israel and Lebanon, is closed owing to political hostility. How does one take a bomb from Syria across the Israeli border to Haifa? Further, how does one smuggle an A-bomb through Israeli without the Israelis finding out? Israel is a "one-hit state" that would be crippled by a nuclear strike. Surely they would notice this in real life, but this is a movie so we can suspend disbelief.

Cabot and Ryan travel to Russia to perform some arms control inspections, as the Russians (like the Americans) are pledged to dismantle a number of warheads. Ryan notices the absence of three Russian nuclear scientists. Grushkov gives the reasons for their absence instantly, but Cabot knows the information is erroneous thanks to his Russian source, code-named "Spinnaker." Cabot and Spinnaker maintain a communications back channel between the U.S. and Russian governments, exchanging information when there is a mutual interest or need.

The film is playful at times with comic relief. As Ryan flies out to Russia on short notice, he has to cancel a dinner date with Cathy Muller. On the plane's cell phone, Ryan fumbles for an excuse. Cabot says its okay for Ryan to say he works for the CIA. She hangs up in disbelief. Cabot gently laughs at Ryan getting blindsided. To make up for it, Cabot promises Ryan two tickets for the White House correspondents' dinner, "the hottest ticket in town." Ryan can go to the hotel desk and pick them up—they will be under the name of John Clark.

Well, guess that means John Clark is not going to the White House correspondents' dinner. Instead, Cabot dispatches him to Russia to locate the missing Russian nuclear scientists. (Ryan and Cathy Muller are attending the dinner, watching the president do a bit of inept stand-up comedy, a nice piece of verisimilitude, when the movie's Chechen crisis breaks out.) Cabot sends Ryan to the Ukraine to catch up with Clark and give him the most current information about a suspected covert weapons lab located by the shore of the Kremenchug Reservoir. Ryan presents the latest satellite photos on a handheld computer. Clark is mildly ticked as he muses over Ryan's gadget. Wish I had one of those, he says. I don't even have e-mail. In the Zodiac, Clark seats Ryan up front and makes sure he is hitting the swells to splash Ryan silly as he muses some more.

Wish I could have one to that White House correspondents' dinner. Clark's sense of deadpan humor is drier than a martini.

The boat hits the shore. Clark tosses Ryan a pistol and tells him to make sure no one steals the boat. Into the abandoned plant he goes. Clark sights the three dead scientists, each graced with a few bloody bullet holes. He spots the broken crate, and radiation detection badges. He doesn't spot the two guards who blunder in after him. It would be easy for the two guards to just shoot Clark. But this is a movie, so Ryan gets the drop on the guards and they are disarmed.

The book deals with these developments in many chapters while the movie must make do with a few minutes. The book has one of the Arab terrorists dissecting the bomb. Contact is made with the German terrorists. They recruit an East German nuclear scientist to supervise the rebuilding of the bomb. Of course, they kill him and his recruited assistants once the job is done.

Shipping the bomb proved easier in the book than in the movie. First, shipment was made from Latakia, Syria via Cyprus, thence to the U.S. The terrorists Ghosn and Qati fly into Miami via Mexico City and are met at the airport by the Native American renegade Marvin Russell. Scouting work, safe house, and other arrangements in the U.S. were handled by Russell to facilitate the strike on Denver.

Without the book's bad guys and the interesting logistics of smuggling a rebuilt nuke, showing shipment takes less work. E-mail to a sympathetic far right-wing dockworker alerts him to the arrival of the bomb—shipped to Baltimore from the Ukraine by means and route that needed no establishing shot in the movie. He picks up the bomb (disguised as a cigarette vending machine) and drops it off next to a couple of other vending machines at the football stadium. And yes, it runs on current from a normal wall outlet, timer and all. (Of course, even this useful go-between is killed once his utility is fulfilled, dispatched by an Austrian bodyguard seen earlier in the film strangling one of the more skeptical conspirators.)

Now comes the big bang.

In the movie, the president attends the football game in Baltimore, with his good friend Cabot in tow. Ryan barely gets through to Cabot on the cell phone, telling him there is a nuke in Baltimore ready to explode. Cabot yells at the Secret Service bodyguards to hustle the president out and away. The bomb goes off when the presidential motorcade is a mile or two away, and the blast wave knocks over every vehicle. Ryan, en route aboard a helicopter, also crashes but miraculously survives. A pair of USMC CH-53s picks up the president and hustle him to *Air Force One* or the airborne command post (the film is not clear which). He will have to manage the crisis from above, chatting with Nemerov via the hotline.

In the book, the escalation crisis is more complicated, with the president away at Camp David to watch the Super Bowl, accompanied his national security advisor (and lover, Elizabeth Elliot), who proves not to be very clear-thinking in a crisis. (She will never be mistaken for Condoleezza Rice.) The 1970s-vintage West German terrorists stage their faux battle with U.S. troops in Berlin. Other extraneous events occur beyond the control of Fowler and Nemerov, where they amplify confusion and fuel the escalation.

But the movie neo-Nazis are subtler. A phone call goes to the commander of a naval air regiment, flying the Tu-26 Backfire bomber, optimized for antishipping attacks. The illegally scrambled flight flies over the North Sea, locates a U.S. carrier (USS *John Stennis*, CVN-74), and launches a salvo of cruise missiles. A few get through the antimissile countermeasures and counterfire, hitting the carrier in several places, starting fires. This ship will have to stand in for the USS *Maine*, which is sunk by a stalking Russian attack submarine. (And how were the Russians able to find the carrier, much less one that traveled without an escort or CAP overhead?)

The escalation toward nuclear war is the ticking clock Ryan must race in the movie. He goes to ground zero and finds out the vintage of the plutonium used in the bomb—Savannah River, late 1960s. The bomb is not Russian. He finds a mortally injured Cabot, who barely has enough time to put him on to Spinnaker. Ryan races to the docks to find the bomb's shipping records. He confronts the Austrian bodyguard–hit man, and a pointless fight scene ensues. Maryland state police show up, too, and Ryan cadges a helicopter ride to the Pentagon, where he hopes to cut into the hotline there to present his information and plead for a stand-down between Fowler and Nemerov.

Yes, it happens. Jack Ryan saves the world again.

Once the confusion gets sorted out, dirty deeds are done dirt cheap. Clark slashes the throat of the opera-loving arms dealer in his Damascus apartment. Several "state security types" execute the rogue Backfire squadron commander, who definitely does not look like a pilot. The nicest touch is the head neo-Nazi Dressler (played by Alan Bates), who is fleeing Vienna. His chauffeur starts the car, which does not blow up. Bates gets in. He presses the cigarette lighter in the armrest. As soon as it pops out, the car explodes. (Smoking can be hazardous to your health. Is that the message?) All this happens as Grushkov watches.[5]

The film ends with Nemerov and Fowler signing a treaty at the White House, a stand-in for the treaty signing that took place much earlier in the book. Grushkov is there to heighten the irony, as he offers to talk to Ryan (and yes, Grushkov is Spinnaker). Yes, we should stay in touch, Jack Ryan.

And our hero enjoys a picnic date with Cathy Muller, because that is what he is all about.

Two Thumbs Up? Two Thumbs Down!

All four movie adaptations of Clancy novels are well crafted, commercial but not artful. Clancy has never concentrated on the depth of his characters, and their shallowness is emphasized in the movie versions of his books. Craft compensates for the lack of art, however, as talented actors must make up for the lousy lines and cheesy clichés that are the currency of action-adventure films.

Take *Hunt for Red October* as an example. The lesser characters paint much background color. Scott Glenn plays a deadpan Bart Mancuso. James Earl Jones plays Greer with some puckish insouciance. Sam Neill fakes a decent Russian accent as *Red October*'s first officer. What is there to play with here? There is no role of a lifetime any member of the cast can sink his teeth into. Only good acting can compensate for bad screen writing and journeyman directing. That makes for viewable entertainment, but the plot twists and foreshadowing surprise no one. Perhaps a Clancy novel could be made into a decent TV miniseries, where a twelve-hour run time can be used to really bring out the plot, in all its meticulous techno-detail.

There are some differences in the way Jack Ryan is played by Alec Baldwin, Harrison Ford, and Ben Affleck. Baldwin's Ryan is well-meaning and sincere, but a tad sarcastic. He knows he is out of his element, whether it be facing down the service chiefs at a high-level briefing or the lone Soviet gunman on the *Red October*. He doesn't even know how to handle the helm on the sub, but he manages. Baldwin plays Ryan as just enough of a hero without standing too tall. He's scared, but he doesn't run away.

Ryan, as played by Harrison Ford, is not much different from any other role played by Ford in other films. Ford is more of an everyman figure who has to rise to meet outsized challenges. And yes, he has to get beaten up in some one-sided fight every time he must take action, save the last fight. While Baldwin's style is lively and a tad sarcastic, Ford is more deadpan. Action films require little emotional range, so Ford's acting talent is not taxed. He does his job, much like his character.

Affleck's Ryan is closer to Baldwin's portrayal than Ford's. Smart, enthusiastic and focused, Affleck-Ryan energetically goes wherever he must to get the job done with terrier-like stubbornness. No matter what the obstacles, Affleck's Ryan pushes until he gets through, regardless of the odds.[6]

Keep in mind that what all three actors have in common portraying Jack Ryan: they are movie stars first (and also staunch Democrats). People who lined up to see these four movies were shelling out their bucks to see Alec Baldwin, Harrison Ford, or Ben Affleck. We are not talking about more mature actors exploring the gray world of espionage. This is not Alec Guiness playing George Smiley. This is not Richard Burton in *The Spy Who Came In from the Cold*. Jack Ryan will never be mistaken as the main character in *Reilly: The Ace of Spies*. It would be interesting to see a more serious actor handle the role, just to see what they would bring to it. Jack Ryan is thinly drawn in the book, so there is a lot of room for a serious actor to flesh out and color such a black-and-white character.

The movie format also doesn't do justice to Clancy's book-length plots, which tie together many concurrent threads. Okay, maybe not all the threads are needed, but half the fun in reading such large, shaggy dog stories is to see how many unrelated plotlines tie together in the end. If *Hunt for Red October* were a limited-run miniseries of eight to twelve episodes, would it be better executed? There would be more room for drama, exposition, flashback, concurrent action, and the usual bang-bang, shoot-shoot. Action films demand action throughout. Many of Clancy's books build up to the action. But in Hollywood, the book must bear the sacrifice to make the movie work.

Clancy likes writing about the technology and how it works—or malfunctions. None of that comes out in any of the films. Detail need not be the enemy of a movie, as many heist films from the 1960s often devoted a big chunk of their screen time showing the bad guys planning and rehearsing their elaborate schemes. The best the viewer gets is a little scene showing rogue Russian nuclear bomb scientists rebuilding a nuke in *Sum of All Fears*, or the overhead spy satellite footage of an antiterrorist strike in *Patriot Games*. Not shown is the elaborate nuclear meltdown that totals a Soviet attack sub in *Hunt for Red October*.

Larger fights get abridged. The "battle of Ninja Hill" in *Clear and Present Danger* showed a squad of light infantry twice mauling platoon-sized enemies. This would have made for a great fifteen-minute battle scene, but the movie can't afford to spend this time. The ULA's assault on the Ryan estate in *Patriot Games* was also platoon-sized, but we see little more than five to six bad guys in the movie, and the scene makes do with about ten minutes of predictable action.

All four Clancy movies rely on extensive cooperation from the Defense Department to provide the ships, planes, and troops to make the films "look realistic." Yet little of the realism comes through, as the filmmakers get by with tight shots of a ship here, a helicopter there. In all fairness, it could have been too difficult to arrange for large shots showing fleets and squadrons really mixing it up with the bad guys. Computer-generated imaging, which has come a long way in the past decade, could make up for the lack. Used modestly in *Sum of All Fears*, CGI added a nuke to the A-4 Skyhawk's bomb rack, a nonexistent football stadium on the edge of Baltimore or onion-domed Russian Orthodox churches in the background skyline of the Russian nuclear disarmament plant. One could picture using CGI to paint a major battle in *The Bear and the Dragon* or *Executive Orders*.

Such sweeping fights can distract from the main action required in an action-adventure film, where the bad guy and the good guy must somehow have their one-on-one fight in the end. If Jack Ryan can't be James Bond, will the book still be made into a movie? And will it reflect the author's views on politics and policy?

Only Hollywood has that answer.

They control the camera.

They control the script.

Run end credits.

Fade to black.

Light Reading on the Road to Reykjavík

The War That Never Was could have been the title of *Red Storm Rising*, the one book in the Clancy canon that does not fit into the Jack Ryan time stream. The book dealt with a major front of the cold war—the confrontation between NATO and Warsaw Pact forces in Europe.

The topic is one found beguiling by many authors. General Sir John Hackett tackled it in his *Third World War: August 1985* released several years before that fictional date. As the Russians make their push, RE-FORGER adds a few U.S. divisions to the order of battle as NATO stages a fighting withdrawal across Germany. The NATO counterstroke is successful, but the Russians go nuclear by hitting Birmingham, England. NATO responds by taking out Minsk. The war ends when both sides realize that going on would be suicide.

The book, published in 1978, presumed that the shah of Iran was still in power in 1985, playing a major role in fighting Communist Arab forces threatening Oman during World War III. A pity the real shah was deposed in a theocratic revolution in 1979. Likewise, Hackett has Carter in the White House toward the end of his second term in 1984, with the Soviets refusing to negotiate with him until the fictional president-elect, Thompson, is inaugurated on the following January 20. Hackett crafts a very detailed and highly specific world situation leading up to the three-week war later that summer. It bore no relation to what actually turned out. Gorbachev was already at the helm of the Soviet Union, and the cold war had cooled down a bit despite the continuance of superpower rivalry.

Ralph Peters took a stab at the same topic in his *Red Army*. Here he focuses more on planning, strategy, and human factors. The Warsaw Pact makes it to the Rhine, just as the U.S. counterstroke from Bavaria gets underway. West Germany calls it quits before the Americans can win the war, so the USSR comes out ahead. Peters wrote one of the few books that shows the "bad guys" winning, and he doesn't do it because he likes the Warsaw Pact.

Harry Coyle took a more intimate look at the topic with his *Team Yankee*, the story of a company of M-1 Abrams tanks linked with a platoon of infantry operating M-2 Bradley IFVs. Coyle places his story within the larger scenario of Hackett's *Third World War*, but details the horrific losses that were typically expected should the next war ever happen. Units typically lost a quarter of their strength on defense and half on attack—a far cry from the one-sided drubbings the U.S. has dished out on Iraq.

Clancy's fling with World War III was cowritten with an uncredited Larry Bond, who developed the computerized naval war game Harpoon and later went on to write several techno-thrillers of his own. *Red Storm Rising* is a curious book in that it shows the path not taken in Clancy's literary career. One cannot spot the exact points where one author's work ends and another begins, but the stylistic strongpoints are easily seen in the peaks of action. Clancy's strength has always been framing individual characters in action settings and keeping the action focused at the small-unit level, be it a squad, a team, a ship's crew or a White House staff. Clancy is also a major weapons buff, so any tool of war will get a full write-up of its gee-whiz features.

Bond's approach has a better feel for larger operations—regiments or divisions mounting attacks, squadrons of strike aircraft inundating fleets with cruise missile attacks, convoys fighting their way across the North Atlantic. While Bond does not delve into geopolitics, he touches on enough of it to shade the outer frame of the scenario. There are just enough specific facts to shape the scenario, but not enough details to look wildly obsolete when real life overtakes fiction.

Another Bond trademark is the wrong war/right solution plotline. The national leaders (politicians sitting atop an oligarchy or dictatorship) launch an aggressive war to seize resources or power and the army obeys. Things do not go according to expectations. The nation finds itself beleaguered. The army patriotically ousts the corrupt politicians in a coup d'état and shuts down the war. In each case, the United States (good guys) intervenes or has to fight, is winning toward the end, but not quickly enough. This was not readily apparent in *Red Storm Rising*, but the theme runs through Bond's later works—*Red Phoenix* (war with North Korea), *Vortex* (war with South Africa, complicated by Cuban intervention), and *Cauldron* (France and Germany team up to redraw the map of Europe).

Noticeably absent from *Red Storm Rising* are the upper echelons of U.S. government. Politburo meetings are held throughout the book, but the reader never sees the U.S. president convening any cabinet meetings. Congress is also invisible. So is the UN. There is no scene where an American UN ambassador or secretary of state appears before the Security Council to argue the American case against aggressive war waged by the Soviet Union. (Such a move would appear to be a pointless exercise in diplomacy, but the inevitable Soviet veto would prove the U.S. case.)

Indeed, the highest ranked American in the book is SACEUR—supreme commander for Europe and NATO military chief Robinson. A few admirals and generals populate the upper cast, but for the most part the book is going to center on the actions of a few characters. There is Daniel X. McCafferty (skipper of SSN USS *Chicago*), who bears some resemblance to Bart Mancuso, the fictional commander of the USS *Dallas* in *Hunt for Red October*. Edward Morris (commander of frigates USS *Pharris* and USS *Reuben James*), is the beleaguered ASW commander. Mike Edwards is the reluctant man of action, a trait often associated with Clancy hero Jack Ryan. The stronger stand-in for Ryan, however, is Bob Toland, a naval reservist and intelligence analyst. Another Clancy staple character, the "good Russian," is Pavel Leonidovich Alekseyev, a character the reader can admire with some respect, but not root for since he is working for the "bad guys."

So How Likely Was World War III?

If a NATO–Warsaw Pact conflict was not going to happen in Europe during the cold war, then why the massive buildup of forces? Both sides did take this potential conflict seriously.

It was not known that the cold war was entering its "endgame" period by the late 1970s–early 1980s. At this time, the U.S. stationed Seventh Army HQ in West Germany, controlling VII Corps and V Corps. Each corps had a mechanized infantry division and an armored division. Divisions averaged around ten to eleven battalions each. The mix was almost evenly split between mechanized infantry and armored battalions. A mechanized infantry division would have one more infantry battalion than armored, while it was the other way around for armored divisions.[1]

To this, the U.S. was going to dip into its existing force pool for reinforcements. Slated for deployment to West Germany were the First and Fourth Infantry Divisions and the Second Armored Division, with preplaced stocks of equipment waiting for the troops that were to be flown in. A marine division was also scheduled to go over as well.[2]

The total U.S. force pool was just sixteen active-duty divisions, a far larger sum than the ten divisions the army must use today to police the world's trouble spots. The Marine Corps, then as now, had three divisions. In the reserves was another marine division plus eight more army divisions in the National Guard. It would take six to eight weeks to bring the reserves up to combat readiness, according to the planning of the day.

To be fair, the U.S. was not going to defend Western Europe single-handedly. Denmark, Belgium, the Netherlands, West Germany, the United Kingdom, and France had also raised forces and planned for their deployment.

In the NORTHAG area (Northern Army Group), the order of battle showed the British Army of the Rhine fielding four armored divisions, an airmobile division, and a parachute brigade. West German forces amounted to three armored and two mechanized infantry divisions. The Belgians were good for two mechanized divisions and two infantry brigades. The Netherlands deployed two mechanized brigades. Even tiny Denmark promised one mechanized division and two mechanized brigades.

In the AFCENT area (Allied Forces, Central Europe) aside from the U.S. deployments, one also found West Germany fielding three armored and two mechanized divisions plus another five mechanized brigades. France slated the deployment of eight armored divisions, two mechanized brigades, and four infantry divisions.[3]

Include NATO reserves that can be brought to bear seven to ten days after the start of fighting, and another eighty-plus brigades of infantry, mechanized infantry and armor can be sent to the war. This listing leaves out many miscellaneous regiments and battalions that would also play a role in the defense.[4]

The Soviets could start the war from East Germany with thirteen tank divisions and thirteen motorized rifle divisions (MRDs). They could count on Warsaw Pact ally East Germany to kick in two armored divisions and four MRDs. Poland was listed at five armored divisions plus three MRDs. Czechoslovakia's contribution was pegged at three armored divisions and three MRDs.[5]

A mix of first and second line divisions could be fed into the war. Within seventy-two hours, the Soviets could commit one armored, one mechanized, and six airborne divisions, all category I. Within ninety-six hours of war's start, add a Polish airborne division and a Czech airborne brigade, both rated as category II.

Within ten days, the Soviets would be sending to the front two armored and three motorized divisions, rated at category I. Within fifteen days, Poland could commit a pair of MRDs, rated category II.

Counting thirty days from the war's start, the Soviets would be tapping three tank divisions and seven MRDs, all category II. By D+90 days, Poland would be tapped for three MRDs, while Czechoslovakia would send another pair of tank divisions and another pair of MRDs, all category II. By 120 days, the Soviets would be scraping the bottom of the barrel, sending into the fray nineteen armored divisions and forty-eight MRDs, all category III.[6]

The numbers look pretty frightening in black and white, but there are some shades of gray that need to be appreciated. First, Soviet divisions are on average about half the size of their U.S. equivalents—roughly 9,400 men compared to 18,000 men. Estimates also varied during the early 1980s, with NATO able to muster about 84 to 88 divisions total to the Warsaw Pact's 115 to 173, depending on how one counted the units.[7]

Both sides could commit about 12,000 aircraft to the European theater. But the breakdowns are revealing. NATO could commit about 140 F-14 Tomcats from its (U.S.) carrier battle groups, plus 96 F-15s (also U.S.), 250-plus F-16s (U.S. and its allies), 650 F-4 Phantoms (U.S., Britain, and West Germany), 80 Tornadoes (Britain, West Germany), 105 Mirage IIIEs (France), and 150 Jaguars (Britain, France). The Warsaw Pact would be sending up 775 MiG 15s and MiG 17s, already obsolete by the 1980s; 944 MiG 21s (Vietnam era); 125 MiG 27s, and 48 MiG 23s.[8] However, this does not count Soviet naval aviation, where the Bears and Backfires plus the sub force get to refight the battle of the Atlantic in *Red Storm Rising*. About two hundred of these planes were estimated in service by 1980, while the number of Bears configured for reconnaissance was put around twenty-five.[9]

This was typical of the cold war, as the U.S. and USSR spent billions to maintain parity—and stalemate. For if one side should slacken, an advantage would appear for the other, making the first strike a tempting option. As it was for nuclear weapons, so too the rule of stalemate would play out in Europe for NATO and the Warsaw Pact.

On the nuclear front, NATO had 5,460 nuclear weapons handy, divided between warheads that could be delivered by aircraft (3,200), seaborne ballistic missiles (1,896—U.S. Poseidon and UK Polaris), and land-based missiles (98–France). Of that number, include 108 Pershing II ballistic missiles and 96 Tomahawk ground-launched cruise missiles, which gave the U.S. the ability to retaliate against a Soviet strike on Europe without dragging the continental U.S. nuclear force into the exchange. In short, the U.S. would not be forced to trade New York and Washington for Frankfurt and Brussels. The Soviet arsenal pointed toward Europe consisted of 2,327 warheads, of which 900 were mounted on the SS-20 IRBMs.[10]

Was there ever a time when all this force was nearly used?

Yes. At least once that we know of.

This incident occurred in late 1983, when a NATO command exercise called Able Archer nearly triggered a preemptive first strike by the Soviets. By this time, the Russians adopted a strategic mind-set that NATO would start the war, using the Pershing II as a first-strike weapon that could take out the Soviet leadership. As the NATO exercise proceeded from November 2 to November 11, release procedures were practiced for tactical nuclear weapons. As the Soviets already had a doctrine for masking actual operations under the cover of exercises, their panic was understandable. This fed into an ongoing KGB operation that year called "operation RYAN." The name has nothing to do with Clancy's Jack Ryan, but was the Russian acronym for nuclear missile attack—*raketno yadernoye napadenie*. Russian KGB agents assigned to RYAN were told to look for any signs of an impending attack.

NATO monitors picked up a huge increase in message traffic between Soviet leadership and forces in the field indicative of an imminent nuclear attack. The Soviets were also vigilant for signs of the NATO first strike that never came. After a few days, Able Archer wound down. The Soviet and Warsaw Pact units stood down from heightened alert. As historian Robert O'Connell quipped, "We had been eyeball to eyeball—only this time one side was hallucinating and the other was dozing. . . . History was on cruise control. The war scare of 1983 might have been the end."

Then Secretary of State George Shultz was surprised to hear the Soviets publicly voicing their fear of a first strike aimed at decapitating the leadership, just a month after Able Archer's conclusion. In January 1984, the Soviets sent several Delta-class SSBNs on a cruise off the East Coast of the U.S. as a show of force. Discreet American diplomacy reassured the Soviets that no first strike was contemplated. A public statement by President Reagan calling for a peaceful resolution of differences helped to defuse the crisis further.[11]

From Silliness Comes Seriousness?

Clancy and Bond frame the book's opening with an event that can alter the strategic balance of power between the U.S. and USSR. A small gang of Islamic fundamentalist Azeris infiltrate a very large oil refinery, seize the control room, open the valves, and destroy the control panel— all this while engaged in a shoot-out with the facility's guards. It's a one-way trip for the terrorists. But the action destroys about one-third of Soviet energy production, including close to half of all gasoline production. The Soviet Union will not be able to recoup the loss for at least two to three years, according to newly minted energy minister Sergetov, a technocrat who is a junior nonvoting member of the Politburo. The

Politburo assesses its situation. Lacking foreign reserves, the USSR would have to import oil from the ideologically hostile West. However, the United States could choose not to sell the oil, really screwing the Soviet Union. The solution lies southward: the rich oil fields of the Middle East. Invading Iran or the oil states of the Persian Gulf is the answer to the Soviet oil shortage, and would deprive the West of at least one major source of oil.

Does this scenario sound far-fetched yet? This answer has two parts that add up to "maybe not." Imperial Japan found itself in a similar resource dilemma in the late 1930s. The United States objected to Japan's invasion of China, and as relations deteriorated between 1937 and 1941, the U.S. imposed an oil embargo on Japan. About one year of oil reserves was all that was left before the Japanese economy (and war machine) ground to a halt. One solution backed by the Imperial Japanese Navy was to go south and seize the oil fields of Malaya and the Dutch East Indies (now Malaysia and Indonesia, respectively). This would put Japan at war with the Dutch government in exile (the Nazis already occupied the Netherlands in 1940) and Britain (too busy fighting for its life in Europe). But the American-occupied Philippines lay astride Japan's sea-lanes to the south, so it too would have to be neutralized. To become self-sufficient in oil, Japan would also have to go to war with the United States, which possessed an economy that was thirty times larger than Japan's. In a classic misreading of a foreign culture, Japan chose war, hoping that a quick victory against a culturally weak, peace-loving U.S. might yield a settlement before America could mobilize its economy to fight the war. Again, this assessment had some grounds in reality, as isolationism was a major voice in the domestic public debate over armaments, alliances, and America's outlook on World War II. In truth, the war did not turn out as Japan had hoped. Six months of whirlwind victories produced an empire that could give Japan economic self-sufficiency. But it also damned Japan to a long war of attrition against an implacable and angered United States. Japan was destroyed and defeated.

The Bond-Clancy scenario also had another root in reality. During the 1970s, the CIA forecast that Soviet energy production would peak and decline in the 1980s, which could force the USSR to seek resources elsewhere by force. This was one factor that formed the foundation of the Carter Doctrine, which declared the Persian Gulf to be an area of vital interest to the United States. Central Command was established to intervene in this area should the Russians ever lunge southward. The likely scenario was a Russian invasion of Iran to capture the oil fields hundreds of miles south of the Russo-Iranian border. As the Iranian Revolution degraded Iran's military, it was assessed that a modern mechanized force would not be meaningfully opposed.

For some reason, that was not the outcome of the Iran-Iraq War, where Iraq enjoyed the advantage of modern Soviet weapons and plenty of them. They could not cut through Iranian lines to seize the very same oil fields, located less than one hundred miles from the Iraq-Iran border. The Soviet nightmare scenario, hinted at in *Red Storm Rising*, never came to pass.[12]

Soviet grand strategy in the book calls for the Warsaw Pact to neutralize NATO in Europe to permit a free hand to take the oil in the Middle East. War cannot be waged without a political reason. The Russians need to fabricate one. A bomb placed in the Kremlin by a West German agent cuts down a group of visiting Young Pioneers from Pskov. In a closed society that was the Soviet Union, where tight security was the rule, this is a bit of a stretch. The KGB really planted the bomb, but this is kept secret. Again, far-fetched? In the late 1990s, powerful bombs in the middle of the night felled several Moscow apartment buildings. The crime scenes were quickly bulldozed and Chechen separatists were blamed, quickly providing Russia a reason to reinvade and reestablish its dominion over Chechnya. However, these crimes were never "solved." The wrecked buildings were never treated as a crime scene. Evidence was never gathered. The usual suspects were rounded up. The Russian government has a lot of experience lying to its people. Could the Russian security service kill their countrymen and blame it on the Chechens?

It sounds too far-fetched for the average American to believe, unless he was a compulsive conspiracy theorist.

With a pretext made in Moscow, Russia mobilizes for war.

While the Soviet foreign minister proposes an agreement to reduce nuclear arms, U.S. intelligence is picking up many weird signs that do not add up to peace in the weeks leading up to mid-June in this unspecified year in the mid-1980s. Private micro-allotments of land to peasants are more than doubled. (Impending food shortage?) Diesel-electric subs are absent from their patrol areas, while battery factories in the USSR are working on three shifts. (Are batteries being replaced?) Soviet sub deployments in the Mediterranean are altered so that the returning and relieving subs are in the North Atlantic at the same time. (A threat to REFORGER?) The USS *Chicago*, on patrol in the Barents Sea, spots Soviet SSBNs moving to the nearby White Sea. (Protecting the SSBN fleet for a second strike, if need be?)

Intelligence analyst Bob Toland reads these arcane tea leaves, delivers his hunches to his higher-ups in the navy, and the admirals quietly decide to increase the tempo of training, inspections, and exercises, just in case. As the United States picks up signs of increasing Soviet readiness (class B reserve divisions are mobilized), it goes to DEFCON 3. (Defense Condition 1, or DEFCON 1, is war).

Now wait a second.

Do analysts really have this much clout?

That depends on where they sit.

The Pentagon is chock-full of military officers and young analysts brandishing PhDs who spend a lot of time (and money) trying to figure out what the bad guys are going to do next. The likelihood of one analyst coming up with a magic finding that rapidly cuts its way through the many echelons of command to the threshold of national decision is downright rare.

Within the Pentagon, analysts are forever giving briefings to future and current flag officers. The oral briefing, and not the written report, is the preferred method for transmitting information in the military's uniform culture. As a good brief gets noticed, word is passed up to each echelon of the military's bureaucracy to get the briefing repeated for them.[13]

It may take months for a brief to make its way up to the Joint Chiefs of Staff. Real-life Pentagon analyst Thomas Barnett put it this way: "In the movies, it's just one dramatic scene, but in real life it is more a matter of plugging away, month after month, even when a lot of people think you have a screw loose."[14] In Barnett's case, the magic brief was a forecast of the Soviet navy's collapse in the early 1990s and the need for the navy to extend an olive branch to its bankrupt rival. It took six months for Barnett's brief to percolate to the top of his service and become a topic for a White House policy review.

Advice can also come from sources close to the top. Take the Defense Policy Board as an example. This bipartisan body was formed in 2001 by current Defense Secretary Donald Rumsfeld. It consists of about thirty members drawn from former government and military officials, among them former Secretary of State Henry Kissinger, former CIA Director James Woolsey, former Air Force Chief of Staff Ronald Fogelman, and former Vice President Dan Quayle. This body made the headlines in the run-up to the second Gulf War when former Assistant Secretary of Defense Richard Perle resigned owing to an apparent conflict of interest that would have arisen from the war he advocated.[15]

Sometimes the advice can come from informal groups. One example occurred in 1968, when President Johnson convened the so-called "wise men" to review the Vietnam War. These were foreign policy experts and appointees from previous Democratic administrations, including former Secretary of State Dean Acheson. (Recommendation: quit the war.)

Another example was the CIA's "team B" study of Soviet capabilities and intentions done between August and December 1976 under the direction of then CIA director George H.W. Bush. In the weeks leading up to the study, the CIA had revised upward its estimates of percentage of gross national product the Soviets spent on their military from 6–8 percent to 11–13 percent. The report reasoned that more rubles had to be spent to produce the then current armament given the inefficiencies of the Soviet economy.[16] Then the figure for the Soviet Union's economic growth that year was trimmed from 4–5 percent down to 2–3 percent, with defense spending increases still pegged at 4–5 percent.[17]

When the team B group of outside analysts was assembled, it was going to review the same data as CIA analysts, focusing on the accuracy of Soviet ICBMs, the ease or difficulty bombers would have penetrating Soviet airspace, and Soviet strategic capabilities and intentions. Team B concluded that Soviet missiles were just as accurate as U.S. ICBMs, to within $\frac{1}{15}$ of a mile. (The CIA analysts disagreed, citing lack of evidence.) Team B also noted that Soviet airspace could be penetrated by low-flying aircraft (a finding that would have some impact on B-1 bomber funding).

But most galling to the CIA analysts was team B's findings on Soviet intentions. Team B asserted that among Soviet goals were the interdiction of the sea-lanes to prevent oil shipments to the West from the Middle East; the disruption of U.S. power projection from the sea; the successful defense of Soviet nuclear capabilities from U.S. nuclear subs; and the development of a superior nuclear force capable of a successful first strike. CIA argued back that the evidence was lacking.[18] Team B concluded that the Soviets were intent on achieving strategic dominance over the U.S. in the next decade.

Team B's findings came after President Gerald Ford's defeat in the 1976 presidential election, and for the most part were not acted upon by the incoming president, Jimmy Carter. Eventually, team B's findings found their way into policy in the form of President Ronald Reagan's five-year $1 trillion defense spending plan.

When it comes to analysts influencing policy, we must grant another free pass to Bond and Clancy for the sake of dramatic license. The bureaucratic battles fought over intelligence and defense spending are lengthy, arcane, and dry. Explaining all the policy options would put the reader to sleep before the first war shot was fired. So forgive the authors for skipping the boring parts. The story would not be exciting if they remained true to real life. That is the sad truth about fiction.

Time to Start World War III

Meanwhile, back in the novel . . .

In the face of growing war preparations by the enemy, the U.S. puts REFORGER into operation. REFORGER stands for *return of forces to Germany*. An annual exercise, REFORGER practiced the airlift and sealift of additional supplies and reinforcements to Europe, much needed in the event of a major war. Clancy and Bond give NATO only five weeks of stocks on hand to fight the war, so resupply is crucial. Airlift can move men to meet up with prepositioned equipment, but any more equipment plus supplies must move by sea.

In effect, REFORGER becomes the strategic replay of the battle of the Atlantic. For the third time in a century, the U.S. and Britain must secure the sea-lanes to support a war in Europe. Only now the submarine threat will come from Russia, not Germany.

Red Storm Rising will concentrate on the action, as befitting a novel. It's much more exciting to read about the sub captain who is stalking a warship, or a frigate captain trying to kill a sub before it attacks his merchant convoy. That is just as true for any war memoir. Countless books were written about or by U-boat aces in the North Atlantic, American sub captains in the Pacific, or British destroyer captains who hunted the hunters. In truth, the aggregate sea battle is much more boring—but deadlier. In both world wars, all those merchant ships were carrying vital war supplies, without which Britain would have folded. The problem was best described by Winston Churchill: "The only thing that really frightened me during the war was the U-boat peril. . . . It did not take the form of flaring battles and glittering achievements . . . it manifested itself through statistics, diagrams and curves unknown to the nation, incomprehensible to the public."[19]

So how well did the battle of the Atlantic turn out in its two previous incarnations?

In World War I, German U-boats had only limited range compared to their World War II successors. Hunting merchant ships, they stuck to the waters north and south of Ireland, where all merchant traffic had to pass if it was bound for Liverpool or London. In the first round of unrestricted U-boat warfare in 1914–1915, Germany blunted British imports by only 8 percent. Resuming the strategy in 1917, Germany managed to cut Britain's imports by 20 percent. Britain resorted to the convoy of merchant ships. The destroyers were equipped with hydrophones (which listened for the sub's engine noises) and depth charges. Using these weapons, the naval escorts fought off the U-boats, just as their more advanced successors did a generation later.

Now take note of Churchill's "statistics, diagrams and curves." By war's end, Germany had sent 373 U-boats to sea, losing 178 of them. For each U-boat lost, 32 merchant ships were sunk, totaling 5,708 ships. But shipbuilding kept up with the losses. The world merchant fleet was larger in 1918 than in 1914, despite the scourge of the U-boat.[20]

In 1939, Britain would face the same grim equation. It imported half of its food, and needed to import fifty-five million tons of goods per year to support its economy. Its merchant fleet now numbered 3,000 ships (plus 1,000 coastal vessels) and had 220 escorts to protect them. Germany would start the war with only fifty-seven U-boats, not all of which were suitable for combat in the mid-Atlantic. Yet the Kriegsmarine planned for three thousand U-boats to be built to strangle Britain.[21]

Churchill had every reason to be frightened by the U-boat threat. By mid-1942, merchant ship sinkings outran the launching of new ships by 10 percent. But American entry into the war, increased cooperation between Britain and the U.S., and improved technology and aircraft pushed the U-boat menace into the mid-Atlantic by mid-1943, then snuffed it out. By this time, the Allies had lost 2,452 merchant ships. But the German Kriegsmarine came out worse, losing 696 of 830 U-boats.[22] It was a near-run thing. Britain suffered partial strangulation, its populace getting by on tight food rationing, its armies in North Africa supported by a roundabout supply line around Africa that was twelve thousand miles long. Add to this a delay in the buildup of U.S. forces in Britain and desperate efforts to support the USSR with war supplies to make up for lost or relocating factories. Those convoys also had to take roundabout routes or had to fight their way through.

In the fictional third battle of the Atlantic, the Soviets would execute a strategy that could throttle REFORGER, blunting valuable resupply and replacements as the land battle raged in Europe.

One key for the U.S. to hold the Atlantic secure is Iceland, an important anchor of the SOSUS line. SOSUS was an array of passive sonar microphones anchored along the sea bottom between Greenland, Iceland, and the United Kingdom (referred to as the GIUK Gap). In the book, the Soviets ready a large barge freighter to carry an air assault regiment tasked to take the airfields at Reykjavík and Keflavík, to be quickly reinforced by long-range aircraft flying in the remainder of the division. Taking Iceland robs NATO of an important mid-Atlantic air base, allowing the Soviets to project air power over the sea-lanes. Taking Iceland also removes the SOSUS line from action, which also allows Soviet subs to enter the Atlantic freely to throttle REFORGER.

In come the Soviets. The surprise attack is supported by a massive salvo of air-to-ground missiles launched by Tu-16s and Tu-26s that take out the control tower at Keflavík as well as any aircraft on the ground.

At this point, 1st Lt. Michael Edwards, an air force meteorologist, is introduced as one of the book's hero characters. As Keflavík is attacked, he grabs a portable satellite telephone and hightails it, along with several marine guards. For the remainder of the book, Edwards and his small band will wander over the rocks of Iceland, avoiding contact with the Soviet paratroopers while phoning in observations to their intelligence handler.

Mike Edwards and Bob Toland have one common trait with Jack Ryan: the reluctant man of action. Prior to becoming president, it was not uncommon to find Jack Ryan leaving his desk to do something that had to get done when no one else was around. We saw this humble analyst and military historian in shoot-outs with Irish terrorists, Russian agents, and Colombian narco-gangsters, arranging defections of a Soviet sub and a KGB chairman to boot. Toland finds himself in similar waters, planning counterstrikes against Soviet naval aviation to win the third battle of the Atlantic. Likewise, Edwards treks across the Icelandic wilderness with satellite phone in hand, getting on-the-job training as an operative in Special Forces and providing strategic intelligence. That's mighty good for a humble meteorologist.

Losing Iceland has a strategic impact disproportionate to its size. Aside from losing the SOSUS line, Iceland in the hands of the enemy reopens the mid-Atlantic gap. In World War II, this was the area in mid-ocean south of Greenland and Iceland that was beyond the reach of land-based aviation, which proved to be a rich hunting ground for U-boat wolf packs. Not until the introduction of the B-24 in an antisubmarine role did the Allies have a weapon that could close the gap and threaten submarines. In *Red Storm Rising*, the Soviets run their attack submarines through the Denmark Straits between Iceland and Greenland to get to the North Atlantic, while a similar air corridor opens up over Iceland permitting Backfire raids on REFORGER convoys.

As Keflavík falls, the *Nimitz* is escorting an inbound marine amphibious unit (MAU—about the size of a battalion) to Iceland (and yes, Toland is aboard). Bond's background as the designer of Harpoon, a computerized naval war game, comes into big play at this point in the narrative. Soviet Tu-142 Bear F aircraft come in first, using onboard surveillance radars to acquire the exact location of the U.S. carrier group. Tu-16 Badger bombers launch a salvo of AS-5 Kelts upon reaching the outer edge of U.S. radar coverage. The Kelts are slow-moving plane-like antishipping missiles and are woefully obsolete, but they show up as incoming aircraft on the American radars. F-14s are scrambled and sent to intercept the inbound raid. Salvos of AIM-54 Phoenix missiles fired by the F-14s destroy the incoming swarms of useless missiles.

Red Storm Rising was written in 1986. This tactic was used in battle in 1991. At the start of the first Gulf War, the U.S. launched 39 BQM-74 drones. Equipped with radar reflectors, the drones would show up on Iraqi radars as Coalition aircraft, prompting Iraqi air defenses to fire up their targeting radars and fire SAMs. This act would unmask the location of the SAM batteries to F-4G "wild weasel," A-6 and A-7 aircraft, which would fire HARM radar homing missiles to destroy the radars.[23]

Back to the fictional war. As the F-14s are distracted, faster Tu-26 Backfires attack the carrier battle group from another side, loosing a volley of AS-6 Kingfish. No American carrier since World War II has ever taken a hit in hostile action (though there have been a couple of spectacular accidents). Yet in the book, the carriers *Nimitz, Saratoga*, and *Foch* are damaged by the attack. It has long been a contentious hypothetical argument throughout the 1980s whether the large aircraft carrier was truly vulnerable and obsolete. Submarine advocates long contended that an attack sub could penetrate the escort ring and get a shot at sinking a flattop. But the saturation missile attack was the most likely scenario the navy feared. As the cold war never became hot, we will never truly know beyond war-gaming whether such a thing would have come to pass.

In the event of a third world war NATO could have fought the third battle of the Atlantic defensively or offensively. Defensively, the carriers would have done their job screening the Atlantic convoys against Soviet air and sub attacks. Offensively, the navy would have taken its carrier battle groups into the Norwegian Sea and Barents Sea to strike at Soviet bases in the Kola Peninsula. During the Reagan administration, the navy was gearing up for the offensive option.

Crafting the Scenario

The authors keep World War III simple in this book. They use no more political detail than needed to frame the outline, while avoiding too many specifics that could date the story too soon. Greece stays out of the war. So does Turkey. (This violates NATO's rule that an attack on one ally is an attack on all.) The Russian southern flank is safe. Many Third World nations stay neutral or sympathize with Russia. Forces in

South Korea stay put as North Korea and China stay quiet. Japan is pressured by Russia to stay out of the war. The USS *Midway* carrier battle group cannot attack Kamchatka alone, so the U.S. does nothing in the Pacific. Diego Garcia is nicked by a missile attack.

Not seen in the first-day recap (or anywhere else in the book) is the use of Polish and East German divisions in the Russian attack. Nor are any French divisions seen. While France pulled out of NATO's command structure, it did have an understanding to coordinate its forces with the alliance. (French ports are definitely used to receive RE-FORGER convoys.)

There is no address by the U.S. president to explain what is happening to the American public. No mention is made of mobilizing the reserves or National Guard. (In fact, the U.S. president doesn't even make an appearance in the story. Congress rates no mention, either.) There is no UN Security Council session on the war. It is hard to believe that a war this big would see no action by any of these actors. The focus is on the war. Politics is kept to a minimum.

Airpower: Playing the Trump Card

While the first two days of the war go badly for the United States at sea, it's a different story on land. A well-planed preemptive strike takes out many bridges, fuel dumps, and transport nodes in East Germany, putting a crimp in the Soviet offensive. The plane that plays the starring role is the F-19 Ghostrider. There is no such airplane by that designation, but this was a necessary fiction. Here's the explanation.

When the F-117 Stealth fighter came off the assembly line in the late 1970s, its existence was classified. Only fifty were built, and their role was primarily as a strike aircraft rather than as a true fighter. Boxy and ungainly in appearance, the F-117 was designed to absorb and dissipate a radar signal rather than return it. The plane has no right angles in its design. Its jet exhaust is ducted to reduce its infrared signature.

When Reagan became president, the F-117 stayed under wraps. The Defense Department stopped releasing accurate weapons specifications on the grounds that it gave too much free information to the Soviets. (In practice, the KGB probably got the information anyway. Domestic political opponents were robbed of the information.) All that was known about Stealth was that it was an airframe that sacrificed performance for near-invisibility on radar. The F-19 is the stand-in for the real thing. The Clancy and Bond construct of a Stealth fighter is a two-seater strike aircraft that carries a mix of external weapons, be they air-to-air missiles or laser-guided bombs. The plane also carries a laser designator to illuminate targets for accurate laser-guided bombs.

Throughout the war, the F-19s spearhead many high-value raids over enemy territory, making their effects felt well beyond their small number. But they sustain losses throughout the war. Toward the end of the book, the single squadron of F-19s is already down by about one-third. In real life, only one F-117 was ever lost in combat. This was the "lucky shot" over Serbia that brought down one of the Stealth fighters during the 1999 Kosovo war. The pilot ejected, survived, and was rescued. The Serbians quickly handed over the wreckage to the Russians.

The F-117 had its combat debut during the 1989 Panama intervention, where a single plane dropped a pair of two-thousand-pound bombs. During the first Gulf War of 1991, F-117s struck Baghdad on opening night and made many high-value raids.

The popular image of the F-117 is that of an "invisible airplane." The first raids on Baghdad belied the image. The F-117 strike force was aided by jamming from a flight of EF-111 Ravens, plus the decoy raids and HARM strikes that confused and degraded Iraq's air defense system.[24] The plane repeated in the same role over Belgrade during the Kosovo war, and flew again during the second Gulf War. Stealth is now a requirement in aircraft design, finding its way into the slow born F-22 and the more likely F-35 Joint Strike Fighter.

Can't Find Jack Ryan to Save the World?

As the fictional war unfolds, a strategic race develops between the U.S. and USSR. Can the Russians move more reserves to the front faster than the U.S. can reinforce NATO? The Soviets are hobbled by the deep NATO air strikes against their bridges and railheads. The U.S. is choked by the Soviet success waging the third battle of the Atlantic. Both sides did not plan on these things happening when the war started. Now they must craft new strategies to deal with unexpected problems.

For the Americans, that effort centers on Toland. Why him? Toland started the book as a Russian-speaking analyst at the National Security Agency and a lieutenant commander in the Naval Reserves. This guy is not Nimitz, even though he served on the carrier of the same name. Posted to northern Scotland, Toland plays a decisive role planning operations for the displaced F-14s to hinder the Backfire strikes that threaten the REFORGER convoys.

Convoy Battles, World War III Style

As the story progresses, an eighty-ship convoy forming in New York becomes the key Soviet target. An entire National Guard armored division plus two weeks of supplies are being transported. If this convoy gets through, NATO's supply shortages will ease considerably and new reserves will help resolve the desperate situation. If the Soviets maul the convoy, not enough supplies and reinforcements will get through to NATO, and maybe the Soviets will get their breakthrough to the Rhine. The Backfires and the subs must deliver the victory.

Clancy and Bond are going to have the convoy fight its way through. Many convoys during World War II were rerouted around U-boat wolfpacks, thanks to the British defeat of Germany's Enigma cipher machine and shrewd signal intelligence work. But there were times when certain Enigma code keys were not broken in time. Such was the problem for two convoys that fought their way through—HX-229 and SC-122. These two convoys were part of the largest U-boat battle during the battle of the Atlantic in March 1942. Both crossed the eight-hundred-mile "air gap" in the North Atlantic, beyond the reach of air cover. Forty-two U-boats were laid out in three patrol lines to intercept the two convoys. They outnumbered the escorts two to one.

After enduring two days and nights of attack, the two convoys made it to the other side of the air gap, now covered by B-24s flying out of Iceland. Of the ninety merchant ships, twenty-two were lost. But the U-boats also took it on the chin. Three were chased away by escorts. Seven were damaged. Aircraft also chased away two U-boats, damaged another seven, and sank two more.

That May, another large convoy battle took place. ONS-5 was stalked by sixty U-boats for about ten days. On one good night, the U-boats sank six merchantmen and were ordered by headquarters the next day to close in for the kill. But seven of the U-boats were sunk in exchange for the loss of another twelve merchantmen. This was not an exchange rate the Kriegsmarine could absorb with any hope of winning.[25]

The convoy battles in *Red Storm Rising* are no less desperate. Now Morris becomes the central character, first in command of USS *Pharris*. The authors first show the *Pharris* as the lone ASW escort in an earlier convoy, bearing grim witness to the Russian Backfire strikes that take out seven merchantmen in a twenty-ship convoy. In a second convoy battle, the *Pharris* has its bow blown off by a Soviet sub it was stalking.

Morris now finds himself in command of the USS *Reuben James*. In the mid-Atlantic, the Bears and Backfires attack again. At first, several Bears are picked off by unexpected encounters with the F-14s from the escorting carriers. But one Bear gets off a message, fixing the convoy's location. The Backfires attack. Three freighters and one escort are sunk.

As the convoy radios it is under attack by Backfires, Operation Doolittle is set in motion. A cruise missile strike launched by five U.S. subs, Doolittle takes out the Backfire bases just as the planes return from another mid-Atlantic attack mission. In some ways the strike is reminiscent of the turning point in the Battle of Midway, when several squadrons of USN dive-bombers pressed their search just five minutes longer and were rewarded by the sight of three Japanese aircraft carriers below. The enemy aircraft lay thick on the flight deck, with plenty of gas and bombs lying around as they refueled and rearmed. All it took was one or two hits to turn each carrier into a flaming charnel house.

Let's Root for the Good Bad Guy

Now let's shift to Alekseyev. He begins as deputy commander of a rear-area theater slated for the Persian Gulf invasion. He is called west several weeks into the war, again to serve as a deputy front commander, as Soviet advances are stymied by NATO's active defense. The Soviet main drive on Hamburg is a slow-moving affair with heavy casualties. The advance westward is slow and bloody up and down the front. Alekseyev understands that to cut casualties and obtain a decision, a breakthrough is needed to restore mobility to the Soviet Army.

Here the story succumbs to dramatic necessity, which of course must sacrifice some reality. A general must command from the rear to retain a "big picture" of what is going on, which would quickly be lost if he were to lead from the front. But leading from the front is what Alekseyev will do, as if he were Rommel reborn. After briefly reminiscing about how simple life was as a divisional commander, Alekseyev goes to Bieben to watch an attack and breakthrough by one tank regiment, with a second regiment in reserve to exploit the breakthrough. The attack fizzles after two hours, with only four kilometers of ground gained. Alekseyev thinks he is facing a NATO regiment instead of the two depleted companies that were holding the line.

To renew the attack, Alekseyev has to draw another tank regiment from the operational maneuver group (OMG) further to the rear, which requires Moscow's approval. Drawing on deep World War II experience, Soviet battle planning finds its strength at the operational level, that intermediate layer between tactics (the actual fight on the battlefield) and strategy (crafting and deploying the forces needed to win wars and dictate political outcomes). The operational maneuver group is a multidivision force whose purpose is to exploit the breakthrough and advance as quickly and deeply as possible. The OMG never participates in the attack that opens up a hole in the enemy line, instead passing through the depleted attacking force.

Getting his breakthrough, Alekseyev aims the armored drive toward Alfeld on the Weser. There a British tank regiment and a force of U.S. mechanized infantry hold the town as assorted Belgian and West German units retreat in the face of a four to five division Soviet advance. No commander is in overall charge. An uncoordinated defense is the best they can muster.

Alekseyev wants the bridges. His lead tank regiment is mauled by antitank guided missile fire from the town. Another thirty tanks are taken out by a NATO airstrike. The Americans north of Alfeld withdraw across the river and cover the bridges from the western bank. The Belgians south of the town lose one-third of their tanks but make it across. The West Germans stay put in Alfeld, while the British withdraw through town.

Alekseyev orders a tank regiment to swing north of Alfeld to take advantage of the American withdrawal, going around the town to drive southward toward the bridges. Refugees clog the streets and are caught in a bloody cross fire between retreating British and Germans on one side and the attacking Russians on the other. This is probably the only instance of civilian casualties in battle ever seen in a Clancy novel, as the author prefers to fight his fictional wars well away from cities. (See the campaign summaries for *Executive Orders* and *Bear and the Dragon* in Chapter Three.)

Alekseyev captures some of the bridges, but that's enough to push the drive across the Weser and toward the Rhine. Here the authors have set up a tightening situation. It all comes down to the big eighty-ship convoy coming out of New York, which carries a National Guard armored division and two weeks of supplies. Will the NATO convoy make it to Europe before the Soviets make it to the Rhine?

The NATO units are depleted. Divisions are fighting at half-strength. The Soviets are burning through all their A divisions, and soon will have to rely on second-rate B and third-rate C divisions to maintain the tempo of their offensive. The Soviets no longer have Iceland to support their mid-Atlantic Backfire attacks. They don't even have their Backfires, which have just been blown apart by Operation Doolittle. To kill the convoy, the Soviets will have rely on their sub force. The convoy will have to fight its way through. It's a replay of the World War II convoy battles, with the Soviets standing in for the U-boat wolf packs.

War at Sea, War on Land

This climactic sea battle takes place as the Soviets drive toward Hameln from Alfeld. They are tapping their B divisions now, which waste one-third faster than their A units. NATO scrapes up a few more brigades, but the fight is getting desperate as both sides are reaching the limits of their efforts.

Intertwined with this narrative is the key convoy's fight to get through to Europe. USS *Reuben James* and HMS *Battleaxe* detect six inbound Soviet attack boats. Each sub hunt is an aggravating mix of tension and patience, as each target must be found, fixed, and destroyed. The two ships and their helicopters destroy two subs, but it takes hours. Other escorts sink two more subs. Only three freighters are lost. The battle eases once the convoy is thirty-six hours out from Europe, safely under the cover of land-based aircraft.

The key convoy is docked at Le Havre, with eight roll-on/roll-off transports off-loading the National Guard armored division. Another amphibious task force carrying a lone marine division is rumored to be going to Europe, but is slated for Iceland, with the carrier USS *Independence* providing escort (and yes, Toland is aboard). Even the Nimitz is out of dry dock, patched up and lacking electronics, but otherwise ready to operate aircraft.

Now the Russians are in for a bit of strategic confusion. They can't reinforce Iceland with more troops (and a powerful surface action group as escort) until the situation in Germany turns for the better. They can't locate a U.S. major amphibious group that can land an entire marine division. Nor do they know the whereabouts of three American carriers, and they are counting *Nimitz* out of the battle.

The fog of war has descended on the Russians.

The U.S. is readying a one-two punch, and the Soviets only glimpse one fist coming at them, in Germany. Alekseyev knows vaguely that a division is assembling to threaten his right flank, but he presses on with the offensive, hoping to gain a victory that will moot any counterstroke.

But the fateful blow comes sooner than expected.

Two provisional divisions are formed from various NATO brigades to support the NG division. The attack, led by the 11th Armored Cavalry Regiment, comes knifing from the northwest to the southeast, toward the Russian crossing at Alfeld, using a little-known pipeline right-of-way that runs as straight as an arrow. The 11th ACR tops the crest near Alfeld and falls upon the Russian rear, ripping out the supply depot, destroying over one hundred trucks, and severing two of the four ribbon bridges needed to cross the Weser. Alekseyev has eight divisions to the west that are cut off.

This move becomes a favorite in both Clancy land battles depicted in *Executive Orders* and *Bear and the Dragon*. Once U.S. units penetrate into the enemy's rear, the lightly guarded support and logistics echelon gets mauled, depriving enemy combat units at the front of much-needed supplies and support. No offensive can proceed if the services in the rear are destroyed.

Facing 11th ACR are several C-class reserve divisions, armed with older T-55 tanks that are at best woefully obsolete. The 11th ACR must hold until relieved. Alekseyev orders two division-sized attacks that are repulsed. The C-class units are easily stopped and bloodied. Within twenty-four hours, a West German Panzergrenadier division supports 11th ACR. Alfeld is held.

Pause here to note that in real life, an armored cavalry regiment has been known to maul a Soviet-style tank unit. In the first Gulf war, 2nd ACR defeated a brigade of the Tawakalna Division of the Iraqi Republican Guard in an encounter battle called "73 Easting."[26]

Returning to fiction, NATO begins focusing its attention on the Soviet fuel supply, sending air units up to seek and destroy any fuel dumps to worsen the Soviet predicament. (Remember, the Russians were trying to win a war with limited fuel reserves.)

The Russians tap Alekseyev to be the next C-in-C West. The Soviets have thirty divisions committed to the war, and another five C-class reserve divisions are en route to the war zone. Alekseyev proposes stripping depleted A-class divisions of their officers and noncoms to stiffen the arriving C-class divisions, and then renew the effort to clear Alfeld, restore contact with Soviet forces west of the Weser, and drive onto the Rhine. The only catch is that Alekseyev must pitch the plan to the Politburo.

The meeting is frightening, as there is talk of taking Russia across the nuclear threshold. Alekseyev wants to attack with ten divisions on a front thirty kilometers wide by twenty kilometers deep, using the refitted C-class divisions. To even the odds, he would also need a maximum of thirty tactical nuclear warheads in the 5–10 kiloton range to clear the line of NATO defenders, thus achieving the breakthrough and exploitation. (The A-bomb that leveled Hiroshima was in the 15–20 kiloton range.) Alekseyev also dances around this issue delicately, as the use of nuclear weapons is a political decision despite their tactical use.

Pause here to dwell on this point.

During the cold war, much planning and exercise was expended trying to incorporate tactical nuclear weapons into doctrine. This was hard to do, as nuclear weapons don't have much of a military history to begin with. (Nukes were only used twice—against Japan by the U.S.) Nukes have even less military utility owing to their destructiveness. The last theoretical iteration of tactical nuclear war occurred in the 1980s, when the U.S. adopted the so-called "neutron bomb," which had a short one-kilometer blast radius while putting out a lot of radiation. If the neutron bomb were used against follow-on echelons of the Red Army, their use would have yielded many killed while leaving buildings and equipment largely unharmed.

We have no way of knowing what the trail of events would have been if another war in Europe went nuclear (even though the Russians nearly started a nuclear war in 1983 by a misreading of events). Many theorists fiddled with "escalation ladders," basically checklists of discrete events that could accelerate the tempo of a crisis, assuming the other side reacted as expected. That threshold is approached in *Red Storm Rising*, but Clancy and Bond won't cross it, even though in real life planners on both sides were aware of the dangers surrounding direct confrontation between the superpowers.

Rather than tossing nukes around Europe, the authors resort to deus ex machina. One of the C-class divisions recently manned by chosen officers from the front is transiting Moscow. These are people loyal to Alekseyev, and they have no trouble pushing past the company guarding the Kremlin to take over the government. The coup d'état installs a more level-headed troika of antiwar Politburo members that negotiates a stand-down in Europe. Hopefully from here, Russia pursues a rational strategy to get along with the world.

We Win?

And so ends another version of the "war that never was." World War III in Europe turns out to be a nonnuclear repeat of World War II. Casualties are heavy on both sides, as divisions are quickly whittled down to half-strength. This may seem perplexing as recent U.S. victories in Iraq, Afghanistan, and Kosovo were monstrously one-sided and decisive. Remember that Clancy and Bond wrote their war story in the 1980s, when the most recent example of mechanized warfare writ large was the Arab-Israeli war of 1973. (The Iran-Iraq War, which was then ongoing, suffered from lack of press coverage to provide a decent source of public information.)

In the 1973 war, armored units on both sides were quickly cut down to mere shadows of themselves in but a day. A good example to cite is Israel's 7th Armored Brigade, which held the northern sector of the Golan Heights. The unit lost sixty to eighty tanks defending this sector after starting out with about one hundred. Syrian losses were far worse, as five hundred tanks and armored personnel carriers were lost when a mechanized infantry division plus two armored brigades tried to bull their way through. "The Valley of Tears," as the battlefield became known, is an extreme example of reinforcing failure, as the Syrians tried to pull off an unimaginative frontal assault against a prepared defensive position. Set aside the outcome for a second and understand that both sides literally smoked over half their forces fighting this battle.[27] The Syrian division was reorganized as a battalion on the following day.

Don't think that the Arabs had a monopoly on failure. On October 8, 1973, the Israelis also pulled off a failed armor attack. Major-General Avraham Adan's division attempted to pierce the Egyptian Second Army line south of Kantara. In what could best be described as a "cavalry charge," unsupported by air strikes, artillery or infantry, Israeli tank brigades got mauled by Egyptian infantry firing cheap Sagger wire-guided antitank missiles. One battalion lost twelve tanks. Another battalion lost eighteen tanks, leaving only five that made it back to the start line.[28]

Real-life examples like this to provide baselines for planning. A hypothetical NATO–Warsaw Pact fight was expected to produce losses at similar levels. Hence the fictional accounts in *Red Storm Rising* of a tank company in 11th ACR defending with only nine tanks out of fifteen and suffering the loss of half in the defense, or the Russian tank regiment at Bieben losing over half its tanks mounting an unsuccessful attack.

The "fog of war" is also present in the book as it shows what warfare would have looked like twenty years ago. The U.S. has AWACS to control the air battle and the Lockheed TR-1, a variant of the U-2 spy plane that electronically records the movement of enemy ground units. Clancy and Bond show an enterprising NATO officer recording the TR-1's data onto a videocassette tape and replaying it on his VCR at fast-forward to show the pattern of Soviet movement, thus allowing some post-recon analysis to make sense of the data. The Russians can't get any aerial reconnaissance going, so they are only dimly aware of a building NATO counterstroke on their right as they drive on to Hameln from Alfeld. Likewise, Alekseyev misinterprets a stubborn defense by a depleted NATO tank company and infantry company as resistance by an entire regiment, based on the losses suffered by the Russian tank regiment in the futile attack.

Today the U.S. still has the E-3A AWACS and the TR-1. Supplementing this, however, is the E-8 JSTARS, which does for ground combat what AWACS does for the air war—detecting anything that moves. Supplementing this is the RJ-135 "Rivet Joint," which is used to detect and record all enemy radio signals. Add to this the Predator and Global Hawk unmanned recon drones, which provide real-time TV images of ground action back to headquarters. Add all these assets up and the battlefield is transparent for the American commander. All these assets burn through the fog of war.

This factor helps obtain different battlefield outcomes when U.S./NATO weapons and tactics are matched against their Russian counterparts. Iraq had an army largely equipped and trained by the Soviet Union. During the first Gulf War, Iraq managed to launch a multi-division attack on the coalition line, resulting in the battle of Khafji. It was a one-sided affair that destroyed several Iraqi divisions that attacked blindly to the south, hoping to overrun Saudi units and take some territory. U.S. air power had no trouble locating and striking follow-on units reinforcing the Iraqi attack.[29]

When the U.S. offensive began in February 1991, the position of every Iraqi unit on the front line was known. U.S. aircraft had no difficulty destroying the Iraqi front line by half before the breakthrough. Be mindful that Iraq was fielding an army that had over forty divisions, while the coalition force only numbered twelve to fourteen divisions. (It should be noted that Iraqi desertions and casualties lessened the combat strength of many units the coalition trounced.)

The disparity was more pronounced by the second Gulf War, when Iraq fielded close to eighteen to twenty divisions, while the U.S. could only bring three to bear. Counting the Iraqi Army out of the picture, the

U.S. still defeated a force of Republican Guard/Special Republican Guard that was still larger. Superiority in sensors and communications allowed brigades to punch far above their weight, transforming each brigade into the equivalent of a division. The U.S. fought at night and amidst sandstorms, even delivering air strikes and artillery strikes accurately, without regard to weather and visibility.

Were *Red Storm Rising* written today (assuming a continued cold war standoff with the USSR), the outcome would be a decisive defeat of Soviet forces long before they could even approach the Weser. A second precondition needed to obtain that outcome would be the outfitting of the allies with the same sensor and communications gear. In fiction, all this takes is a few keystrokes. In real life, it takes billions of dollars and a willingness to spend it. The gap between the U.S. and its NATO allies was particularly glaring during the 1999 Kosovo war, as allies lacked the sensor and communications gear the U.S. had. The allies were relegated to occupation and peacekeeping duties after the U.S. did most of the fighting for NATO.

Another small point worth noting: if the Soviets needed to conquer oil fields to survive, then why not cut to the chase? Iraq's invasion of Kuwait in 1991 proved to be a cheaper and potentially more successful oil grab than the miserable Iran-Iraq War of 1980–1988.

Assume Iraq avoids war with Iran and skip to the mid-1980s. That same Soviet parachute division could have been airlifted covertly into Iraq and used to spearhead a joint operation with Soviet ally Iraq to seize the Rumailla oil field that straddles the Iraq-Kuwait border or the bulk of the Saudi oil fields less than two hundred miles south of Kuwait. Such a scenario would have presented the West with a fait accompli that could not be rapidly undone by the few Western forces in the region. Iraq had a fifty-plus division army that could easily back one to two Soviet airborne divisions dropping in to take an oil field or two.

But doing that would have done away with the reasoning behind *Red Storm Rising*. That would not have been as much fun.

Likewise, the real ending to the cold war was an anticlimax compared to the novel's "surprise" ending. NATO and the Warsaw Pact did not find their Armageddon on the north German plain or the Fulda Gap. Instead, the cold war thankfully ended without a shot being fired by the two adversaries. In 1989, every Soviet satellite in Eastern Europe saw massive street protests, which neither the pro-Soviet puppet governments nor the Soviets themselves had the nerve to crush with tanks and guns. (Okay, protestors in Romania were gunned down on the streets, but they did manage to overthrow their dictator.) It was far different from 1956, when Soviet tanks crushed the Hungarian revolution in a bloody struggle for Budapest, or 1968, when the Prague Spring was snuffed by a multidivision invasion of Czechoslovakia.

Not with a bang, but with a whimper did the Russians lose their Eastern European client states. By August 1991, a few disaffected Politburo hardliners tried to overthrow the government of Chairman Mikhail Gorbachev, but could do little more than to seize his Crimean dacha and hold him under arrest. The coup plotters did not have the support of the army, and the coup fizzled. Russian President Boris Yeltsin signed an order dissolving the Soviet Union that December. The "evil empire" was finally felled by the stroke of the pen and not the sword.

Tale of Two Authors

After *Red Storm Rising*, Clancy and Bond pretty much went their separate ways. Once the authors parted company to write their own books, it was easier to see which part of *Red Storm Rising* was the primary product of which writer. Bond has shown a greater ease writing prose about combat above battalion level. One gets a feel for the operational level of warfare, and the battles show a serious exchange between friend and foe, with victory by the good guys uncertain. The coup d'état by patriotic army officers is another staple of Bond's prose, as wars with North Korea, South Africa, and France/Germany are brought to a grinding halt by this end-of-the-book move. In each instance, the U.S. is winning, but not winning fast enough, and continuing the war will be bloody and expensive (and hard to do in the last twenty pages of the paperback).

Clancy's strength is at the small-unit level. Any action taking place at the conn of a ship or sub, or any action mounted by a several squads or less, gets a good treatment from someone whose reputation is more well known for the "techno" side. Clancy also focuses more on "hero figures" that must rise above themselves to face daunting challenges. Just as Jack Ryan must do things he never did before, Toland fashions war-winning strategies as a lowly commander. (Aren't admirals supposed to do that?) Edwards is not a trained commando, but must become one on the spot with nothing more than a satellite phone and three marines for company.

Like Bond, Clancy also is shameless when it comes to plundering past plots to write the next book. *Debt of Honor* lifts two major plotlines from *Red Storm Rising*. Retired Coast Guard Chief Petty Officer "Portagee" Ortega plays the part of Edwards. Ortega is on Saipan when the Japanese invade (again), and one of his fishing boat clients is a high-tech executive sporting a satellite phone whose signal is boosted with a homemade dish antenna. And yes, they call in Japanese military dispositions to aid in the U.S. counterstrike. The second plot device is the well-timed cruise missile strike by four U.S. subs that scatter cluster bombs all over the air base runways, just in time for returning Japanese F-15s to hit as they land with low fuel and nowhere else to go.

In Clancy's timeline, U.S. main force engagements are usually decisive, inflicting vast casualties on the enemy du jour much as the U.S. did in both Gulf wars. Bond holds back to the older casualty ratios of the Arab-Israeli wars. Units on both sides are worn down in major fights, with winner and loser fighting to the near-death on near-even terms. Battles hang in doubt until a stroke or a mistake tips the balance in favor of one side. Usually it's a well-placed outflanking move. In *Red Phoenix*, Bond has the U.S. delivering the flanking counterstroke against the North Koreans from the mountains, rather than repeating the Inchon amphibious invasion. In *Vortex*, the U.S. invades South Africa from Capetown while the bad guys are busy fighting Cubans invading from the north. And in *Cauldron*, the U.S. stages another cross-Channel invasion, taking France in the rear as it allies with Germany to invade Poland.

One can only speculate how Clancy's books would have turned out if he maintained his partnership with Bond. They complemented each other well in print, with one making up for the lack in the other, much like Lennon and McCartney did writing pop songs. This is marked as the path not taken by both authors, leaving *Red Storm Rising* to stand in curious contrast with their other works.

The Unintended Consequence

A final aside: *Red Storm Rising* was rumored to be Ronald Reagan's sole preparation for his first meeting with Soviet Premier Mikhail Gorbachev in the November 1996 summit conference in Reykjavík, Iceland. At this time, the U.S. and USSR were still facing each other in Europe, ready to fight the war that never was.

So the offer was made by Reagan to scrap all ballistic missiles in Europe and halve the Soviet and U.S. ICBM arsenals. But the U.S. would get to keep the Strategic Defense Initiative, also known as Star Wars, a space-based missile defense still in development. Gorbachev turned down the offer.

One facet of NATO's defense was the possible use of nuclear weapons to destroy any Soviet invasion should the defense of Germany falter. Reagan's offer would have left Gorbachev with conventional superiority in Europe. Likewise, with France and Britain still in possession of their nuclear arsenals, the USSR would also have lacked a regional means to deter a more local nuclear threat.

Clancy was one of Reagan's favorite authors. Reagan's endorsement of *Hunt for Red October* helped make Clancy a bestselling author. Prior to being vice president, Senator Dan Quayle (R-Indiana) advocated for antisatellite missile technology, as it was portrayed in *Red Storm Rising*. "They are not just novels. They read like the real thing," Quayle said.[30] (*Red Storm Rising* is a work of fiction, however.) Even President George H.W. Bush (the elder) made sure he was the first one on his block to get a copy of *Clear and Present Danger* as soon as it came out. Another quote came from Secretary of State Colin Powell, also a former chairman of the Joint Chiefs of Staff: "A lot of what I know about warfare I learnt from reading Tom."[31] As Powell was a career military man who did his tour of duty in Vietnam, this quote is a bit unbelievable.

The fact that statesmen read books is less than astounding. So is it really far-fetched that a Clancy novel might influence policy? How much stranger is that compared to John F. Kennedy taking into account his reading of Barbara Tuchman's *Guns of August* during the Cuban missile crisis? Or George H.W. Bush being swayed by reading Martin Gilbert's *World War Two* during the crisis leading up to the first Gulf War?

Even *Hunt for Red October* played a small role in the cold war. The U.S. Naval Institute got the green light to publish Clancy's novel from Admiral James D. Watkins, then chief of naval operations. While some in the navy feared that the book was going to give the Russians too much information on U.S. subs, Watkins figured out that the book would "psych-out" the Soviet admirals, making them misbelieve that the American navy was more capable than it really was. Watkins admitted that Clancy got about two-thirds of the details right and overstated many U.S. capabilities.[32]

That's the funny thing about books.

Reading them can get you into and out of all sorts of trouble.

Afterword
Famous Last Words

Tom Clancy is more than an author. He is a brand name.

This is not said to malign his body of work. It's just that there is more than one way to sell an author, and the publishing industry has been pretty aggressive in finding new ways to put Clancy's name in front of readers. In short, there are other franchises bearing Clancy's stamp.

There is the Op-Center Series, created by Tom Clancy and Steve Pieczenik, numbering at least ten titles. Tom Clancy also worked with Martin Greenberg to create the Power Plays series, with six titles, as well as cowriting *SSN: Strategies of Submarine Warfare*.

Tom Clancy's Net Force franchise lists six titles.

Clancy has also written nonfiction. *Submarine*, *Armored Cav*,

Fighter Wing, *Marine*, *Airborne*, and *Carrier*. All six books are billed as "guided tours" of these weapons or units.

Four more nonfiction books were cowritten with generals. *Into the Storm: A Study in Command* was cowritten with General Fred Franks, who commanded VII Corps in the first Gulf War. *Every Man a Tiger* was cowritten with General Chuck Horner, an air commander from the same war. *Shadow Warriors* was cowritten with General Carl Stiner, who was commander of U.S. Special Forces. Clancy's latest joint effort, *Battle Ready*, was cowritten with General Tony Zinni, who preceded General Tommy Franks as C-in-C of Central Command and has cast a critical eye on the U.S. invasion and occupation of Iraq.

And let's not overlook several computer video games bearing the Clancy name. It is doubtful he cowrote the coding.

There is nothing wrong with this multiplicity of works. If Clancy makes more money selling his name as a franchise to cowriters, then more power to him. Getting rich is as American as playing baseball. (Come to think of it, major league ball players make a lot of money, too.)

Why were all these works overlooked in this book? Simple. Clancy had to share his voice with other writers. An exception was made for *Red Storm Rising*, as it was cowritten by another practitioner of the techno-thriller genre while the cold war was still ongoing and new threats need not be fabricated.

Through the series of novels focusing on Jack Ryan, and to a lesser extent John Clark and Jack Ryan Jr., Clancy found his vehicle for making his view of the world known while letting his heroes loose to right the world accordingly. Clancy cannot remake the world in real life, but he can in fiction, through his characters.

If the reader were to pick up a major newspaper of record, like the *Washington Post*, *Wall Street Journal*, or *New York Times*, he would see very quickly that the world is a complicated place. The average U.S. president has to make decisions on many issues in real time, not always having the best information, and without the foreknowledge that his decision will yield the best result. In short, a president tries his best while being admired by half the voters and despised by the rest. No problem is easily fixed or solved. How frustrating it is to see this reality.

Fiction doesn't have to be this way, and Clancy plays by that rule.

Not content with the world as he finds it, Clancy reshapes it. Granted, that overhaul occurs a few years after some point of contention has passed from page one. The trade disputes with Japan in the 1980s were a source of frustration for many Americans, especially those who lost jobs to Japanese competition. But Clancy hears that gripe and the U.S. beats Japan in a fictional war written a decade later. The Iranians storm the U.S. embassy in Tehran and take our diplomats hostage in 1979. Lo and behold; the U.S. knocks Iran down a few pegs, again over a decade later in a Clancy novel. Arab terrorists knock down the World Trade Center and try to destroy the Pentagon. But Clancy has the U.S. chasing the hypocritical bad guys on their home turf a few years later.

Fiction can be powerful, literally the stuff that daydreams are made of.

So which world are we better off living in?

In reality, the U.S. finds itself the world's only superpower, and cannot act unilaterally without suffering political friction from its allies and grief from its rivals. Never mind the enemies, they hate us anyway. Every move the U.S. makes can trigger unintended consequences, especially if force is used. Even the best-intentioned intervention can produce a lot of political pain. And our two-party system spends much of its time in a state of foul discord.

But in Clancy's world, there is no great amount of criticism coming from domestic opponents. There is no U.N. Congress follows the president, for the most part. Action speaks louder than words. Results matter more than process. France doesn't try to politically foul up the American use of force. Russia is an ally after being an adversary. The Chinese, Iranians, and Indians don't like us, but we swat them when they get in the way or mess with our friends. There are no complications or shades of gray in any policy decision. The difference between right and wrong is clear and without compromise. Bad guys deserve to die. The innocent should be protected. Liberals are wrong. Conservatives are right, and patriotic, too. And they have a clear worldview that appreciates the use of power and disdains diplomacy as a waste of time.

To get such a world, all one has to do is implement the Jack Ryan Agenda. That is fine for the novelist, but once the storybook is closed, it is the real world we all have to face.

Notes

Two: Clancy's Presidents

1. On a smaller note, Bush dispatched advisors to the southern Philippines to help quash a Muslim jihadist insurgency there.

2. The U.S. aid program is called Plan Colombia, and funnels about $700 million a year to that country in mostly military aid to help the government take back towns and territory from FARC, a revolutionary group that now finances itself by controlling the cocaine trade.

3. A distinction must be made here between the Palestinian extremists in *Sum of All Fears* and their Irish and Colombian counterparts. The Irish ULA aims at the ouster of the British from Ireland, but their agenda is suffused with a quasi-Marxist fight against the ruling class, epitomized by the British royal family. The Colombian drug cartels just want to stay in business, smuggling

cocaine to the U.S. while protecting the trade with brute force from Colombian and U.S. law enforcement. These agendas are small potatoes compared to goading the U.S. and USSR into nuking each other as payback for an Arab-Israeli peace accord.

4. It is not certain that Durling got much of a political honeymoon upon taking office. Clancy's book places the action prior to the Iowa caucuses and New Hampshire primary, so assume events are pegged around 1995–1996.

5. George W. Bush also suffered from events beyond his control, like the Abu Ghraib prison scandal, the daily loss of Americans to Iraqi resistance, and the 9/11 Commission Report. This made for lower approval ratings in the spring of 2004. For a more detailed overview of multiple crises impacting a presidency, see *Washington Post*, Mar. 8, 2004, p. 1, "Foreign Crises Stretch U.S. in Election Year," by Robin Wright and Glenn Kessler.

6. *Washington Post*, Mar. 9, 2004, p. 1, "After Chaos in the Capital, Losses Climbed," by Rick Atkinson.

7. *Washington Post*, Mar. 11, 2004, p. A-27, "Would FDR Run Those 9/11 Ads?," by David S. Broder.

8. George W. Bush was running for reelection as this book was being written. The U.S. suffered more casualties during the nineteen months' occupation and counterinsurgency than in the brief shooting war that was the invasion of Iraq. Bush clearly paid a political price for the long and bloody occupation, which showed in lower approval ratings sometimes dipping below 50 percent. But he managed to get reelected despite this.

9. Ironically, Jack Ryan does not suffer a similar confrontation when he signs an executive order granting U.S. recognition of Taiwan, an event taking place near the end of *Executive Orders*.

10. The 2004 presidential campaign lasted over eight months. It was only in early February when Massachusetts Senator John Kerry became the likely Democratic nominee. Television ads for Kerry and President George W. Bush were already on the air by the end of March. Compared to this, the fictional President Ryan was lucky to have a campaign that lasted less than three months!

11. Zhang Han Sen made influential cameo appearances in previous books. With political talents that could shame Stalin or Richelieu, Zhang persuaded Japan's *zaibatsu* to make war on the U.S. in *Debt of Honor*. He plays a significant supporting role engineering the anti-U.S. unholy alliance between China, Iran (United Islamic Republic), and India in *Executive Orders*.

12. Siberia has long been regarded as a land rich with resources but difficult to extract owing to its harsh climate. As a place to live, it's not popular with

Russians. The nation has only one hundred and fifty million people, and of that only twenty-five million live in Siberia. The region lies across a long shared border with China, a nation of 1.2 billion people.

Three: Weapons

1. The defense buildup, started by President Carter, is associated with President Reagan, whose first term encompassed the bulk of rearmament.
2. See *The American Way of War*, by Russell Weigley, on pp. 471–73, for a concise review of ABM and SALT I.
3. See *The U.S. War Machine*, edited by Ray Bonds, p. 71, for a review of the MX missile-basing scheme.
4. For a brief summation of the "war of the cities," see *Lessons of Modern War, Volume II: The Iran-Iraq War*, by Anthony Cordesman and Abraham Wagner, pp. 363–69.
5. For a detailed analysis of Patriot vs. SCUD, see *Lessons of Modern War, Vol. IV: The Gulf War*, by Anthony Cordesman and Abraham Wagner, pp. 867–77.
6. Israel also had its theatrical part to play. Gas masks were issued to Jewish citizens while none were given to West Bank Palestinians to guard against any possible delivery of nerve gas by the Iraqi Scuds. The gas masks may have provided a psychological security blanket to the Israeli people, but only a full MOPP suit covering every inch of bare skin can protect an individual from nerve gas. As the Iraqis never fired nerve agents at Israel, a painful embarrassment was avoided.
7. *Washington Post*, Jan. 12, 2003, p. 1, "North Korea to Resume Missile Tests," by Peter S. Goodman and Philip P. Pau.
8. *Blind Man's Bluff, The Untold Story of American Submarine Espionage*, by Sherry Sontag, Christopher Drew, with Annette Lawrence Drew, pp. 262–77.
9. The tactic of infiltration via submarine goes back to World War II. A German U-boat once landed a quartet of Nazi saboteurs on Long Island's south shore. Contrast this with a British sub landing then Brigadier General Mark Clark to negotiate with Vichy counterparts shortly before the Operation Torch landings in North Africa in November 1942.
10. Sontag and Drew's *Blind Man's Bluff* provides a good anecdotal history of submarine espionage operations during the cold war.
11. Yes, this is the namesake of that other USS *Maine*, a battleship that accidentally exploded in Havana harbor, providing the U.S. with the needed pretext to start the Spanish-American War in 1898.
12. *Wall Street Journal*, Nov. 20, 1997, p. 1, "Skipper's Chance to Run a Trident Sub Hits Stormy Waters," by Thomas E. Ricks.

13. It is worth noting that many of the real Pearl Harbor battleships fought on after salvage and refit. While the *Oklahoma* and *Arizona* were total losses, *Nevada* made it to Europe in time to deliver fire support for D-day. *California, West Virginia, Tennessee, Maryland,* and *Pennsylvania* were also present at the Battle of Surigao Straits, where they delivered their broadside fire against an oncoming column of Japanese battleships and cruisers.

14. Clancy's fictional air battle for the Marianas resembles its 1944 counterpart, known as "the Marianas Turkey Shoot," when the U.S. Navy shot down over 340 Japanese aircraft while losing only a tenth as many of its own aircraft. See p. 227 of *The Naval Academy History of the United States Navy,* by E. B. Potter.

15. At the time Clancy penned his book, the Indian Navy had two aircraft carriers, *Viraat* and *Vikrant.* Both carriers are refits of British flattops built shortly after World War II. *Vikrant* operated six Sea Harriers and nine ASW helicopters until it was retired from service in the early 1990s, finally decommissioned in 1997. *Vikrant,* ex-HMS *Hermes* of Falklands War fame, still operates, with twelve to eighteen Sea Harriers and seven to eight ASW helicopters and is expected to be retired by the beginning of the next decade.

    India will begin construction of a midsized "air defense ship" in mid-2005, with an expected date of commission in 2011. This ship is expected to operate about twenty-four MiG-29s. India has also purchased the *Admiral Gorshkov* from Russia, one of four Kiev-class light carriers. The Soviets used to a squadron of about a dozen operate Yak-36 V/STOL fighters, roughly comparable to the Harrier. India is interested in refitting the ship to operate the MiG-29.

    Compare these Indian carriers to the typical Nimitz-class carrier, which can carry over ninety aircraft. Sources: *Pakistan Daily Times,* Aug. 14, 2004; *Times of India,* Feb. 14, 2004.

16. The HMS *Sheffield* burned and sank after taking just one missile hit from the Argentines during the Falklands War just four years earlier in 1982.

17. CNN, Feb. 23, 2004. Almost $8 billion was expended on development when Secretary of Defense Donald Rumsfeld killed the RAH-66 program. About 121 RAH-66s were supposed to be built for a price tag of $14.6 billion. Had the army gotten its wish on the Commanche, the program would have run $39 billion and produced 5,023, giving each helicopter a flyaway cost of $12.1 million. When the program was trimmed back to 650, the price per helicopter shot up to $58.9 million—more than most jet fighters.

Upon cancellation, only five RAH-66s were in production. The chopper would have wielded a 20mm gun, an array of 2.75-inch rockets, and an air-to-air missile.

18. The $72 billion F-22 program is competing for aircraft dollars against other programs. The F-35 Joint Strike Fighter is a $200 billion program to produce over 2,700 aircraft (1,763 for the air force, 609 for the marines, about 480 for the navy. Great Britain will buy about 150, and another 2,000 aircraft will be sold to U.S. allies). The plane is expected to replace the aging F-16 at about $30 million per plane, a bargain compared to the nearly $200 million per F-22. The F/A-18 Super Hornet, a two-seater version intended to replace the F-14 Tomcat, is running at $51 billion for the program to build 460 aircraft.

For program price tags, see *Pittsburgh Post-Gazette*, July 13, 2004. For detailed breakdown of the F-35 program, see May 2002 cover story of *Popular Mechanics*. For F-35 foreign purchases, see Associated Press, July 12, 2004, which also slates F-35 delivery date for some time in 2009.

19. For those unfamiliar with World War II history, "Operation Tibbets" is named after then Colonel Paul Tibbets, who piloted the B-29 *Enola Gay* on its fateful mission to drop the A-bomb on Hiroshima in August 1945. While Clancy chose this irony, he had no way of knowing that Tibbets's grandson, Captain Paul Tibbets IV, is a B-2 pilot. For that tidbit, see p. 243 of *Duty* by former *Chicago Tribune* columnist Bob Greene.

The reader should be warned that *Duty* could be strange reading at times. Greene successfully tracks down the elder Tibbets in Columbus, Ohio. The interviews that came of this were both insightful and ironic.

20. If the B-2 program were fully funded, the B-2 build-out would have had a flyaway cost of $258.7 million per plane—just $60 million more than a F-22.

21. Loren Thomsen, a defense analyst for the Lexington Institute, questions the wisdom of retaining the B-1 when it can't operate against any foe possessing a decent SAM-based air defense system. He focuses on this factor as to why the B-1 failed to deliver its bomb load on Belgrade repeatedly during the Kosovo war, while the B-2 always got through. See the August 14, 2001, issue brief on the B-1 made by the Lexington Institute.

22. CNN, Apr. 8, 2003.

23. Predator comes in two models. The MQ-1A model, which can carry two Hellfire antitank missiles, goes for only $4.5 million. The MQ-9 B model is supposed to carry either eight Hellfire or a pair of air-to-air missiles or GPS-guided bombs. Predator is propeller driven, can chug along at 85–140

mph, and can spend up to sixteen hours on station at altitudes up to twenty-five thousand feet. (For details, see December 2003 issue of *Air Force* magazine.)

The RQ-4A Global Hawk, in contrast, is driven by a single jet engine at speeds around four hundred mph, can fly as high as sixty-five thousand feet, and can spend twenty-four hours over an area of interest after a 1,200-mile flight from base. However, flyaway costs have become a problem, as Global Hawk's price tag has gone up from $15–$20 million per plane to close to $123.2 million. (Sources: *Aviation Today*, Aug. 1, 2003; *Space Daily*, Feb. 12, 2003; and *The Washington Post*, Dec. 7, 2004.)

24. China is also expected to acquire almost three hundred SU-27s by 2003 and is also expected to produce two hundred more by 2012 under license. This, along with limited purchases of one hundred S-300 SAMs and ten IL-76 transport aircraft, marks a selective modernization of the Chinese military, not an across-the-board upgrade. See "China's Strategic Modernization," by Michael J. Barron, *Parameters*, Winter 2001–2002.

25. While the Israelis scored an 18.4:1 kill ratio in the 1973 Arab-Israeli war, it still lost forty-two of over one hundred aircraft to crew-served SAMs; Israel lost seventy-seven aircraft to SAM fires of all types. (Contrast this with only fifteen losses to SAMs in the 1967 war.) By 1982, Israel integrated electronic countermeasures (ECM) with advanced command, control, communications, and intelligence (C3I) to produce near-total air superiority over the Syrians, yielding a 90–0 win over the Syrian Air Force. For detailed explanations, see *The Lessons of Modern Warfare, Volume I: The Arab-Israeli Conflicts, 1973–89*, by Cordesman and Wagner, pp. 85–90 and 193–203.

26. For the details behind those figures, see *War in a Time of Peace*, by David Halberstam, pp. 51–55 and page 471.

27. *Arabs at War*, by Kenneth M. Pollack, pp. 436–41.

28. *Arabs at War*, pp. 441–43.

29. *The Art of Maneuver*, by Robert Leonhard, pp. 267–73.

30. *Lessons of Modern War, Volume IV: The Gulf War*, by Cordesman and Wagner, pp. 759–60.

31. For a detailed examination of Russo-Japanese border disputes in the 1930s, turn to *Nomonhan*, by Alvin D. Coox, pp. 92–119. Much of the skirmishing took place over ground later contested by the Russian and Chinese armies in the late 1960s.

32. *The Chinese War Machine*, edited by Ray Bonds, pp. 112–13.

33. *Diplomacy*, by Henry Kissinger, pp. 721–32.

34. Indeed, Clancy touches on the effect of Goldwater-Nichols on his fictional CINCPAC, Bart Mancuso, in *Bear and the Dragon*. Here you have an ex-

perienced submarine commander trying to make sense of the air and land dimensions of his theater command with the help of staff from the other service branches.

Four: Terminate with Extreme Prejudice

1. For a brief summation of the Phoenix Program, see *Vietnam: A History*, by Stanley Karnow, pp. 601–02.
2. *Every Spy a Prince*, by Dan Raviv and Yossi Melman, pp. 189–92.
3. BBC, Jan. 3, 2003, and Sept. 20, 2000. Bulgarian prosecutors closed an investigation into Markov's killing by the Bulgarian KGB after twenty-five years had elapsed without a resulting arrest or indictment. However, a Bulgarian intelligence officer was sentenced to a short jail term after destroying ten volumes of documents pertaining to the Markov assassination.
4. BBC, Apr. 21, 1999. The item quotes an article in *Konsomolskaya Pravda* providing details on Dudayev's assassination.
5. While the high-powered flashgun is a figment of Clancy's overactive imagination, it does tie in with the concept of nonlethal warfare being developed by the Pentagon. Such weapons under development include stun bullets, burn rays, slippery stuff, exploding nets, and vehicle-arresting nets. For more details, see "The Quest for the Non-Killer App," by Stephen Mihm, *New York Times Magazine,* July 25, 2004.
6. *Ike's Spies*, by Stephen Ambrose, with Richard Immerman, pp. 308–16.
7. *Warriors of the Night*, by Ernest Volkman, pp. 75–82.
8. *Wall Street Journal*, Aug. 2, 2002, p. 1, "Inside al Qaeda's Afghan Turmoil," by Alan Cullison and Andrew Higgins.
9. *Washington Post,* Feb. 22–23, p. 1, "A Secret Hunt Unravels in Afghanistan" and "Flawed Ally Was Hunt's Best Hope," both by Steve Coll.
10. BBC, June 14, 2000.
11. *Wall Street Journal*, Aug. 10, 2004, p. 1, "Ravaged Colombia Sees Glint of Hope As Killings Fall Off," by Jose de Cordoba. Uribe's Colombia has received about $700 million a year, mostly in military aid, to fight drug production and restore civil government in villages and towns taken over by FARC. The U.S. has invested $3.3 billion since 2000 in the Colombian drug war, which is being fought mostly by Colombians.
12. That sole fatality was Lieutenant Colonel Yonatan Netanyahu. His brother, Benjamin Netanyahu, became better known as Israel's former UN ambassador, later headed the Likud Party, and became prime minister in the late 1990s.
13. *Airborne Operations*, edited by Philip de Ste. Croix, pp. 210–15.
14. *Airborne Operations*, pp. 215–17.

15. *Washington Post*, Dec. 28, 1994, p. 1, "French Say Hijacking Target Was Paris," by Sharon Waxman.
16. *Newsday*, Apr. 26, 1997, p. 1, "Rescue in Peru: 126 Days," by Diana Jean Schimo, Calvin Sims, and Sheryl Wu Dunn.
17. CNN, Oct. 26, 2002.
18. BBC, July 29, 2004.
19. *New York Times*, May 4, 1993.

Five: Secondhand Clancy

1. Clancy is not thrilled with seeing his books turned into movies. "Giving your book to Hollywood is like turning your daughter over to a pimp." *New Statesman*, Sept. 24, 2001, "He Is the Most Popular Novelist on Earth, Whose Images of Catastrophe Animate the Modern American Psyche— Tom Clancy—A Critical Essay," by Jason Cowley.
2. This is a bit of a stretch. The Soviet Union was officially atheistic, so how does a communist sub captain get his hands on a Bible to read from Revelations?
3. *Wall Street Journal*, Jan. 22, 1992, p. 1, "To Tom Clancy, The Real Bad Guys Work In Hollywood," by Meg Cox.
4. The key visual clue is found in the same way by Harrison Ford's character in Ridley Scott's *Blade Runner*.
5. Okay, this scene wasn't in the book, but it looked way cool. It also copies from the end scene of a Mafia comedy, *The Gang That Couldn't Shoot Straight*, when the mob boss also blows up as soon as the car door is slammed shut. (You expected him to blow up when the car is started.)
6. Evidently, Clancy is partial to Affleck's portrayal of Ryan, but not for artistic reasons. "He [Affleck] was down at the house a while back. He would not consent to taking the part without getting my blessing, which I thought was a remarkably generous thing for him to do," said Clancy in an interview with CNN. See CNN, August 9, 2002.

Six: Light Reading on the Road to Reykjavík

1. *U.S. War Machine*, pp. 81–85, p. 260.
2. *The Myth of Soviet Military Supremacy*, by Tom Gervasi, p. 451; United States Ground Forces Reinforcement Schedule, 1981–1985. A more detailed list of U.S. forces in Europe can also be found on p. 453.
3. *The Myth of Soviet Military Supremacy*, pp. 442–45.
4. *The Myth of Soviet Military Supremacy*, pp. 459–64.
5. *The Myth of Soviet Military Supremacy*, pp. 468–69.
6. *The Myth of Soviet Military Supremacy*, pp. 473–75. Category I divisions

are ready for combat, ready to go within twenty-four hours with 100 percent of personnel and equipment and four days of combat supplies. Category II divisions have all weapons and vehicles, but are 50–75 percent combat effective and can be manned by reservists within three days. Category III divisions are at only 20–50 percent manned, have one-quarter of their equipment in mothballs, and the stuff is older and obsolete. They can be manned and ready to go within eight to nine weeks of mobilization. For more details, see *Claws of the Bear*, by Brian Moynahan, p. 358.

Note that this breakdown is similar to the class A, B, and C divisions that Clancy and Bond refer to in *Red Storm Rising*.

7. *The Myth of Soviet Military Supremacy*, p. 188.
8. *The Myth of Soviet Military Supremacy*, pp. 204–05.
9. *Russian Military Power*, edited by Ray Bonds, pp. 90–91.
10. *The Myth of Soviet Military Supremacy*, pp. 435–36.
11. This account of Able Archer is a composite drawn from *What If*, edited by Robert Crowley, pp. 394–95, and Sontag and Drew's *Blind Man's Bluff*, pp. 340–45.

This was by no means the only direct confrontation between the U.S. and Soviet Union. There was the Berlin blockade of the late 1940s and the Cuban missile crisis of 1962.

12. For details on the Iran-Iraq War to use as a benchmark, see *Arabs at War*, by Pollack, pp. 182–93, and Cordesman and Wagner's *Lessons of Modern Warfare, Volume II: The Iran-Iraq War*, pp. 76–107.
13. For a good description of the briefing culture, check out pp. 161–62 of *Boyd*, by Robert Coram. "It is obvious that most people can read and assimilate information faster than they can learn something by listening to a dog and pony show. But the military culture is an oral culture and the bedrock of that culture is the briefing."
14. *The Pentagon's New Map*, by Thomas Barnett, p. 16.
15. CNN, Mar. 28, 2003.
16. *New York Times*, May 19, 1976.
17. *New York Times*, October 6, 1976.
18. *New York Times*, Dec. 26, 1976, p. 1, "New CIA Estimate Finds Soviets Seek Arms Superiority," by David Binder. The article listed team B's members as: Richard Pipes, professor of Russian history at Harvard University; Thomas W. Wolfe of the RAND Corporation; retired Lieutenant General Daniel O. Graham, former head of the Defense Intelligence Agency; Paul D. Wolfowitz of the Arms Control and Disarmament Agency; General John Vogt, USAF, retired; and Professor William van Cleve, USC, former delegate to the SALT I talks. The CIA research team was led by its national-

intelligence officer for the USSR, Howard Stoertz. The story quoted by name Pipes and Soviet skeptic former air force chief of intelligence Major General George J. Keegan. No CIA source was quoted by name, though many were quoted without attribution.

One thing to be mindful about when rereading cold war analysis of Russian arms and intentions: If the analysts are conservative, the Russians are very dangerous and the U.S. must spend more on defense to stay ahead of them. If the analysts are liberals, then the Russians aren't as powerful as we think they are and current defense spending is sufficient. Neither analysis proved 100 percent correct. But the Soviets never publicized their military operations and expenditures, so educated guesswork was the best intelligence our money could buy.

19. *The Second World War*, by John Keegan, p. 104.
20. *The Price of Admiralty*, by John Keegan, p. 220.
21. *The Second World War*, p. 105.
22. *The Second World War*, p. 121.
23. *The General's War*, by Michael R. Gordon and Bernard E. Trainor, pp. 113, 114, and 217.
24. *The General's War*, p. 220.
25. *The Price of Admiralty*, pp. 261–63.
26. *The General's War*, pp. 390–92.
27. *Arabs at War*, pp. 489–91.
28. *The Arab-Israeli Wars*, by Chaim Herzog, page 251.
29. *The General's War*, pp. 267–88.
30. "Paperback Fighter," by Scott Shuger, *Washington Monthly*, November 1989.
31. "He Is the Most Popular Novelist on Earth, Whose Images of Catastrophe Animate the Modern American Psyche—Tom Clancy—Critical Essay," by Jason Cowley, *New Statesman*, Sept. 24, 2001.
32. See the notes in *Blind Man's Bluff*, page 478.

Bibliography

Tom Clancy novels, in order of publication:

Hunt for Red October, Naval Institute Press, Annapolis, Maryland, 1984

Red Storm Rising, G.P. Putnam's Sons, New York, 1986

Patriot Games, G.P. Putnam's Sons, New York, 1987

The Cardinal of the Kremlin, G.P. Putnam's Sons, New York, 1988

Clear and Present Danger, G.P. Putnam's Sons, New York, 1989

The Sum of All Fears, G.P. Putnam's Sons, New York, 1991

Without Remorse, G.P. Putnam's Sons, New York, 1993

Debt of Honor, G.P. Putnam's Sons, New York, 1994

Executive Orders, G.P. Putnam's Sons, New York, 1996

Rainbow Six, G.P. Putnam's Sons, New York, 1998

The Bear and the Dragon, G.P. Putnam's Sons, New York, 2000

Red Rabbit, G.P. Putnam's Sons, New York, 2002

The Teeth of the Tiger, G.P. Putnam's Sons, New York, 2003

Other books, publications and articles:

Ambrose, Stephen E., and Richard H. Immerman, *Ike's Spies: Eisenhower and the Espionage Establishment*, Doubleday, Garden City, New York, 1981

Atkinson, Rick, "After Chaos in the Capital, Losses Climbed," *Washington Post*, Mar. 9, 2004

Barnett, Thomas P.M., *The Pentagon's New Map*, G.P. Putnam's Sons, New York, 2004

Barron, Michael J., "China's Strategic Modernization," *Parameters*, winter 2001–2002

Binder, David, "New CIA Estimate Finds Soviets Seek Arms Superiority," *New York Times*, Dec. 26, 1976

Bonds, Ray, editor, *The Chinese War Machine*, Salamander Books, London, 1979

Bonds, Ray, editor, *Russian Military Power*, St. Martin's Press, New York, 1980

Bonds, Ray, editor, *The U.S. War Machine*, Crown Publishers, New York, 1983

Broder, David S., "Would FDR Run Those 9/11 Ads?," *Washington Post*, Mar. 11, 2004

Coll, Steve, "A Secret Hunt Unravels in Afghanistan" and "Flawed Ally Was Hunt's Best Hope," *Washington Post*, Feb. 22–23, 2004

Coox, Alvin D., *Nomonhan*, Stanford University Press, Stanford, California, 1985

Coram, Robert, *Boyd*, Little, Brown, Boston, 2002

Cordesman, Anthony C., and Abraham R. Wagner, *The Lessons of Modern Warfare, Volume I: The Arab-Israeli Conflicts, 1973–1989*, Westview Press, Boulder, Colorado, 1990

Cordesman, Anthony C., and Abraham R. Wagner, *The Lessons of Modern Warfare, Volume II: The Iran-Iraq War*, Westview Press, Boulder, Colorado, 1990

Cordesman, Anthony C., and Abraham R. Wagner, *The Lessons of Modern Warfare, Volume IV: The Gulf War*, Westview Press, Boulder, Colorado, 1996

Cordoba, Jose de, "Ravaged Colombia Sees Glint of Hope as Killings Fall Off," *Wall Street Journal*, Aug. 10, 2004

Cowly, Jason, "He Is the Most Popular Novelist on Earth, Whose Images of Catastrophe Animate the Modern American Psyche—Tom Clancy—A Critical Essay," *New Statesman*, Sept. 24, 2001

Cowley, Robert, editor, *What If: The World's Foremost Historians Imagine What Might Have Been*, Berkley Publishing Group, New York, 2000

Cox, Meg, "To Tom Clancy, The Real Bad Guys Work in Hollywood," *Wall Street Journal*, Jan. 22, 1992

Cullison, Alan, and Andrew Higgins, "Inside Al Qaeda's Afghan Turmoil," *Wall Street Journal*, Aug. 2, 2002

Gervasi, Tom, *The Myth of Soviet Military Supremacy*, Harper & Row, New York, 1986

Goodman, Peter S., and Philip P. Pau, "North Korea to Resume Missile Tests," *Washington Post*, Jan. 3, 2003

Gordon, Michael R., and Bernard E. Trainor, *The General's War*, Little, Brown, Boston, 1995

Green, Bob, *Duty: A Father, His Son, and the Man Who Won the War*, Harper-Collins, New York, 2000

Halberstam, David, *War in a Time of Peace*, Scribner, New York, 2001

Herzog, Chaim, *The Arab-Israeli Wars*, Random House, New York, 1982

Karnow, Stanley, *Vietnam: A History*, Viking Press, New York, 1983

Keegan, John, *The Price of Admiralty*, Viking Penguin, New York, 1988

Keegan, John, *The Second World War*, Viking Penguin, New York, 1989

Kissinger, Henry, *Diplomacy*, Simon & Schuster, New York, 1994

Leonhard, Robert, *The Art of Maneuver*, Presidio Press, Novato, California, 1991

Merle, Renae, "The Price of Global Hawk Surveillance System Rises," *Washington Post*, Dec. 7, 2004

Mihm, Stephen, "Quest for the Non-Killer App," *New York Times Magazine*, July 25, 2004

Moynahan, Brian, *Claws of the Bear*, Houghton Mifflin, Boston, 1989

Pollack, Kenneth M., *Arabs at War*, University of Nebraska Press, Lincoln, Nebraska, 2002

Potter, E. B., *The Naval Academy Illustrated History of the United States Navy*, Gallahad Books, New York, 1971

Raviv, Dan, and Yossi Melman, *Every Spy a Prince*, Houghton Mifflin, Boston, 1990

Ricks, Thomas E., "Skipper's Chance to Run a Trident Sub Hits Stormy Waters," *Wall Street Journal*, Nov. 20, 1997

Schimo, Diana Jean, Calvin Sims, and Sheryl Wu Dunn, "Rescue in Peru: 126 Days," *Newsday*, Apr. 26, 1997

Shuger, Scott, "Paperback Fighter," *Washington Monthly*, Nov. 1989

Sontag, Sherry, Christopher Drew, and Annette Lawrence, *Blind Man's Bluff*, PublicAffairs/Perseus Books Group, New York, 1998

Ste. Croix, Philip de, editor, *Airborne Operations*, Crown Publishers, New York, 1978

Thomsen, Loren, Issue Brief by Lexington Institute, Arlington, Virginia, Aug. 14, 2001

Volkman, Ernest, *Warriors of the Night*, William Morrow, New York, 1985

Waxman, Sharon, "French Say Hijacking Target Was Paris," *Washington Post*, Dec. 28, 1994

Weigley, Russell F., *The American Way of War*, Indiana University Press, Bloomington, Indiana, 1977; republished by Macmillan, New York

Wright, Robin, and Glenn Kessler, "Foreign Crises Stretch U.S. in an Election Year," *Washington Post*, Mar. 8, 2004

Other citations were obtained from:

Associated Press

Aviation Today

BBC

CNN

New York Times

Pakistan Daily Times

Pittsburgh Post-Gazette

Popular Mechanics

Space Daily

Times of India